More Praise for *Correction*

"In *Correction*, Ben Austen investigates America's painful criminal-justice crossroads with a necessary urgency and an inspiring moral clarity. Are human beings capable of change? Is forgiveness actually possible? Do we as a society really want justice or revenge? Austen bears down on these questions with engrossing immersive reportage and transcendent heart and soul. The result is invaluable—and unforgettable."

—Robert Kolker, author of #1 *New York Times* bestseller *Hidden Valley Road*

"*Correction* is nonfiction storytelling at its finest. The award-winning journalist Ben Austen follows the harrowing fifty-year journey of two men convicted of horrific crimes, and their path to parole. And yet the question of whether they will be released, or of their innocence, is really a poignant and powerful story about our guilt for building the most punitive and shameful punishment system in the world, and our willingness, as a society, to change."

—Khalil Gibran Muhammad, author of *The Condemnation of Blackness*

"In *Correction*, Ben Austen masterfully brings to life the very real human conditions that underlie an otherwise opaque and cumbersome US parole system, one fraught with holes that seem to swallow up its own efficacy. As readers, we're compelled to ask why closure or redemption should be so hard to come by. A powerful work about a poorly understood phenomenon in our country."

—Amanda Williams, artist, 2022 MacArthur Fellow

ALSO BY BEN AUSTEN

High-Risers: Cabrini-Green and the
Fate of American Public Housing

Correction

Parole, Prison,

and the

Possibility of

Change

Ben Austen

FLATIRON
BOOKS
NEW YORK

www.flatironbooks.com

Grateful acknowledgment is made for permission to reproduce from the following:

"Freedom Is a Habit" by Carl Sandburg. Copyright © 1943 by Paula Steichen Polega and John Steichen. Reprinted by arrangement with Paula Steichen Polega, John Steichen, and The Barbara Hogenson Agency, Inc. All rights reserved. For more information about Carl Sandburg, visit www.nps.gov/carl.

Timeline design by Nadxieli Nieto

Library of Congress Cataloging-in-Publication Data

Names: Austen, Ben, author.
Title: Correction : parole, prison, and the possibility of change / Ben Austen.
Description: First edition. | New York : Flatiron Books, 2023. | Includes bibliographical references and index.
Identifiers: LCCN 2023006824 | ISBN 9781250758804 (hardcover) | ISBN 9781250758811 (ebook)
Subjects: LCSH: Parole—United States. | Corrections—United States. | Punishment in crime deterrence—United States. | Prison—Moral and ethical aspects—United States.
Classification: LCC HV9304 .A96 2023 | DDC 364.60973—dc23/eng/20230314
LC record available at https://lccn.loc.gov/2023006824

Our books may be purchased in bulk for promotional, educational, or business use. Please contact your local bookseller or the Macmillan Corporate and Premium Sales Department at 1-800-221-7745, extension 5442, or by email at MacmillanSpecialMarkets@macmillan.com.

First Edition: 2023

10 9 8 7 6 5 4 3 2 1

For my parents, Ernestine and Ralph, and my brother, Jake, and for Danielle, Lusia, and Jonah—the family we made together

And let us once again assail your ears,
That are so fortified against our story

—Hamlet, Act 1, Scene 1

A Partial Timeline of

Prisons and Parole
in the United States of America

1790   The Walnut Street jail in downtown Philadelphia begins its conversion into the country's first state prison for Pennsylvanians convicted of crimes and sentenced to confinement

1829   Eastern State Penitentiary opens in Philadelphia with the belief that forced isolation and silent contemplation will lead to "penitence"

1870   National Prison Association resolves that prison sentences should be indeterminate, meaning parole boards should decide long after sentencing when someone is worthy of release

1876   Country's first prison "reformatory" opens in Elmira, New York, for males sixteen to thirty, focused on rehabilitation and earned release

1880   30,659 people in prisons in the United States

1884   First state parole system created in Ohio

1891   Federal prison system established

1904   57,070 in prison

1910   United States establishes a federal parole commission

1927   Parole instituted in all but three U.S. states: Florida, Mississippi, and Virginia

1925   91,669 in prison

1939   Because of prohibition, the country's ill-advised "war on alcohol," and the economic hardships of the Great Depression, U.S. prison numbers nearly double, before falling again

1939   179,818 in prison

1945   133,649 in prison

1954   National Prison Association changes name to the American Correctional Association—prisons reclassified as "correctional facilities," guards as "correctional officers"

1955   185,780 in prison

1965   210,895 in prison

1970   Twenty-seven prison uprisings occur across the country; strikers at California's Folsom Prison demand "an end to indeterminate sentences whereby a man can be warehoused indefinitely, rehabilitated or not"

1970   196,441 in prison

1971	Hundreds of state troopers and officers storm New York's Attica Correctional Facility, killing twenty-nine incarcerated men and ten prison staffers
1972	196,092 in prison
1973	204,211 in prison
1973	The U.S. prison population grows by 8,119 people from the previous year, a 4 percent rise. Incarceration rates have remained relatively stable in the twentieth century, but from here the prison population increases every year until 2009
1975	240,993 in prison
1976	Maine is the first state to abolish discretionary parole, the process of being released by a parole board. People released from prison by other means remain on conditional supervision also known as parole
1977	California abolishes discretionary parole for all crimes other than murder. Indiana abolishes discretionary parole
1978	Illinois ends discretionary parole, except for those convicted prior to 1978
1979	New Mexico abolishes discretionary parole
1979	291,610 in prison
1980	220,438 people on parole (on conditional supervised release after prison)
1982	Minnesota abolishes discretionary parole
1982	385,343 in prison
1983	Florida abolishes discretionary parole
1984	Washington abolishes discretionary parole
1985	465,236 in prison
1985	277,438 on parole
1985	Of all admissions to state prisons, 23.4 percent are people who violated the terms of their parole. Mass incarceration creates the collateral epidemic of mass supervision, with the latter feeding the former
1987	Federal prison system ends discretionary parole for all future offenses
1988	U.S. incarceration rate is 244 per 100,000 people
1989	Oregon abolishes discretionary parole
1990	Delaware abolishes discretionary parole
1990	775,030 in prison
1990	531,407 on parole
1993	Kansas abolishes discretionary parole. Washington is the first state to enact a "three strikes and you're out" law, mandating long prison sentences for habitual offenders, even if the third offense is relatively less serious; twenty-three other states and the federal government quickly adopt similar statutes

1994	The federal Violent Crime Control and Law Enforcement Act incentivizes more incarceration, offering states billions for new prison construction if they lock up more people for longer periods of time. One of the criteria: states must enact "truth-in-sentencing" statutes mandating people in prison serve at least 85 percent of their convicted sentence
1994	1,055,073 in prison
1994	690,159 on parole
1994	Arizona and North Carolina abolish discretionary parole
1995	Virginia abolishes discretionary parole. Of all admissions to state prisons, 33.7 percent are parole violators
1996	Ohio abolishes discretionary parole
2000	Wisconsin is the last state to abolish discretionary parole
2000	1,391,261 in prison
2000	725,527 on parole
2005	1,527,929 in prison
2005	784,408 on parole
2008	California's Supreme Court rules that the original crime can't be the sole reason to deny someone parole. Release rates in the state soon triple
2009	U.S. incarceration rate 754 per 100,000 people; Black male incarceration rate 4,347 per 100,000
2009	1,617,970 in prison
2010	451,000 people sent to prison for violating the terms of their parole or probation. Michelle Alexander's *The New Jim Crow* published
2012	4,790,700 people in America on parole or probation, one of every fifty adults
2012	1,483,900 in prison
2015	Barack Obama becomes first sitting president to visit a federal prison
2017	Campaign for Smart Justice, ACLU's strategy to cut U.S. prison population by half, launches in all fifty states and the District of Columbia
2018	First Step Act, bipartisan criminal justice reform bill that blunts some of the crueler edges of federal incarceration, signed into law. First steps lead to decarceration only if other steps follow
2020	1,215,821 in prison
2020	862,113 on parole
2023	Mass incarceration turns fifty

Note: All prison and parole figures are from the Bureau of Justice Statistics. The BJS started collecting parole data from all fifty states, the federal system, and the District of Columbia in 1980.

Correction

Introduction

Why Do You Deserve Parole?

In the former rail hub of Galesburg, near the border with Iowa, Johnnie Veal sat in the prison's school building, between flags of the United States and the state of Illinois. He was wearing a surgical mask and an oversize short-sleeved blue shirt, his bare arms rested innocuously on the lacquered desk in front of him. Across from him a monitor was perched atop a rolling AV tray. Johnnie concentrated on making his body a statue. He had been locked up since he was a teenager in 1970; he was now past the age at which most people retired. A half century of incarceration. A lifetime. The screen in front of him flashed white and recomposed into a grid of panels, faces at different angles and distances filling each box. Inside one of them was Johnnie's pro bono lawyer. In others, his fiancée, his grandson, a reporter. The most important face belonged to a delegate from the Illinois parole board, who was on the video call to interview Johnnie and make a recommendation whether to release him from prison.

"Johnnie, can you talk about why you believe you are deserving of parole," his lawyer prompted.

Johnnie took his time to reply. He reminded himself to stay relaxed. He wasn't supposed to sound rehearsed. He shouldn't overthink his answers. What could he possibly say after all these years that would equal free?

I was one of the people on the call; Johnnie's lawyer had asked me to serve as an expert witness. It was November 2020, eight months into the Covid-19 pandemic, and by then most of us were experienced with Zoom or some other online videoconferencing. Not Johnnie. He had prepared for the interview by watching a thirteen-inch television in his cell. Studying the people on TMZ, he noted how the remote hosts of the celebrity gossip show engaged one another despite their separate isolations. He analyzed guests of news programs who appeared from their home setups. Johnnie saw that speakers who looked away from the camera tended to come across as shifty or insincere. "Like a hunting dog each time a rabbit jumps out of a bush, chasing it," he'd say. So he trained himself. Peering at a mark on his cell wall, he practiced speaking without breaking eye contact.

"I have done everything possible up under your guidelines, up under your old law, to rehabilitate myself, to show that I am worthy of a risk parole assessment, to show that I am trustworthy enough," Johnnie told the official from the parole board. He locked his sights on the camera affixed to the monitor in front of him. "I have earned the right to be paroled."

A parole hearing isn't a trial. A trial is where a court determines guilt beyond a reasonable doubt. Where the convicted are sentenced. Parole board members are like a jury without a judge, civilians appointed to decide whether a long prison sentence should or shouldn't come to an end.

Not only is a person's fate in the balance. But parole, at the back end of the criminal system, also tells the story of everything that came before it. The stories of a crime and decades in prison. Of victimization and rehabilitation. Of childhoods and lives ruined. Parole is a result of each preceding decision and policy choice. It contains the whole of criminal justice. Parole conveys the story of the country in all its fevered conceptions of safety and punishment.

This book tells the prison and parole sagas of two men: Johnnie Veal and Michael Henderson. It is interested not only in whether their long prison terms will—or even should—come to an end. The book is also a history of American incarceration. And it tells the stories of several other people embroiled in the corrections system or trying to change it.

Like Johnnie, Michael Henderson entered prison in the early 1970s, at a time when the United States incarcerated a total of 200,000 people. In 2023, with mass incarceration in America turning fifty, that number seems quaint. The prison population has increased nearly six-fold. Two hundred thousand doesn't even amount to the number of women the country currently locks up. In federal and state prisons today, there are more than 200,000 people alone serving life without parole or sentences so long that they amount to the same thing. The United States, a single country, locks up a quarter of the world's incarcerated people.

Despite our gross overreliance on prisons, it's not clear what a prison term is supposed to accomplish. We don't actually know why we punish. Apart from clichés—*paying a debt to society*; *you do the crime, you do the time*—there is no consensus in America on what constitutes retribution or atonement. What must someone who commits a violent crime do to get a second chance?

Parole hearings are opaque and riddled with inequities. They also wrestle with the most profound questions underlying the country's values around crime and consequences. Parole presupposes that change—a correction—is possible. Parole is this extraordinary pivot point in the country's shifting conceptions of justice. By studying the parole process, we can see how the United States created the crisis of mass incarceration, and how we might find a way out.

I had researched Johnnie for *High-Risers*, a previous book I wrote about Cabrini-Green—the crime he was in prison for had transformed the Chicago public housing complex. But while reporting and writing that book, I didn't think to contact him. Some fifty years had passed since the crime. The truth is no one I spoke to even talked about a seventeen-year-old from 1970 as a person still sitting in a prison cell. The American criminal system fosters that disconnect. Prisons are remote and largely inaccessible, communication is made difficult and sometimes forbidden, and the tough-on-crime rhetoric that became ubiquitous during Johnnie's and Michael's incarcerations normalized the erasure of people like them. People were taken "off the streets," "sent away," tossed "out." They were given "life."

The delegate from the parole board asked if Johnnie wanted a message conveyed to the other board members. Johnnie pondered the question for a few moments.

"I ask the board to look at my totality of experience, my totality of growing from a seventeen-year-old to a sixty-eight-year-old."

"I could do that," the board member told him.

They said their goodbyes, and the boxes on the screen disappeared.

1

The Ideal of a True Prison System

Michael Henderson borrowed the .38 snub-nose revolver from his younger brother. He tucked it into a pouch cinched around his waist, but all that evening the gun beckoned him like a secret he couldn't keep. This was in the summer of 1971, on a Friday night, in East St. Louis, Illinois, a declining industrial city across the Mississippi from its Missouri namesake. Michael was eighteen and, at that point in his life, rarely thought beyond the next distraction. Some days he toted a briefcase to the local community college and pretended to study, a ruse to talk to female foreign exchange students. Once, he and his buddies found a Ford Galaxie with Florida plates and keys still in the ignition. They filled the tank and took turns racing the streets of East St. Louis, teasing whoever was behind the wheel that the police were around every corner. When a state trooper really did appear, Michael dashed off with the other boys. The officer fired at Michael's back. One of the shots caught him in the thigh, passing clean through his leg, and he limped home. Michael had escaped the finality of the trooper's extra-judicial justice. Later, at the hospital, he was arrested and eventually sent to juvenile detention.

On that summer night in 1971, with the juvie stint behind him, Michael and two friends ended up in front of the Delisa Lounge, a tavern that opened its basement on weekends for parties. By midnight, he was drunk on cheap wine. The occasional car zipped along State Street in front of them. The lounge's parking lot was full but the crowd was down-stairs, and Michael could hear the music thumping inside. A lone DJ on break leaned against his Cadillac, smoking a cigarette. Then a white kid pulled into the gravel lot in a black-and-red car with two Black teenage passengers. White people in that part of the city were increasingly rare, and Michael didn't know the three boys. They said they were partying with friends and ran out of beer. Would Michael buy them more if they gave him the money? Here was the next distraction.

Michael purchased two six-packs of Pabst Blue Ribbon and a pack of Juicy Fruit. He passed the beer and the gum through the open car window. Then he asked for a tip. At least a couple of bucks. One of the passengers had gone inside to check out the party. The other one in the back seat said no. For Michael, that was the only cue he needed. It was reason enough to reveal his secret. He pulled the small gun from its pouch and held it inside the driver's window.

"You going to pay me or what?" he snapped, hard-boiled.

Michael intended only to scare the boys with the revolver. But at the sight of the gun, the guy in the back seat panicked. "Drive!" he yelled, and the driver responded. The car jerked backward; the gun went off. For years to come, that's how Michael would describe it, slipping into a passive voice, as if the .38 fired on its own. The car swerved, then smashed into the DJ's Caddy. The passenger in the back jumped out and disappeared. Michael fired a second shot into the air, involuntarily, he said. Like a spasm.

The driver, who was later identified as Richard Schaeffer, dragged himself from the car. Schaeffer was seventeen and from a whiter and wealthier suburb. He had a job that summer working for the East St. Louis Housing Authority. In the fall, he was going to enter a new high school. Gasping for air, he stretched out along the gravel.

In the Delisa Lounge parking lot, Richard Schaeffer died.

PEOPLE WHO LAND in a criminal courtroom or a cell will often say they "caught a case." The expression is elusive, meant to evade fixed mean-ing. It's a catchall, you could say, to match the sweep of the American criminal system. The verb "catch" can be fully active, as in catching a ball, suggesting an admission of guilt, of *doing* the crime. Or it could be used like "ensnared," the way one is caught in a trap. *They put this case on me.* You could also talk about catching a case in the way you caught a virus. Which is to say, it happened sort of incidentally, from negligence or exposure. The verb was not uncommonly a way to dodge responsibility, or at least to be vague enough to leave options open. But "catching a case" could be a declaration as well that you're simply one of the six million people in the United States caught up in the machinery of the country's vast corrections apparatus.

In 1983, a dozen years after the shooting, Michael was led into a small room and seated across a table from two men and a woman, each of them in business attire. He was an inmate at a maximum-security prison in southern Illinois. The three officials had the authority to parole Michael; they could release him from custody with conditions before the completion of his sentence. Michael had a vague understanding that the members of the parole board would make a decision after interviewing him and reviewing his conduct while incarcerated. He was aware that he would have to give a convincing account of the case he caught.

Michael entered prison with an eighth-grade education. At the start of his freshman year of high school, he'd tussled with a group of white kids who were harassing a bookish Black student. When the white boys returned in three cars, carrying chains and bats, a gym teacher put Michael in her car and shuttled him home. The teacher probably saved his life, but Michael never went back to school. At fourteen, he lied about his age and started working as a welder.

In prison, Michael completed an adult basic-education course. He took additional classes and worked jobs in data entry and on a painting detail. He bolstered his vocabulary through repeated readings of *Word Power Made Easy*. By 1983, at twenty-nine, Michael had already developed his tendency to philosophize, to slip into disquisitions on the universal and the humanistic. He had an actor's strong-featured expressive face, with eyebrows like marquees and soft brown eyes that onlookers often thought shimmered with heartfelt emotion. Michael came across as thoughtful and sincere. "Witty and sagacious," he liked to say.

Yet the murder Michael committed still baffled him. The events of an otherwise unremarkable night in 1971 following one after another—the gun, the boys arriving at the liquor store, Michael's threat turned tragic. He tried to communicate to the three members of the parole board how foolish and immature he was at eighteen. He had taken the gun with him, brandished it and pulled the trigger, and over the chance at maybe a dollar or two. But in trying to explain to the parole board how this crime fit into some larger story of an appropriate punishment and his own rehabilitation, Michael found himself drawing a distinction between the harm he'd caused that could never be undone and who he was fundamentally as a human being. Yes, he committed a murder. But, he insisted, he was *not* a murderer.

The three parole board delegates had with them what is called the "statement of facts." The file contained the state's version of events. They could see, for instance, that the first bullet Michael fired entered the victim's back left shoulder, passed through his rib cage and his left lung. It pierced the lower left section of his heart and lodged itself in his spine. The delegates also read that Michael didn't turn himself in after the shooting. He ran. His aunt lived a half block from the tavern, but he took a circuitous route, bounding up State Street and doubling back. He hid the gun inside a vase in his aunt's living room. Two boys were lounging on the stoop next door. On his way out, Michael traded shirts with one of them and took a hat from the other. In this modest disguise, he returned to the scene of the crime. The parking lot was now a riot of people: the Delisa crowd, police, and paramedics. Realizing he might have killed the driver, Michael beelined back to his aunt's house. He retrieved the gun and dropped it down a sewer.

For two years Michael avoided having to answer for the crime. But the pair of boys on the porch who gave Michael the hat and shirt eventually caught cases themselves. In exchange for reduced charges, they traded information about the killing of the white boy at the Delisa. Michael's buddies who were with him outside the tavern talked as well. "I asked Michael why he shot him," a friend told East St. Louis detectives. "Michael said, 'I don't know, he just pulled off and I shot him.'" In 1973, Michael was working at the American Car and Foundry Company, welding parts for railcars. He and his wife, Joyce, were the parents of three children with a fourth on the way. Michael was in lockup—arrested for driving without a license—when he was charged with Schaeffer's murder.

What is the punishment for a teenager who thinks nothing of carrying a gun, who on some random Friday night kills another teenager? Michael Henderson took the life of another human being. An irreversible crime. A venial sin. A breach of a social contract, one in which we must abide by certain laws and moral codes to ensure our mutual safety. Michael avoided taking responsibility for the murder. How much prison time would equal justice? What could he do during his incarceration to earn back his liberty?

A county prosecutor decided that a fair punishment for Michael would be a prison term of no less than seven years and no more than twenty-one, so long as Michael agreed to plead guilty and avoid a trial. What was the systematic study behind the seven to twenty-one years? The balancing of the scales of justice? There wasn't one. What did Schaeffer's family think about the negotiated plea? As is customary, the prosecutor didn't consult them. This is primarily how the criminal system works. Today, more than 95 percent of all criminal cases end in a plea deal worked out by a prosecutor, but even then few cases reached a determination by a jury or a judge.

Michael rejected the offer. He'd convinced his grandmother that he didn't kill anyone. His mother said maybe Michael's little brother who was always getting in trouble could have done something like that, but not Michael, who seemed so caring and clever. Michael couldn't bring himself to disabuse them of these lies. He believed, too, that he could convince a jury to acquit him. For better and worse, it was part of Michael's nature to expect that things would work out. The prosecutor sweetened the offer, carving another year from the maximum term. Twenty years, at most, would equal justice. Still, Michael fought the charges in court.

"You have been living according to the law of the jungle, and that is what you are not supposed to do," a judge told him in the courtroom. Michael had killed someone. The complicated act of criminal justice—of holding him accountable and keeping his community safe—was made only more problematic by the judge categorizing him, or all of Black East St. Louis, as savage. A jury found Michael guilty. The power to set his prison term shifted from the prosecutor to the judge. Those who turn down a plea deal often faced what's called a trial penalty, an inflated sentence meant as a warning to others to accept what's offered them. The judge said, "We don't need people like that in society, and I am going to take you out of the mainstream." He sentenced Michael to one hundred to two hundred years.

Michael appealed the sentence as excessive. "The average person would say, 'Who'd you kill, the president?'" he'd protest. A second judge let the decision stand, although he agreed that Michael's protest had some merit. A term of a hundred or two hundred years made no biological sense. It was an impossible minimum and maximum, like something out of the Old Testament or science fiction. But the appellate judge pointed out that the sentence was *indeterminate*. With an indeterminate sentence, it wasn't the trial judge who got to decide how long Michael stayed in prison. It was left up to a parole board to determine when the punishment would end. And, in theory, it would also be up to Michael, since he could demonstrate through his behavior and understanding of his crime that he no longer posed a threat to society. That he was remorseful, reformed. Eligible for parole consideration after less than eleven years, he would have an opportunity to show a board that he was deserving again of freedom.

PAROLE, THE PRACTICE of releasing someone from prison early based on their good conduct and then afterward monitoring them for a time, dates back to the early nineteenth century in Europe and Australia. The term comes from the French for "word of honor" or "oath," as in, *If we free you, do you give your word, your* parole, *that you'll keep off the battlefield? Or return when summoned?* In the United States, the policy has its origins in an 1870 conference in Cincinnati, Ohio, the first congress of the National Prison Association. Hundreds of delegates representing twenty-four states came together there to remake the country's prisons. Rutherford B. Hayes, the Ohio governor who would soon be president, welcomed them: "Prison discipline ought to be placed upon the only solid and sure foundation—a foundation whose chief cornerstone is the golden rule: 'as ye would that men should do to you, do ye also to them likewise.'" The United States was only five years past the Civil War and the abolition of slavery. With the rise of industry and the arrival of large numbers of immigrants from Europe, cities in the North were booming—and so was poverty, inequality, and, therefore, crime. The Progressive Era embrace of science and technology as the means to modernize American institutions—everything from public education to housing, sanitation, food safety, and working conditions—was also being applied to punishment. The representatives of the National Prison Association shared the general opinion that prisons were necessary. (The Department of Justice was founded in 1870 as well.) But they felt just as certain that discipline in the United States had in many respects failed.

In early America, punishments were largely inflicted on the body of the offender and carried out as spectacle. Those deemed guilty of a punishable offense were placed in stocks or tied to whipping posts or branded or hanged from gallows. Enslaved people, considered property, were punished outside any system of justice as a way to reinforce the social order of chattel slavery and white supremacy. Crimes committed against enslaved people or Indigenous Americans—theft, rape, torture, murder—were not legally crimes. For white men who broke laws, other forms of punishment existed, including forced labor, the confiscation of property, and banishment from society. But the public rituals of revenge served a societal function. They were carried out not only to shame or harm offenders. They were directed as well at the onlookers who were to understand that whatever moral balance had been disturbed by a crime was now restored, any outrage done. The observers were made aware, too, that they better abide the laws or face a similar fate. By the 1800s, many of these punishments had come to seem medieval; they were uncivilized and inhumane. Their reform came in the construction, in the early nineteenth century, of the country's first penitentiaries. England had established its first "house of correction" three centuries earlier, a physical structure where petty criminals could be held for a time—and also put to work. In the United States, too, punishment would no longer be administered publicly; it wouldn't involve a display of physical suffering. It would occur now in private, behind prison walls, in cells. The punishment was the loss of one's liberty.

By 1870, it was clear that the reform the penitentiary provided in America was in need of a correction. Taking away a person's liberty was by itself supposed to be a big deal. We are a nation whose Declaration of Independence enshrines liberty as an inalienable right. But the horrid conditions of incarceration meant that people also suffered physically and mentally. As its name suggests, the penitentiary was intended to make its occupants reflect and feel penitent. Yet solitary confinement and imposed silence were forms of torture that drove people mad. New York's Sing Sing Prison, opened in 1826, popularized the brutality of marching men with their legs chained to one another in a shuffling lockstep. In the Southern states after emancipation, new "Black Codes" criminalized all sorts of behavior that was illegal only when committed while Black. Tens of thousands of freed Black people were being arrested on charges of vagrancy, idleness, gun possession, and "mischief," and interned to prison work camps. Incarceration rates in the South remained low relative to the North, since most forms of social control were built into the daily life of Jim Crow laws and the reality and terror of lynchings. But the racial demographics of who was locked up flipped. In 1865, the incarcerated population in the South was overwhelmingly white; by the end of the century, it was overwhelmingly Black. In the years and decades after emancipation, the practice of forced, unpaid prison labor became a new form of slavery. The Virginia Supreme Court made that equivalency explicit in law, ruling that an incarcerated Black person "is for the time being a slave of the State." Northern prisons also exploited the forced labor of incarcerated people, often in factories and industries built into the penitentiaries. The widespread practice of contracting out prison workers led to abuses and corruption. Northern prisons in the Progressive Era were still predominantly white, with immigrants from Europe and native whites making up the vast majority of admissions. Reforms were embraced without having to confront deeper racial prejudices. There existed in this moment, as the historian Khalil Gibran Muhammad notes in *The Condemnation of Blackness*, "a hopeful vision of white criminality."

The Progressive Era reformers viewed the carceral system through a scientific lens—crime was a disease, punishment was its cure. They saw that penitentiaries, as they existed, did little in the way of preparing those removed from free society for a successful reentry. That wasn't as it should be. "The supreme aim of prison discipline is the reformation of criminals, not the infliction of vindictive suffering," the National Prison Association asserted in its new "Declaration of Principles." Imprisonment was supposed to keep society safe by incapacitating the dangerous and deterring other would-be lawbreakers. The reformers in Cincinnati, though, believed that punishment should also minister to the imprisoned; by rehabilitating those who committed crimes, future crimes would be averted.

Possibly the most influential paper at the 1870 prison congress, "The Ideal of a True Prison System for a State," was delivered by the superintendent of Detroit's city jail, its house of correction, a forty-three-year-old named Zebulon Brockway. Brockway had worked in jails and penitentiaries his entire adult life, beginning as a twenty-one-year-old guard at the Connecticut state prison. He had considered the cases of many incarcerated men. He believed that individuals with free will "voluntarily elect and deliberately do wickedness," but he concluded that more often than not their circumstances had led them to commit crimes. They were usually young, ill-educated, indigent, poorly paid, foreign-born, or abusers of alcohol. The way to improve American prisons, Brockway proclaimed in Cincinnati, was to change how these people were sentenced.

It was an advance of Enlightenment thinking to conceive of a prison sentence as a unit of time. A judge considering a criminal act quantified the appropriate punishment in terms of days, months, years. The sentences were determinate, that is, their length and conditions were determined at trial. Brockway said that if the goal of punishment was preventing crime *and* reforming the incarcerated, then it defied reason to set a fixed date of release before someone even entered a prison. A judge or a prosecutor who predetermined the date at which a person would be rehabilitated made about as much sense as a doctor deciding on a surgery before examining a patient. "No man, be he judge, lawyer or layman, can determine beforehand the date when imprisonment shall work reformation in any case," Brockway declared. A prison term that was too short returned someone to full citizenship who remained a threat. A prison term too long meant the justice system lost its claim on being just, and those inside who were already "cured" became disenchanted and desperate. It would be better to have a mechanism in place to continually evaluate people in prison, to encourage their pro-social behavior. "The remedy cannot be had, the public sentiment toward the law cannot be changed, so long as a *determinate* sentence is imposed at the time of trial," Brockway said.

The logical solution, the just solution, according to Brockway, was the sort of indeterminate sentence imposed on Johnnie Veal and Michael Henderson a hundred years later. What Brockway proposed to the first congress of the National Prison Association was the modern system of parole. At trial, a judge could set a minimum and maximum range of imprisonment. But the actual date of release would be decided in the years ahead by a board—"guardians," Brockway dubbed them. A trial, he noted, was a moment of high emotion and prejudice, as people were still reacting to the crime. The guardians, however, could look beyond the crime, and with dispassion assess an individual's growth in the intervening years. Under this system, judges and prosecutors would lose some of their power to set the terms of a punishment. But discretionary parole would result in a more accurate determination of when someone had come to understand right from wrong, when they'd learned to overcome the disadvantages or compulsions that got them locked up in the first place.

Brockway proposed a points system in which an incarcerated person's good behavior would allow them to graduate to more favorable classifications, not unlike today's maximum-, medium-, and minimum-security prisons. There would be clear incentives for someone to behave and take classes and better themselves. Upon release, they would remain under some form of state supervision for a period of time. Ireland and one of the British penal colonies in Australia had implemented a similar "mark system," in which reaching various work requirements and levels of good conduct led to one's release. The conference in Cincinnati voted to adopt Brockway's proposal as one of the tenets of the modern prison system. "Sentences listed only by satisfactory proof of reformation should be substituted for those measured by a mere lapse of time."

Six years after the 1870 congress, the country's first prison "reformatory" opened in Elmira, New York, for males between the ages of six-

teen and thirty, and Brockway was hired to run it. In addition to basic
education, the Elmira Reformatory offered classes on morality, religion,
and philosophy. Those doing time there could learn trades, training to
make brushes or metal pots; they could work on a weekly prison newspaper. The men who behaved well earned merits and moved up to a
classification from which they could be released, while those deemed
crooked or quarrelsome were moved down. Once a board sent a person
home, he had to check in periodically with the equivalent of a parole
officer for another six months.

In little time, this model took off and was turned into law across the
land. The spread suggested both the logic and humanity of a prison system focused on second chances, on returning people to rightful citizenship who demonstrated positive change. In 1884, Ohio, the host of the
prison conference, became the first state to rewrite its sentencing laws
and establish a parole agency. By the turn of the century, half the states
had created a system of parole. The federal government established a
parole commission in 1910. By the 1920s, every state except Florida,
Mississippi, and Virginia was sending people to prison with indeterminate sentences.

In the years ahead, the National Prison Association changed its
name to the American Correctional Association. Penitentiaries and
prisons in each state were reclassified as "correctional" facilities. Guards
became "correctional officers." Philosophically, prisons were supposed
to do more than warehouse and punish people convicted of serious
crimes. A prison's mission was to correct them.

A SCENE FROM the movie *The Shawshank Redemption* begins with a
point-of-view shot looking out of a prison cell. The bars screech open
and clang, and the camera moves down a dark corridor until it reaches
a door. The door opens into a bright office and, inside, five figures are
sitting around a small work table. Four white men and a white woman
are each reading from thick stacks of papers. The camera turns around
to reveal the viewer: Ellis Boyd Redding, a Black man in his sixties
known in Shawshank Prison as Red. He wears a blue prison uniform
faded nearly to white, suspenders, and an inmate identification number

printed above his heart. Red is played by the stately actor Morgan Freeman, who in this scene looks like he superglued his lips shut so as not to
scream. It's 1967, and Red sits down before the parole board. Like Johnnie Veal, he's been in prison most of his adult life, and the parole board
has denied his release year after year. Red awaits the same perfunctory
questions that will lead, invariably, to the same rejection.

"Your files say you've served forty years of a life sentence. Do you feel
you've been rehabilitated?" a board member asks.

"Rehabilitated?" Red repeats the word as if about to spit out rotten
food. "Well, now, let me see. You know, I don't have any idea what that
means."

"Well, it means you're ready to rejoin society—"

Red cuts the younger man off, saying he knows what the board
thinks it means. At each previous parole hearing, he's come before the
board and shared his story of remorse and reform. The board members
either haven't believed him or haven't cared. Red is done with them.

"To me it's just a made-up word," he says. "A politician's word so that
young fellas like yourself can wear a suit and a tie and have a job. What
do you really want to know? Am I sorry for what I did?"

"Well, are you?"

"There's not a day goes by I don't feel regret. Not because I'm in here
or because you think I should." The shot zooms slowly in on Freeman's
face and the deep, heavy-lidded pools of his eyes. "I look back on the
way I was then. A young, stupid kid who committed that terrible crime.
I want to talk to him. I want to try to talk some sense to him. Tell him
the way things are. But I can't. That kid's long gone. And this old man is
all that's left. I got to live with that."

The camera reverses to show the face of the board member, who is
listening, really listening, and then returns to Red.

"*Rehabilitated?*" Red continues, his anger rising. "It's just a bullshit
word. So you go on and stamp your form, sonny, and stop wasting my
time. Because to tell you the truth . . . I don't give a shit."

The room falls silent, so quiet that the sound of notes being written
by hand becomes audible. And then the screen fills with a hand pressing
a stamp into an ancient mugshot of a twenty-year-old Ellis Boyd Redding, inking the word "APPROVED."

The Shawshank Redemption is a beloved film, frequently topping lists of all-time favorites. Set almost entirely in a prison, it's a compelling portrait of human dignity and what amounts to perseverance. For many people, the film is also what comes to mind when, or if, they think about parole. Part of the movie's enduring appeal, though, may be that it's careful not to demand more from its viewers. The film was released in September 1994. That same month, the largest and most draconian crime bill in United States history was signed into law. The film offers no commentary on the present conditions of U.S. prisons. There's no questioning the country's embrace of long-term incarceration. The movie's plot takes place between 1947 and 1967, and even the pointlessness of locking up a person like Red well into old age is relegated to some notion of the unenlightened past before the civil rights movement. The cruelty and indifference, they were *from back then, when we didn't know better.*

From 1970 to 1980, however, the number of people in state and federal prisons in the country doubled from 200,000 to nearly 400,000, an unprecedented growth. Then, over the next decade, the number doubled *again.* The year *Shawshank* hit theaters, the prison population topped a million for the first time ever, a fivefold increase from *back then.* And public officials were clamoring for more. The numbers peaked in 2009 at 1.6 million, a 700 percent climb from the 1970s, with another 770,000 confined in local jails. In the country's history, there was nothing like it. Worldwide, there was no equivalent. The 1994 Violent Crime Control and Law Enforcement Act, supported by politicians from both parties, treated real-life Reds who were convicted of violent offenses as if they were existential threats to the country, as if they were beyond the "redemption" of the movie's title. The new law funneled billions of dollars to local law enforcement for tougher policing and imposed longer and more certain prison sentences; it also excluded anyone in federal or state prisons from receiving the federal Pell Grants that are used to pursue higher education. In the years before the bill, there were 350 college-degree programs in prisons across the country; several years after the law, there were just eight. The crime bill treated "rehabilitation" like it was a bullshit word.

In 1983, Michael Henderson had served far less time than the fictional Red. Similar to the movie, the members of the parole board asked Michael about his rehabilitation. They assessed his years of captivity and his merits and demerits during that time. Michael had not been idle. "Considering the length of Mr. Henderson's sentence," the prison wrote in a memo to the parole board that year, "his overall adjustment has been stable, while the resident is generally cooperative with staff." The board members recognized that Michael was a teenager at the time of his crime. And they couldn't help themselves—they found him engaging. The officials commended him for his candor, but they also had to consider the victim, Richard Schaeffer's grieving survivors, and the balance of a moral ledger, one that matched punishment to offense. These calculations were as monumental as they were intuitive. They were also susceptible to politics and subjective views on public safety. Were the board members able to identify with the parole candidate? Was crime, in general, up or down and how was the public reacting to it? Did the people harmed by a crime or their family members protest release or show up at the hearing? Any of those external factors could determine whether a person went free. At Michael's hearing, the board members decided that his punishment was not yet equal to his crime.

"Your parole is denied at this time," the board ruled, slipping into passive voice.

The board wanted to encourage Michael. They couldn't say how much more time in prison would be enough. But he'd have another shot at parole in twelve months, and he'd have periodic reviews after that. The three board members instructed Michael to attend Alcoholics Anonymous. As Brockway might have put it, they told him to continue bettering himself. He needed to mind the rules and avoid disciplinary infractions. Michael had been locked up long enough to know that he'd catch tickets regardless of his behavior. Some rules in prison were impossible to follow when you needed to eat or avoid danger, and some guards meted out punishments because they could. But Michael was nonetheless heartened.

"It gave me an incentive to correct myself," he said.

2

Indeterminate Sentence

O fficer Edward Poppish, Chicago Police Department, Eleventh District, and I'm here to oppose the release of Johnnie Veal."

"Officer Olsen, Chicago Police Department, Tenth District, here to oppose the parole of Johnnie Veal."

At the start of Johnnie's parole hearing in Springfield, the members of the Illinois Prisoner Review Board watched as some twenty-five police officers stood, one after another, to introduce themselves. In uniforms, service revolvers on their hips, a sea of blue.

"Officer Carlos Santiago, Chicago Police Department, here to oppose the release of Johnnie Veal."

It was March 2018, just after nine in the morning. The officers had bused down from Chicago, a three-hour drive. Few of them were alive in 1970 when the two policemen were gunned down at Cabrini-Green. But they'd heard about Sgt. James Severin and Officer Anthony Rizzato from older colleagues, on police message boards, or in news reports about the cop killer's most recent bid for release. Some had seen the memorial to the two slain men inside the Eighteenth District police station. But the lack of familiarity with the case was also the point of their presence. They were the embodiment of the police creed that a fallen officer is *never* forgotten. They needed to show the members of the parole board that there was no expiration date on honoring officers killed in the line of duty.

By the sleepy standards of the parole board, the crowd at the public hearing was enormous, and the proceedings had to be moved a few blocks from the board's cramped offices to the Illinois State Library. Johnnie had secured a pro bono lawyer, a Chicago civil rights and criminal defense attorney named Sara Garber. She was there and introduced herself. As did a professor who taught Johnnie in a class at the prison, and several others who championed his release. But those in opposition to parole dwarfed the supporters. Along with the Chicago Police officers, there were two state legislators, officials from the Fraternal Order of Police and the Police Memorial Foundation, veterans of the Chicago Police Department ("I was a survivor of the day that Johnnie Veal killed Severin and Rizzato"), and one of James Severin's nieces, now in her sixties herself, who said her family had never missed a parole hearing in thirty-five years and would continue showing up generation after generation until both Johnnie and his codefendant died in prison.

The twelve members of the parole board present that morning were a motley group. Aurthur Mae Perkins, from Peoria, earned her GED at the age of thirty-eight, followed quickly by her bachelor's and master's, and became one of the longest-tenured principals in the city's public schools—a street would be named in her honor. Pete Fisher, a former police chief in central Illinois, was one of four people on the board who'd worked in law enforcement. According to a report by the nonprofit media outlet Injustice Watch, Fisher had voted against parole 160 times, and for release only once, and that for a man whose maximum sentence was soon expiring no matter what. By law, the parole board included roughly the same number of registered Republicans and Democrats, and the board was racially diverse as well. Kenneth Tupy, one of three former prosecutors on the board, had a bushy white goatee and was a member of the Knights of Columbus, the Benevolent and Protective Order of Elks, and the Noon Lions Club. Virginia Martinez was from a mostly Mexican and Mexican American neighborhood in Chicago; in 1975, when she and a friend passed the bar, they became the first two licensed Latina attorneys in Illinois history. Board members came from all over a state that stretched from the Great Lakes nearly to Tennessee. Each time a former high school guidance counselor named Wayne Dunn opened his mouth, his drawl and twang were a lesson on just how much southern Illinois was *the* South. The governor appointed the members to six-year renewable terms, with the state senate voting to confirm the appointments. In some states, serving on the parole board was a part-time job. It was full-time in Illinois, and board members earned $89,443 a year.

The United States has fifty-one separate criminal justice systems, and parole proceedings differ in each state as well as federally. In California, pairs of commissioners conduct hearings inside the prisons, interviewing parole applicants and listening to protests before making a ruling. In Georgia and Texas, investigators alone venture inside the prisons to talk with candidates, and they later give an account of the interviews to the voting members of the parole board. In New York, even before Covid, those up for parole testify via videoconference, sitting alone in a designated room in the prison as they speak to a TV screen. Illinois, which restricts parole eligibility to a small portion of its prison population, stopped holding full hearings inside prisons in the early 1980s. Since then, only one board member goes into the prison to interview an applicant. That person then reports back to the rest of the board during a monthly public hearing in Springfield, sharing firsthand impressions of the petitioner and a recommendation on parole suitability. The board member who interviewed Johnnie this time was a former prosecutor and Republican state legislator named Tom Johnson.

When they'd met at the prison a few weeks earlier, Johnnie described to Johnson a curriculum he was developing with a nearby college. It was for people like him who were growing old behind bars and who'd missed the lives, and deaths, of many of their loved ones on the outside. Johnnie said longtimers needed a forum to work through their grief and shame. They needed help to keep from going on a rampage or giving up. "How do you do a bit when you're traumatized, raped, beat down, when you lose your mother and sister, when you're under stress of the Department of Corrections?" Johnnie called the initiative Project Sound Off. "People expressing themselves, or *sounding off*, on all the things that affect your life just sitting in a cell," he said. For those serving long prison terms, the lucky among them might leave prison at the age of fifty or sixty or seventy. Sound Off was intended to prepare them for the distinct challenges of reentry in older age. But the rest of them had to face the grim reality that they'd likely die behind the prison walls. Johnnie tried to convince men at the prison—as well as himself—that a slow death in a cell didn't mean their lives lacked meaning and dignity. "The life I lived inside has value," Johnnie would say. In Sound Off, they put together their own legacies, something they could pass on. They assembled picture albums and packets of their certificates and academic achievements. They composed short autobiographies, commemorating major events and milestones in their lives that might otherwise go unnoted. They prepared their last wills and testaments. They indicated where they wanted their belongings sent, and what they wanted done with their bodies.

Johnnie went before the parole board for the first time in 1980, a couple of years before Michael Henderson. In 2018, Johnnie needed the support of seven of the twelve members of the Illinois Prisoner Review Board, a majority, to leave prison. In his eighteen previous parole attempts, he'd never received a single vote in favor of his release. Not one. Garber joked with Johnnie that his chances might improve if in his sixties he looked less muscular and spry. His neat goatee was speckled with gray, his middle had thickened, but Johnnie still played double-headers in the prison's softball league against men a third his age.

At the parole hearing in Springfield, Johnson related his findings to his colleagues. "Mr. Veal appeared to be in good health, was fully engaged, and very articulate," he said. Johnson was charged with retelling the story of Johnnie's crime, an account based on the statement of facts that police and prosecutors assembled for trial. "These two men, the evidence showed, were lying in wait with .30-30 rifles to assassinate the walk-and-talk officers." Johnson said the murders were "an outrage against society." The other board members listened intently, jotting notes or checking documents. They'd have an opportunity to ask questions and deliberate before voting for or against parole.

Johnson went on to enumerate Johnnie's many accomplishments. In prison, he'd earned twenty-five certificates—as a paralegal, in computer coding, in business management. He was accredited as a tutor. He was a skilled flautist and guitarist, and he recently defended a female staff member from another incarcerated man, a guy in his thirties who, a report noted, broke Johnnie's jaw. Johnnie believed people were fundamentally good, that "it's their experiences, a trigger, that makes them turn left rather than go right." He'd shrug off this fight as part of life: "He advanced toward her, and I stepped between them . . . and, you know, I did what I had to do, and it wasn't no big deal, a scuffle's a scuffle."

Johnson recognized that Johnnie had achieved what he had in prison despite the dangers and uncertainties, the lack of programming, the unhealthy food, the inadequate medical care, the isolation, and the repeated parole rejections.

"In my interview with Mr. Veal and my review of the entire record here," the board member said, "Mr. Veal is certainly a very, very different person today than he was at age seventeen."

Johnnie's transformation, while dramatic, was not uncommon. The age distribution for crime is something that criminologists across the political spectrum agree on as fact. The Bureau of Justice Statistics and countless studies show that arrest rates for violent and nonviolent offenses peak when people are in their late teens and early twenties. From there, criminal behavior drops steadily. Nine in ten homicides are committed by those under thirty-five. Among the prison population as a whole, about a third of the people who leave are arrested again within the first six months of their release, and within three years around 40 percent are returned to prison. But the arrest rate for anyone over fifty is small, less than 2 percent. And for people Johnnie's age, sixty-five or older, it is near zero.

The truth is that the United States could let out nearly everyone in prison over fifty-five and see very little statistical change in crime. Yet the country is doing the exact opposite. The number of older people in state and federal prisons is increasing faster than any other age group. How could anyone claim that the point of incarceration was to incapacitate the truly dangerous when there are more people older than fifty-five in U.S. prisons (165,000) than there are people in the high-crime range of eighteen to twenty-four? Many of these older prisoners were convicted of violent crimes when they were young, and they are now serving extremely long sentences or life without parole. Geriatric health care in prison is both disgraceful and expensive. It costs, on average, three times more to incarcerate an older person than a younger one.

With over two dozen uniformed police officers and the relatives of

the murdered cops staring at him, Johnson admitted that he was struggling with his vote. He had on the one hand the assassination of two
police officers in 1970, and on the other the extent to which Johnnie
had changed during his half century of incarceration. He wasn't sure
whether the scales had tipped toward mercy.

In Illinois, the parole board is guided in part by the state constitution, which affirms that the purpose of incarceration is "restoring the
offender to useful citizenship." The board, therefore, is in the business
of corrections. State law also instructs board members to deny parole
to anyone who still appears to be a danger and unable to abide by the
lawful conditions of his or her release. They should vote against a candidate's freedom as well, the law says, if "release at that time would
deprecate the seriousness of his or her offense or promote disrespect
for the law." Most states use variations of the same language. But it is
a paradoxical loophole. Crimes don't become less serious over time. A
murder remains a murder, and an offense by its very definition always
disrespects the law.

Johnson mused aloud whether it was time to parole Johnnie. He
said, "If somebody is going to serve that forty-seven or fifty years, I
believe that the public would certainly understand that that's a lifetime
for most people."

Johnson, who was seven years older than Johnnie, would be dead
in nine months, from cancer. His obituary in the *Chicago Tribune*, in
December 2018, began by noting how he had "evolved from an assistant
county prosecutor to a backer of what's now known as criminal justice
reform, frequently questioning the moral and monetary costs of imprisonment while advocating rehabilitation over incarceration." In 2011, he
was one of four Republicans in the state senate to vote with Democrats
to abolish the death penalty in Illinois. At the parole hearing in 2018, he
pointed out that Johnnie was convicted on the theory of accountability,
for planning and assisting with the crime, not for pulling the trigger.

"He was seventeen. At the time, he had a ninth-grade education, was
involved with gangs. He's remorseful to the extent of understanding the
grief that was caused by the incident." Johnson said Johnnie was not a
danger to others. By any actuarial measure, and based on his conduct
over the past twenty years, Johnnie posed no threat to re-offend.

"Would it bring disrespect to the law?" Johnson questioned. "I struggle with that. Everybody can have different views with that."

Garber, sitting in the audience, wondered for the first time if Johnnie might have a shot at making parole.

JOHNNIE WAS NOT at his parole hearing that morning. He was at Hill Correctional Center, about a hundred miles away in western Illinois. He wasn't nervous. Johnnie didn't get nervous. But he hated feeling powerless as his future was being decided. He could do nothing to affect the outcome. "I'm not in a position to drive," as he put it.

Johnnie dealt with these concerns, as he did with most things, by staying in constant motion. He taught a morning health class to other guys at the prison on hepatitis and HIV. He worked a shift in the laundry. When he first met Sara Garber at Hill a few months earlier, in the tiny room reserved for attorney visits, he flooded her with documents, his bounty of degrees and certificates. Before she even sat down, he was passing her the legal briefs he'd composed in his cell on an ancient Brother typewriter. He explained to Garber that he mentored, tutored, organized activities. "My accomplishments are greater than the average man's," Johnnie would say. He hoped there was a chance this year that the parole board might judge him on his time served and rehabilitation. "They made me the supervillain. I'm not Dracula. I'm not the boogeyman." But the morning of his parole hearing, he refused to dwell on any of that.

When Johnnie first entered prison, in 1972, he was nineteen and had spent the previous eighteen months leading up to his conviction in the Cook County jail. He was, according to his processing papers, five foot ten and 161 pounds. The uniform he'd been issued hung loosely on his teenage frame. He was in a maximum-security prison called Stateville, and Johnnie found himself staring up at a galaxy of cages. The cells were stacked five stories high; each tier stretched longer than a city block. The cages were also at that moment all open. Roaming about in the adult prison were grown men. A number of them now circled Johnnie and the other new arrivals, looking them over as if shopping for items they'd be back to purchase later. "Fresh fish!" men whooped.

Johnnie once saw a documentary about a sardine run. Sardines spawned in the cool waters off Africa and then migrated in enormous shoals that darkened the ocean with their numbers. The sardines, on their journey, were an invitation to predators. The tiny fish were set upon by sharks and humpback whales, by dolphins and seals, by game fish and dive-bombing birds. The feeding frenzy created its own violent churn. In Stateville, Johnnie feared he was the sardine.

Johnnie and the other newbies were still being window-shopped when a commotion drew everyone's attention to an upper tier. Two men in their prison blues were fighting. A guard rushed over to break it up. The fighters turned on the officer. Johnnie watched as the inmates tried to wrestle the guard over the railing to drop him five stories to his death. Other guards raced up the stairwells, waving clubs and hollering. Suddenly Johnnie's throat clenched as he breathed in fire. He'd swallowed the pungent mace that was filling the cellblock. An officer hovering overhead on a catwalk locked and loaded a rifle. Johnnie felt in his spine the echo of the metal engaging, the clicking and cocking. Then the thunder of a warning shot filled the cell house. Johnnie dropped like a stone.

That was day one. Johnnie thought, even at nineteen, that he'd seen everything growing up in Chicago public housing. In the weeks that followed, he witnessed brutality with a casualness and regularity that shocked him: Walking to the workshops, a man stabbed. On the yard, the weight bar used to crush the windpipe of a guy on the bench press. A man struck in the head with a metal pipe and reaching instinctively to hold in his brain matter. There was some version of prison that existed on paper in which Johnnie was supposed to use his punishment to reflect and reform. He was in a "correctional facility," after all. But rather than being reformatories, American prisons are criminogenic: they cause criminal behavior. Johnnie had more imminent concerns than building a résumé to present at a parole hearing in ten years. He focused narrowly on the choices he faced in prison, which as he saw them then were really only two—survival or annihilation.

Johnnie survived. He'd received hundreds of disciplinary tickets during his first decades of incarceration. He spent years in segregation. But in 2018, his petition to the parole board exhibited how much he'd transformed. "He have advised me to get my GED and give up some of my bad habits and make a 180° for the good," a man locked up at Hill with Johnnie wrote in one of many glowing testimonials. Another, from a young man who was being preyed upon sexually by a fellow inmate: "I felt it wasn't no one else I could have turned to. As my mentor Mr. Veal had took on my problems as his own and went to go talk with this individual." That individual, it turned out, didn't appreciate the talking-to. Later that night, during chow, the guy charged into Johnnie's cell, attacking him. For defending himself, against a man twenty years his junior, Johnnie earned a disciplinary ticket—it was one of only three violations in the nine years prior to the 2018 hearing.

Garber wanted to emphasize to the board that this ticket, rather than a mar on Johnnie's record, revealed the exceptional content of his character. He risked his own well-being to protect the vulnerable. Johnnie downplayed it to her, though. A lifetime behind bars had taught him to be cagey. Once something was said out loud in prison, you no longer controlled it, the words could travel and be used against you. When pressed to speak about himself, Johnnie's default was to deflect, to explicate impersonally, to analogize as if teaching from some jailhouse *The Art of War*. "How can I say this?" he said of the different ways he'd plotted to foil prison rapists. "I got cattle on my ranch. If your cattle get mixed up with my cattle, they still my cattle. If I take them by force, now I got to fight you and everyone else on the ranch. I'm risking the chance of an ongoing battle. That's all it is—gauge your wars. Fight the good fight."

Around lunchtime, when the parole hearing in Springfield had certainly ended but Johnnie had yet to get word, he went to play music. His band, Concrete and Steel, got practice time once a week, and he wasn't going to miss it to sit in his cell and stare at the wall. Before prison, Johnnie hadn't touched an instrument, but he took a class inside with a jazz trumpeter who came in as a volunteer. The musician started Johnnie and the other men on an African thumb piano, a kalimba. He showed them an eighteen-stringed sitar, and what seemed like every other instrument known to humanity. Johnnie got good on the saxophone and flute. He was a natural. Things came easily to him. As a boy, he ran track competitively, mastered karate, tae kwon do, Ping-Pong, and really everything he picked up. His current prison didn't allow wind instruments, supposedly for health reasons, so Johnnie played the guitar and bass. He worked with the program officer at Hill to organize concerts for Christmas and Black History Month. The force of Johnnie's determination drew people into his orbit. He had a glinty stare that remained imposing even as he smiled. His silences seemed charged with planning. He was not a follower, and he moved through the prison hunch-shouldered with the single-minded purpose of a boulder. Each year at Hill, Johnnie helped pull together a battle of the bands. He played for the prison population at graduations and holidays. Garber shared with the parole board a letter of appreciation given to Johnnie by the warden: "Thank you for everything you do as an inmate mentor. You have single-handedly helped to change the mindset, attitude and lives of other offenders."

The summer Johnnie was sixteen, in 1969, he traveled with his family to the farm in Mississippi where his mother grew up. His girlfriend, Leora, came along, and so did their newborn, a girl they named Lawanda. Their home on Chicago's Near North Side, Cabrini-Green, was a massive public housing development, with upward of fifteen thousand mostly Black people balled together in a fist of twenty-three towers. The entire complex, 3,600 homes, covered fewer than five city blocks in each direction, a mere seventy acres. The property in Mississippi wasn't that much smaller, and it was for only their one family. The land contained forty or fifty peach trees, fields of blackberries, butter beans, and peas. The city kids picked the crops as if for sport. Holding her granddaughter that summer, Johnnie's mother announced that the girl's fair skin was the same color as the peaches, and from then on that's what everyone called her. Peaches.

Johnnie caught his case the summer after that Mississippi trip. On July 17, 1970, a Chicago police sergeant named James Severin went to check out a report of gunfire coming from one of the Cabrini-Green high-rises. Severin was thirty-eight, a thirteen-year veteran of the force. He had worked the security detail protecting Martin Luther King Jr., in 1966, when the civil rights leader turned his attention from voter suppression in the South to racist real estate practices in the North. King had found more than enough to protest in Chicago. Residents of one

Chicago suburb responded to marchers with shouts of "white power," Nazi flags, bricks, and bottles. Severin now led a goodwill community-relations unit of eight officers at Cabrini-Green. They walked the neighborhood and tried to make themselves available to the people who lived in the housing development.

It was seven at night that July, an hour before the end of Severin's shift, and he took one of his patrolmen with him to investigate the shots fired. Officer Anthony Rizzato had joined the Chicago Police Department four years earlier, signing up along with his twin brother. Severin and Rizzato entered a park surrounded by towers. They crossed a baseball diamond. A woman in front of one of the buildings waved to Severin, and he waved back.

At the crack of the first rifle shot, Severin clutched his chest. A hole appeared there, the size of a baseball. He toppled forward. Rizzato, ten feet behind him, turned to help, or maybe tried to run for cover. He didn't get far. Another shot spun the younger officer around, a complete about-face. He took two or three more steps, and then fell. The coroner who examined the bodies that night reported that each man's service revolver remained holstered. "They didn't know what hit them," he said.

Johnnie was seventeen that summer. Along with other teenagers in his high-rise, he had joined the Cobra Stones, an affiliate of the Black P. Stone Nation, then Chicago's most powerful Black gang. He and another Cabrini-Green resident, twenty-three-year-old George Knights, who was known by his middle name, Clifford, were charged with the ambush and execution.

"Can you conceive of a worse, a more heinous crime?" a prosecutor asked at trial, underscoring the point that the slain policemen were there to help the community. "We talk about retribution. It's a high-sounding word for punishment, to fit the crime. You do an act, you deserve a punishment. Your child goes into the sugar jar, you slap her hand. You kill a couple of innocent human beings, you deserve what our law, the law of Illinois, says is a proper punishment, and that happens to be death."

Johnnie and his codefendant escaped lethal injection, but barely. They were each sentenced to indeterminate prison terms of 100 to 199 years.

Throughout Johnnie's trial and decades of incarceration, he maintained that his was a case that caught him. He insisted that he didn't shoot the two officers. He didn't deny being in the Cobra Stones, nor firing guns across a narrow strip of blacktop at other boys from Cabrini-Green who fired back at him. The kids in the high-rises facing Johnnie's had joined gangs of their own. Johnnie had played games against them growing up; he could pick them out of a crowd by their batting stances or their gait as they sprinted to catch a football. By their late teens, however, these boys were attempting to kill one another nearly every day. "We were ghetto thugs trying to survive, fighting other ghetto kids," Johnnie would say. Yet he insisted he had nothing to do with the murders of Severin and Rizzato. "The police weren't even on my radar."

As Johnnie waited for his lawyer to call with news from Springfield, he took advantage of an opportunity to venture from his cell, to "play on the streets," as he called it. He made his way to a bank of phones and dialed Darlene Holmes. Johnnie found a way to call her three times a day—before she left for work in the morning, during her lunch break, and before she went to bed at night. He bartered for other people's phone time when he exhausted his own. Darlene had also grown up in Cabrini-Green, in a neighboring high-rise, and she and Johnnie had been sweethearts as children back in the 1960s. She'd married a Cook County sheriff and raised a family. After her husband died, she moved to a small city in western Kansas, where she worked as a fitness specialist for cancer patients. She and Johnnie never fell out of touch. They wrote letters and phoned. Around the time they turned sixty, in the 2010s, they decided to get serious. They weren't getting any younger, Johnnie teased. She started to take the train in from Kansas, using her vacation time so she could stay an entire week. They'd sit in the visiting room and talk for hours. Darlene was a health nut, but Johnnie's vice was junk food, and he'd devour candy bars from the vending machines as they laughed about the past. They were permitted to hold hands and even kiss. On the day of Johnnie's hearing, they talked on the phone about the life they would lead if he somehow made parole. She was thinking about retiring from her job, and they used their minutes to imagine whether they'd live in Kansas or move elsewhere. "I'm an Illinois boy," Johnnie said. They joked about how boring their days together would be—she liked to go to bed early; he might sneak out for ice cream—and how that's what made it so appealing.

WHEN MICHAEL AND JOHNNIE were starting their long, indeterminate sentences, the United States had been at war with itself for more than a decade. Public figures assassinated, cities consumed by riots. Revolts against the daily tyrannies of the racial and social order, against the Vietnam War, against police brutality and practices that funneled minorities into the criminal justice system. Johnnie was fifteen in 1968, when Martin Luther King was assassinated in Memphis. Cabrini-Green, like other Black neighborhoods in Chicago and in cities across the country, erupted in rage and destruction. Military jeeps circled the development as guys in the high-rises took potshots at targets below. Johnnie ran the streets with other kids, taking a pair of shoes from a local business. Chicago's mayor at the time, Richard J. Daley, ordered police "to shoot to kill any arsonists," "to shoot to maim or cripple anyone looting any stores." By 1970, the pitched battles on American streets had jumped the prison walls. Prisons and jails had also become hotbeds of protest.

From 1970 through 1972, the country experienced more than a hundred separate prison uprisings. In the fall of 1970, for instance, those locked up at Northern California's Folsom State Prison went on strike for nineteen straight days; nearly all of the 2,400 men incarcerated there refused to work or participate in activities in protest of the conditions at the facility. Two hundred miles south, in California's Soledad Prison, an expert marksman in a guard tower broke up an altercation between white and Black inmates by shooting only the Black men, and a group at the prison went on a hunger strike to demand a fair investigation. When the guard was exonerated, a riot broke out at the prison and in the melee a correctional officer was killed. Soledad pinned the death, falsely, on three of the prison's most vocal Black protestors, including an activist named George Jackson. The case of the "Soledad Brothers" became a lightning rod for a growing movement that linked the rights of people in prison to the fights against the country's racial caste system and stark historical divides. Angela Davis, a philosophy professor and prisoner activist, emerged as one of the leaders—and symbols—of the Soledad Brothers Defense Committee. "During all of the rebellions across the country, the prisoners have indicated that their oppression is not simply a matter of overcrowded prisons, filthy conditions and guard brutality," Davis wrote in a book she managed to cocdit from inside a women's detention center, after her own arrest for purchasing guns used in a courtroom takeover to try to free the Soledad Brothers. "It is centered in the institutionalized racism and class discrimination of the judicial system itself."

The largest of the prison uprisings occurred at Attica, a New York State penitentiary thirty miles outside Buffalo. On September 9, 1971, more than half of the 2,200 men held at the prison gained control of the facility, taking dozens of staff hostage in the process. The protestors delivered a list of ultimatums—*The Attica Liberation Faction Manifesto of Demands*—which was modeled after a document crafted by the strikers at Folsom the previous year. The majority of the men imprisoned at Attica were Black and Latino; all of the guards in the western New York facility were white. Over four tense days of negotiations, the men inside the prison met with lawyers and shared their stories with the media, and the public became increasingly aware of their cause. "We are men, we are not beasts," one of the leaders of the uprising announced, reading from a prepared declaration. All the while, the number of law enforcement officers congregating outside the prison grew, many of them carrying their personal firearms and itching to use them. New York governor Nelson Rockefeller refused to meet with the men inside Attica. Then on September 13, 1971, Rockefeller ordered that Attica be retaken by force. More than five hundred New York State police, joined by sheriff's deputies, state park police, and corrections officers, stormed the prison. Many officers had removed their name tags and other identifying information. None of the incarcerated men had a firearm. But the officers reported later that as they entered the prison yard they saw inmates attacking the hostages, slitting the throats of the captured guards and even castrating them. The officers said they were forced to fire their weapons in desperation to save hostages and to defend themselves.

An official narrative of the prisoners as homicidal brutes took hold. The words of a state trooper who helped recapture the prison became a New York *Daily News* headline: "I Saw Seven Throats Cut." Governor

Rockefeller's account of "cold-blooded killings by revolutionary militants" was repeated by other news outlets. The *New York Times* reported the next day, "The deaths of these persons by knives and gunfire reflect a barbarism wholly alien to civilized society." The officers' version of events, given credence by the media, was a total fabrication. No throats of hostages were cut, as autopsy reports later showed. Troopers went in guns blazing, firing rifles and spraying shotgun blast into clouds of tear gas for minutes on end. They shot guards as well as prisoners, the latter, in some instances, in the back, in the head, or multiple times at point-blank range. All the while, "You will not be harmed" blared over loudspeakers. More than a hundred people inside the prison were shot. Thirty-nine people were killed, including ten staff members, all of them by officers during the takeover. The imprisoned men who survived the raid were tortured by vengeful state troopers, prison guards, and even medical staff. The New York commission appointed to uncover the truth of what happened at Attica wrote, "With the exception of Indian massacres in the late-nineteenth century, the State Police assault which ended the four-day prison uprising was the bloodiest one-day encounter between Americans since the Civil War."

Johnnie was not politicized by the atrocities at Attica or by other high-profile prison uprisings. "I didn't know what civil rights was, let alone the Bill of Rights or the Constitution," he would recall. "I still didn't have a political bone. I was dumb as a box of rocks."

But much of the rest of the country began to pay attention to this burgeoning prisoner rights movement. So what did the movement want? Legal representation for people in prison and adequate medical care. The right to organize and protest without retaliation. Minimum wage for their labor inside prison. An end to solitary confinement. The ability to visit with loved ones. But among the chief demands was also getting rid of parole. When thousands went on strike at Folsom, they insisted in their manifesto "an end to indeterminate sentences whereby a man can be warehoused indefinitely, rehabilitated or not." At California's San Quentin, the prison newspaper *The Outlaw* wrote that doing away with indeterminate sentencing was "more paramount than any facet of reform in relation to the penal system." The newspaper called indeterminate sentences "Death Time," lobbying for a return to fixed terms. "If a man or woman has a flat three years to do, and knows that most other people who committed the same act are looking at the same three years, it is possible to kick back, think it over, get what you can from what's there, and make plans for getting out." Those awaiting the end of their prison terms through parole found themselves at the mercy of parole board members who could be racist, corrupt, lazy. The finish line of a sentence could be moved again and again as a way to discriminate against or punish racial minorities, political activists, women, or anyone deemed different or unsavory. The protestors at Attica wrote in their list of demands, "In a world where many crimes are punished by indeterminate sentences and where authority acts within secrecy and within vast discretion and given heavy weight to accusations by prison employees against inmates, inmates feel trapped unless they are willing to abandon their desire to be independent men."

Taking their cues from people inside prison, many on the outside started to look more closely at parole as it was practiced in the country. They found it oppressive and unfair. The American Friends Service Committee, a Quaker organization that had long been involved in anti-racist and civil rights work, published a book in 1971 based on hundreds of interviews with incarcerated people. *Struggle for Justice: A Report on Crime and Punishment in America* concluded that parole eligibility was used to keep "the powerless in line" and likened the uncertainties of the parole system to a form of torture. The New York State Special Commission on Attica called parole hearings and indeterminate sentences "by far the greatest cause of prisoner anxiety and frustration." How could people in prison trust a criminal justice system to rule on their release if that system abused them, deprived them, and then lied about it to the public? The revelations about Attica led to the formation in New York of the Citizens' Inquiry on Parole and Criminal Justice, chaired by prominent concerned citizens, among them Ramsey Clark—who led the Department of Justice under President Lyndon Johnson—the documentary filmmaker Frederick Wiseman, the playwright Arthur Miller, and Coretta Scott King. The group observed parole hearings in the state and interviewed both candidates coming up for parole and commissioners making the decisions. "The parole system has virtually no rules, standards, or mechanisms to ensure consistency and fairness," the inquiry wrote in its book-length re-port, *Prison Without Walls*, published in 1975. "The criteria used by the parole board are numerous, ambiguous, inconsistent in purpose, and, in some cases, illegal." The group determined that the parole system, as practiced in New York State at least, was "beyond reform" and "should therefore be abolished."

Many judicial scholars joined the denunciations. With indetermi-nate sentencing, parole board members decided the actual end date of a prison term. Judges had adapted to this loss of power by issuing ever-longer prison terms, like the 100 to 199 years given to Johnnie. "Buck Rogers time," people in prison called these sentences, referring to the old science fiction comic strip set in the twenty-fifth century. Judges wanted to send a message that they thought a crime was serious, but these fantastical ranges became meaningless—and highly misleading. They gave the illusion of life sentences. The public was never going to understand how a person given an indeterminate sentence of two hun-dred years could be paroled in twenty. Crime victims felt cheated. The system seemed unjust, and ungoverned.

"There is an excess of discretion given to officials whose entitlement to such power is established by neither professional credentials nor performance," Marvin Frankel, a prominent judge and pioneering le-gal scholar, wrote of parole boards in 1972. Compared to courtrooms, parole hearings operated in secrecy and without formal checks. There was nothing like judicial review to reconsider a parole determination. And as far as a candidate's worthiness to go free, it wasn't clear what parole boards measured, or how these decisions were reached, or that board members could be trusted with this awesome power. The offi-cials on parole boards weren't professionals with years of training in the law. They weren't required to have specialties in psychology or behav-ioral science. Parole boards based their profound decisions on periodic interviews with incarcerated individuals and were supposed to assess someone's crime, time in prison, and the complexities of their emo-tional and psychological development in meetings that lasted, in many instances, all of a few minutes. As political appointees, moreover, they might be disinclined to make unpopular rulings, since the blowback could cost them their jobs. The legal expert Kenneth Culp Davis wrote in 1973, "If a board member is in such a hurry to get to his golf game that he votes in sixteen cases without looking inside the files, no one under the board's system can ever know the difference, even though the personal liberty of sixteen men may be at stake. How could a board member have less incentive to avoid prejudice when his decision can never be reviewed?" Frankel said that indeterminacy in sentencing had become lawless—"a wasteland in the law."

A century earlier, also at a moment of national reckoning on human rights, Zebulon Brockway had introduced the "ideal" of indeterminate sentencing as a way to make the country's prisons more modern and just. Yet even during Brockway's tenure at Elmira, his reformatory was investigated for "cruel, brutal, excessive, degrading and unusual punishments"—for placing men there in solitary, for shackling them to doors, and for disciplining them with a leather whip called a "prison strap." Over the next hundred years, conditions in American prisons remained oppressive. "Prison 'time' does not rehabilitate. On the contrary, it corrodes," *The Outlaw* editorialized in the 1960s. "Correctional officers" weren't trained to "correct" people, to prepare their charges for reentry through counseling or therapy. They were there only to guard and police. Culturally, rehabilitation in the country's prisons was never really attempted. Nor had states invested adequately in psychiatrists to do diagnostic work, caseworkers to monitor progress, or actual teachers and classes for the incarcerated to achieve or demonstrate their emotional and social advancement.

Brockway and other Progressive Era reformers believed that prisons could best serve society by turning lawbreakers into law abiders, by treating incarcerated people with education, training, and counseling. Rehabilitation meant preparing individuals in prison for a safe return to full citizenship. But now the very people sentenced under these provisions saw parole not as a way to win release; it was another con to keep them locked up longer. In a complete reversal, people behind bars were willing to risk their lives to do away with indeterminate sentencing. Prison reformers now wanted to end the second chance provided by parole.

* * *

AT JOHNNIE'S HEARING in Springfield, the chairman of the parole board interrupted Tom Johnson at one point, with polite formality. "If I may," he said. Craig Findley was seventy, with cottony white hair, a cottony voice, and a boyish face. He'd served on the Illinois parole board since 2001, longer than any of his peers. He was a former state legislator, and the son of an eleven-term U.S. congressman. The father and son both practiced a moderate Republican politics that, by the midpoint of Donald Trump's presidency, seemed as obsolete as rotary phones and video rental stores. "Politics ends with the water's edge, and we're one country, one people, and we have to find common cause," Findley would say. He lived in Jacksonville, a small city in central Illinois named after Andrew Jackson, and he served on the chamber of commerce and the board of the public library, and played trombone in the city's symphony orchestra. During his time in the state legislature, Findley viewed himself as a "law-and-order" guy. He summed up his beliefs from that time: "People commit crime, there's a price to pay." He supported the sort of tough-on-crime sentencing laws that would contribute to incarceration in the United States going mass. In Illinois, the prison population went from 5,600 people at the start of the 1970s to nearly 50,000 by the 2010s. Black people made up less than 15 percent of Illinois residents, yet Illinois was one of twelve states in the country in which more than half the people in prison were Black.

When Findley joined the parole board, though, he started to meet people in prison serving long sentences, and his ideas changed. He'd say, "I saw humanity in them that I wouldn't have known had I not taken on this job." He'd say, "It's hard to understand how incarcerating a person past the age in which we think there's no likelihood of the criminal committing the same crime is of value to society." At hearings, Findley administered the proceedings like an attentive host, explaining rules and procedures and ensuring that everyone felt duly respected. After heated exchanges between board members, he tended to validate each of the conflicting viewpoints. He'd say, "We're all informed by our own experiences," or "Both sides were very capably represented today," or "I don't see further incarceration, in my view, serving any useful purpose, but I respect that others may disagree," or "I think we're at the point that we're not going to persuade someone else how to vote. We have to decide for ourselves what is the proper thing to do." He'd instruct them to vote their conscience. At one hearing, Findley echoed Brockway's claims in 1870, expounding on the value of parole. He told his colleagues, "The trial court could never know what became of this nineteen-year-old murderer. That is for the board to consider."

At Johnnie's hearing, Findley said that it had been his job to listen to the victim protests at a separate session not open to the public. "It was grueling," he said. "All of the family members of the two slain officers spoke passionately that they've not been able to overcome the grief of their loss." He explained to everyone in attendance that the law in Illinois gives victims or their survivors a right to be heard at parole proceedings. The board was obliged to factor in their suffering when considering the suitability of ending a punishment. He said he took scrupulous notes during the protests, and he began to check them to ensure he didn't miss anything. He believed a total of fourteen members of the Severin and Rizzato families testified. "Each talked as though the crime occurred yesterday."

Findley could have discussed the victim testimony with the other board members in an executive session closed off to visitors, as was often done. But in this high-profile case, with more than two dozen police officers present, he chose to share what it was like to wrestle with the history and ramifications and politics involved in some of these crimes. Findley read from a letter submitted by a police officer who worked at Cabrini-Green in the 1980s: "I feared ambush, beatings in the stairwells and shootings, rock throwing and falling debris. I prayed that God and the good police would look after me." Johnnie last set foot in Cabrini-Green in 1970, seven years before this officer started on the job, but Findley said the words still provided a picture of what Chicago public housing was like. "They were horrible places," but inhabited, he said, "by some good people." The parole board chairman added that Chicago's current police superintendent, Eddie Johnson, grew up at Cabrini-Green around the same time as Johnnie, moving away when he was still a child. Eddie Johnson had also testified at the protest hearing. "When he was a young boy," Findley related, "Johnnie Veal burned his older brother with a flare."

Findley, as board chairman, voted last. As a personal rule, he rarely expressed an opinion that indicated ahead of time whether he was for or against parole. He didn't want to influence the outcome. But now, in his own courteous way, Findley was saying he felt strongly enough to tip his hand. Tom Johnson, who had sounded lenient, would get to speak again and present his recommendation. Findley, though, believed it necessary to impose a different point of view. He talked about a murder of another Chicago police officer a month before Johnnie's hearing. Commander Paul Bauer was downtown, in February 2018, for meetings with city officials, when he chased a fleeing suspect. He caught up with the man, and the two struggled, tumbling down a flight of stairs. The suspect shot Bauer in the head, chest, and neck. Findley recognized that equating the two crimes against police officers, a half century apart, was problematic. But, he insisted, it was also unavoidable. "While Mr. Bauer's death has nothing at all to do with the case before us of Mr. Veal, it was very much in the words and, I think, the thoughts of those who testified against him," Findley said. Bauer's murder had also deeply affected Findley. Although the last Cabrini-Green tower was demolished in 2011, Bauer had been commander in the same district where Severin and Rizzato served; Bauer was in charge of the Cabrini-Green neighborhood fifty years later. Findley underscored the connection, saying Bauer was doing the same work to bring order and peace to the area.

If a parole hearing were more like a trial, then this would have been when Johnnie's lawyer objected, on the grounds of relevance. A judge would have likely ordered that any reference to Commander Bauer be stricken from the record. None of that happened, of course. At Johnnie's protest hearing, the director of the Chicago Police Memorial Foundation testified that Johnnie should remain in prison "so we can be a little safer and honor Paul Bauer."

Findley had been quoted in one of the Chicago newspapers saying neither Johnnie nor his codefendant would ever get out of prison. At the start of Johnnie's hearing, he apologized, calling his remark "intemperate" and "potentially prejudicial." It was totally unlike him to speak out of turn like that, and he wished he hadn't said it. "Frankly, I could not know whether Mr. Veal will be paroled today or in the future. It's impossible to know." All he knew was that today, he would cast his own vote against Johnnie's parole.

"I've voted to parole more long-serving inmates than anybody on this board," he said. He believed in second chances and rehabilitation. He believed there was a reason that prisons were called correctional facilities. "But there are some cases that I just can't overcome. And this is one of them. I can't support Mr. Veal. Please take the roll."

GARBER REACHED JOHNNIE by phone not long after his hearing. She shared the bad news first. The board again rejected his parole application. The vote, in fact, was unanimous, twelve to zero. Even Tom Johnson in the end couldn't get past Johnnie's assertion of innocence, saying Johnnie still took no responsibility for the murders. Garber was a fast talker, plowing ahead as if punctuation marks didn't exist, and she narrated the day's events at a breathless clip. She described the police who filled the chamber. "It was so fucked up," she shouted. She explained how Findley brought up the recent murder of Bauer and the protest testimony of the current Chicago police superintendent.

"A flare?" Johnnie repeated. He couldn't believe that in 2018 they were trying to say he burned the police chief's brother in the 1960s. "I never saw a flare in the neighborhood," he said.

Garber told Johnnie she had some good news. She said the parole board took the question of his rehabilitation seriously. They weren't blinded by the crime. For the first time in four decades, the board acknowledged the fact that he was convicted for plotting the murders, not as a shooter. The board members still believed Johnnie guilty. That he was responsible, in some way, for the murders of two police officers. But Garber insisted the day was also a success. They got some traction with the board. They moved the needle.

Which meant Garber believed Johnnie had a chance of winning his freedom at his next parole hearing. Board members were not bound legally by precedent as in court cases; a fact recognized at a prior hearing could be ignored at the next. But Garber still felt they had something to build on. Johnnie wasn't due to appear before the board again until the end of 2020. But they needed that time to prepare. They had a lot to do in the upcoming three years. Garber had plans to recruit law students to comb through Johnnie's trial transcripts. She wanted to track down any surviving witnesses of the police shooting in 1970. She would request redacted police reports, publicize the case, and reach out to Johnnie's codefendant, getting him a lawyer in the process. His next hearing would be his twentieth. Johnnie would have spent fifty years in prison. Huge, round numbers. Garber felt that had to count for something in a justice system that saw time as its measure of punishment.

Johnnie listened to his lawyer in silence. It didn't take long for his pragmatism to kick in. The gears of his mind started to turn, the teeth catching. He saw what Garber saw. The parole board had never before recognized that he was convicted on accountability, that even the courts said he wasn't the shooter. That was a big deal. And Johnnie was motivated by the way Garber laid out a battle plan. He was competitive, and this was a political fight. Garber had worked on Johnnie's case for less than six months; he started to imagine what they could do together over the next three years. He said he had to reinvent himself again, change directions. He couldn't do the same thing at the next hearing and expect a different result. That was the definition of crazy. He wasn't the same person at sixty-five as he was at sixty-two or fifty-nine, and he'd be different three years from then. He had to show them that he was continually growing as a person. That the years mattered.

When Tom Johnson came to Hill to interview Johnnie, the two of them had connected. The parole board member was eager to learn more about Johnnie's accomplishments, and Johnnie felt seen. But as they ended their conversation, Johnson said something that stuck with Johnnie. He offered what was meant as a lighthearted compliment.

"We might need you more in prison than we need you out."

3

Taboo

Michael Henderson, being young, unimposing in size, and unwilling to humble himself, attempted to project a toughness upon entering prison that he didn't fully possess. Menard Correctional Center was enormous, a maximum-security fortress, with 1,500 men corralled together in a zoo of cells. Formerly Southern Illinois Penitentiary, the prison was built with "convict" labor in 1878 on the banks of the Mississippi, in a rural county seventy miles downriver from Michael's hometown of East St. Louis. A couple of months before Michael's arrival, in 1974, sixty men seized control of a cellblock and took several guards hostage. Outraged by conditions at the prison, they delivered a list of demands to the warden, among them the right to socialize on the yard, an end to the traumas of solitary confinement, and the creation of a functioning grievance system so they wouldn't have to resort to rioting to be heard. Just a year earlier, a different group of men also protested their treatment at Menard, barricading themselves in the commissary and holding a sixty-year-old guard captive. They were objecting to the prison's wretched food and medical care. That standoff ended when state police filled the commissary with chemical gas. "They treated me well," the freed correctional officer admitted. "They were calling the guards 'pigs,' but they were saying to me, 'Mr. Sheets, are you alright?'"

Michael was, by his own design, a loner. He refused to join any group whose obligations might compromise his free will. When Black

Panthers offered him books by Huey Newton and H. Rap Brown, he respectfully declined the overtures. He said no thank you when members of Black gangs from Chicago and East St. Louis tried to recruit him. His preferred approach was to recede into the shadows, where he could size up a place and its people. "Know everyone before they know you" was his golden rule. Going it alone, though, presented its own dangers. In a little more than a decade, Menard's population would be two-thirds Black. But in the early seventies, the facility was still two-thirds white and known as a "hillbilly" prison. According to the state's own director of prisons, roughly half of those white inmates were members of supremacist gangs, guys with tattoos of swastikas or double lightning bolts, the symbol of the Nazi SS. Menard's staff was entirely white as well. The FBI at the time was investigating a group of white guards for disseminating racist literature, along with a prison chaplain who was suspected of recruiting for the Ku Klux Klan.

Michael had been inside a maximum-security prison once before. Years earlier, when he was in juvenile detention, he was taken with other boys on a field trip to one of the state's penitentiaries. On arrival, they were introduced to men doing hard time. The lesson was designed to scare them straight. Juvie, ostensibly, was meant to reform boys and girls, steering them clear of a life of crime and future incarceration. That was the theory. In practice, what youth prison did most effectively was prepare Michael for the adult version. He served time in a juvenile facility known as "Little Joliet," as if it were the junior varsity to the varsity prison in the same Illinois city. He had an instructor in juvie, a hulking, brutal type, who taught physical education and insisted that his charges learn to fight. After night cleanup, the man marched the boys down to the basement. They were ordered to clear the furniture and the bumper pool table. The teenagers were paired off, and other boys formed a ring around them. The staff cheered as the teens were forced to box. If someone tried to retreat, elbows and boots repelled him back into the fray. For Michael's first bout, he was pitted against a much taller boy, a white kid. The instructor crouched down to glare into Michael's eyes. "If you don't go in and fight, I'm going to beat your ass myself." Michael had every reason to believe him. The teenagers chanted and jeered, and the boy with the longer reach peppered Michael's face with blows. Michael had no other choice but to come back for more. That was the lesson. Once a fight started, it could end only in extreme violence.

Michael learned in juvie a particular code of conduct and how to abide it. He earned a nickname as well. The other boys called him Taboo, because he tended to do what was forbidden. One night, another teen dripped out the ink from a pen and with a needle scratched a jagged tattoo of the new name on Michael's forearm. He would forever be Taboo.

Part of surviving in Menard, Michael discovered, was finding a way to make money. The state gave him—along with a pair of shoes, a white T-shirt, white socks, and a prison uniform—a job in the cafeteria that paid him about thirty dollars a month for his labor. When Michael was sentenced to prison for up to two hundred years, he and his wife, Joyce, ceased communication. She resented being left alone by Michael's crime to manage the large family they'd started together, to pay for the house and furniture they rented, to handle it all without him. And Michael knew she couldn't wait for him. Michael's mother helped with the children, and she brought them along two at a time on her visits to prison. Michael hated that he couldn't help support them. But he couldn't even afford to help himself. At Menard, he was always hungry. He was parched. The food was a disgusting institutional gruel that came with the added insult of never being enough. "One dip, no lip," the staff barked at anyone in the chow line insolent enough to ask for more. Other guys at the prison stocked up at the commissary, on chips and fruit pies and candy bars that they snacked on in their cells. Michael fantasized about food. He needed to do something to get money. So he devised a plan. He'd win it gambling.

During the year he spent in county jail awaiting trial, Michael played every kind of card game. A man constitutionally disposed to expect the best outcome for himself, he thought of gambling and winning as synonyms. Now he only needed a stake to bet with. He sold the extra pair of shoes he'd walked into prison on. He got two cartons of cigarettes, two bricks, the equivalent of less than ten dollars. He handed one of the cartons to his cellmate, keeping the other for himself. He figured with two of them betting, they would double their chances. Then he looked for a mark. They were on a gallery with other cafeteria workers, and a guy four cells away named Dave had a deck of cards and agreed to play a rummy game called tonk. They dealt the cards on the yard. Hand after hand, Dave laid down spreads of three and four of a kind, he revealed long runs of sequenced cards. Dave couldn't lose. He racked up points, which equaled cigarettes, which were the same as dollars. Michael's cellie lost his stake first. Michael and Dave continued their game back on the cellblock, where Michael was cleaned out next.

That night, Michael and his cellie replayed the card game, going over what went wrong and what could have been. Michael was out a pair of shoes with nothing to show for it. He was more broke than before. To cheer Michael up, his cellie said he had some acid that a family member smuggled in to him during a visit. He offered to share. They put the purple microdot on their tongues and waited for the high to kick in. Their living space was about the size of a small bathroom, six-by-eight feet, with barely enough space for a bunk bed, a metal toilet fused to a sink, a miniature table, and a pair of stools. When one of them went to use the toilet, the other one had to hop up on the beds to let him pass. Realizing they'd be up all night, they started looking for things to do. They called to Dave, a couple of cells away, and asked to borrow his deck of cards. They might as well practice and get better. On the little table, they played tonk and other games.

Back in East St. Louis, Michael's uncle had supplied him with acid, among other things, and as teenagers Michael and his friends did so much mescaline and orange sunshine that people called them the "Black Hippies." They dosed and smoked pot and hitchhiked. They lingered at a pool hall for what felt like days. One of them would eventually talk shit about who was the fastest, and then they'd all be outside sprinting up Bond Avenue, feeling like they were floating several feet above the road. They'd wander over to a nightclub and wind up in a fight. Michael and his uncle left East St. Louis for a while to work in a meatpacking plant up north, in Aurora, Illinois. Michael had never experienced anything like it. The cattle in endless streams corralled into chutes. The chorus of their moos growing desperate and deafening. The whoosh of the kill shot as bolts fired into their skulls. The overwhelming smell of shit and blood and death. The animals were sheared in half, the two identical parts folding open like a reflection in a mirror. It was Michael's job to haul the enormous carcasses into a freezer, hundreds of them, and to clean the blood that spilled in rivers. He'd be soaked in it. The uncle had a girlfriend up there who caught him cheating on her and stabbed him, and that's why Michael had to come home.

Michael looked down at the playing cards on the table in his cell. He noticed splotches of dark ink staining the back of the cards. Now that he saw it, everything became clear. The cards were marked. That's how Dave had beaten them. That's why he was eager to play for money. Michael was shouting it across the cells before he knew it.

"You cheated us, Dave!" Saying that he was holding the evidence in his hands, Michael flung the cards onto the gallery for all to see. "You better have my money in the morning!"

Michael understood too late what he'd done. By threatening Dave publicly, by calling him out across the cellblock, the challenge was out there. Michael now needed to back it up. That was the code. If he didn't, he'd be considered weak, and that reputation would follow him like a shadow. He'd be targeted. He'd become an object that others in the prison tried to use for their own amusement or benefit. Michael figured Dave knew the code as well and would attack him first. He needed to act fast.

Michael had befriended two white guys in the county jail, brothers who now worked in Menard's kitchen. He went to them first thing the next morning and said he needed a knife. They gave him a short blade, and Michael slipped it under his sleeve and headed to the dining hall. He waited beneath a guard tower, a blind spot on the way to the toilets. Michael worked himself into a fugue, his breaths coming in rapid gulps. He was adrenalized. He told himself there was no turning back. And then he saw Dave, who spotted Michael and took off in the opposite direction. Michael chased after him. Dave darted around chairs and tables, and in the middle of the cafeteria he slipped on the waxy floor and fell. Michael leapt on top of him. The two of them struggled on the ground. Michael did all he could to free his right arm with the blade. He rolled and punched down. By the time the guards pulled them apart, Michael had stabbed Dave more than once. The wounds were shallow enough not to be life-threatening, and Michael was given a year in seg-regation, a separate unit apart from the general population. He was also sent to a psychiatrist, who asked why he acted out so violently. But as Michael understood it, he was in prison, he had no choice.

Months into Michael's time in segregation, his cellie showed up for an unrelated infraction. By then Michael had landed a job as a gallery worker, mopping and serving food on the isolated wing. The job was prized for its freedom of movement. As Michael made the rounds, he spoke to his former cellmate for the first time since the stabbing.

"Man, Taboo, you almost killed that dude. And for nothing."

"What? For nothing?" Michael reminded him that Dave had cheated them. Dave took Michael's money.

His cellie was shaking his head. He explained that the cards weren't marked. The acid had kicked in. Michael had been hallucinating.

"We were tripping."

IN 1870, ZEBULON BROCKWAY had argued that parole, on the back end of the criminal system, could act as a necessary check on all that preceded it. A delegate at the National Prison Association congress, the warden of a Rhode Island penitentiary, agreed, complaining about inconsistent sentences handed down by courts. He explained that one man at his prison was serving sixteen years for stealing a forty-five-dollar horse, while another stole a horse worth two hundred dollars and got only six years. Today, parole boards maintain that power to act when sentences are egregiously or arbitrarily long, when punishments are cruel or un-usual. At a parole hearing I saw in Illinois, in 2019, the board members reviewed the case of Sherman Morisette, a Vietnam veteran who'd been in prison since the early 1980s. Unlike Johnnie's hearing, no one from the public cared enough to show up to support or oppose Morisette's release. Thirteen board members were seated elbow to elbow around a wood table in their regular conference room, in an office building a sightline away from the state capitol. They hunched over laptops and case files and coffee cups. A stenographer at a small desk typed out notes. A state trooper, who smiled and bobbed hellos, wandered in and out of the hearing. Apart from a pair of upright flags and a state crest carved from a block of cedar, the little room was as bland and unadorned as a tax preparer's waiting room. The tiles of the low-drop ceiling were the same beige as the walls. The room's size made it uncomfortable for visitors, and there were continual plans to move into the larger storage space where the long histories on each parole candidate were kept, but the renovations never got started.

Morisette's crime was robbing a cabdriver. He had a gun but didn't use it, and no one was hurt. He was sentenced under a habitual offender law, a "three strikes and you're out" statute that mandated long prison sentences for a third felony even if the last one was relatively less serious. Morisette had previous convictions for theft, armed robbery, and possession of marijuana. For the new strike, he was given life without the possibility of parole. He was ruled "out," banned from the free world forever. Thirty-five years later, the Illinois governor, recognizing the doctrine that a punishment should be proportional to the crime, commuted Morisette's sentence to one that allowed him to come up for parole consideration.

"He's got how many arrests? It didn't sound like all that many," asked Donald Shelton, a retired police officer and the parole board's only Black Republican.

"Five, six . . . seven," a board member named Edith Crigler, a social worker from Chicago's South Side, counted.

"And he's not killed anybody?" Shelton was incredulous.

"Nope."

"And he's been in prison for thirty-five years?"

The board's vote was swift. Thirteen to zero to grant release. A wrong righted.

At another hearing, the board learned about the medical treatment in an Illinois prison of a man named Orville Miller. Miller, sixty-five, had undergone surgery two years earlier for an enlarged prostate. But his treatment was either botched or insufficient for what ailed him. The board members heard that Miller had been bleeding rectally ever since. The prison gave him pads to sit on. The pain kept him from sleeping. He rarely left his cell, relying on other men on his cellblock to bring him food. A board member wanted to make sure she was getting this right. "The pads are capturing the bleeding? There's something medical that has to happen to actually stop the bleeding?" Yes, that was correct. But the Department of Corrections denied him any additional procedures to treat or even to identify what was wrong. The board did review the case that Miller caught—a murder more than forty years earlier, when he was twenty-two. But his need for immediate medical care made the offense seem almost beside the point. All but one board member voted for parole.

In most cases, though, parole boards were not identifying miscarriages of justice and trying to correct these problems. In the 1970s, in fact, people in prison made it plain that parole boards *were* the problem. Assessments by parole boards were inconsistent, opaque, and rife with bias and discrimination. Indeterminate sentences were extended indefinitely with no recourse. Imprisoned people wanted parole abolished. At Menard, Michael didn't fall in with guys who called themselves "political prisoners," who quoted Angela Davis and demanded an end to indeterminate sentencing. While he didn't know a lot then about the uprisings at Attica or at any other prisons, much of the country did.

At the start of the 1970s, something extraordinary was happening in the United States. What occurred behind the prison walls was suddenly made visible to the world beyond. The public started to care about the rights of the incarcerated. Americans immersed themselves in books and reports about the futility and brutality of the carceral system. *Soledad Brother: The Prison Letters of George Jackson*—released in 1970, a year before Jackson was killed by prison guards in what officials claimed was an attempted escape—sold 400,000 copies. Attica became a proper noun for the nightmare of incarceration. "We're all mates with Attica State," went the refrain of a John Lennon song from 1972. Or consider the movie *Dog Day Afternoon*, how Al Pacino's bank robber, seeing a hundred police officers with guns trained on him, chants "Attica!" and the crowds in Brooklyn take up the battle cry—a word that now unites them against all forms of authoritarian oppression. Moments like this in America are extremely rare and, we're reminded, fleeting. The turmoil on city streets and in cellblocks had created a window of opportunity to reimagine the system of corrections. The realm of the possible had temporarily expanded.

In California, lawmakers passed an "Inmates Bill of Rights," guaranteeing that people in prison maintained the rights of citizenship except those "reasonably related to legitimate penological interests." The

amended California penal code ensured that the incarcerated were allowed to marry, own property, and communicate privately with legal
counsel. In 1971, the Justice Department created a national advisory
council to improve criminal justice in the country. Richard Nixon was
president. And yet the group recommended putting a stop to the building of any new prisons and closing many existing ones. "The perva-
sive overemphasis on custody that remains in corrections creates more
problems than it solves," the council wrote in its report. It called for
greatly reducing the use of jails for adults and eliminating any need
to hold youths pretrial. The commission believed that people who
broke the law, in most cases, could be held accountable *without* being
sent to prison. "Too often we have perceived them as the stereotype
of 'prisoner' and applied to all offenders the institutional conditions
essential only for relatively few. Hence, the report stresses the need for
development of a broader range of alternatives to the institution, and
for the input of greater resources of manpower, money, and materials
to that end."

In Illinois, the outcry over inhumane prison conditions and unfair
punishments reached the governor's mansion. In 1973, a new governor won office, an anti-machine Democrat named Dan Walker, who
as part of his outsider campaign walked across the entire state, a total
of 1,197 miles. Walker recruited the commissioner of the Minnesota
Department of Corrections, a maverick in the field named David Fogel,
to transform the state's prisons. Fogel was a controversial pick to run
the prison system. Two years earlier, just weeks after the massacre at
Attica, Fogel testified at U.S. congressional hearings on prison reform.
He described how those incarcerated in Minnesota were permitted to
wear their hair long and dress as they pleased. They were given access
to free legal assistance and an ombudsman whose job it was to investigate complaints of abuse or lost privileges. He talked about a furlough
program he established that connected people behind bars with their
communities on the outside and assisted with their eventual reentry.
When Fogel took the commissioner job in Minnesota, he spent several
days locked up in one of the state's facilities to understand the experience. A sociologist by training, he grounded his practices in an almost
radical empathy. While in college, he led a chapter of the Student Non-

51

violent Coordinating Committee, the primary youth arm of the civil rights movement, and as a young father he dragged his children with him to Jim Crow Arkansas to register Black voters. As part of his academic work, Fogel conducted "psychodramas," pulling together police officers, judges, prison guards, and imprisoned people and having them all swap roles. He maintained that prisons throughout the country, facilities like Attica or Menard, needed to operate far more compassionately and lawfully, so that they inflicted no additional punishment beyond the temporary loss of someone's liberty.

In Illinois, while all agreed that prisons were in crisis, not all saw Fogel, a bearded liberal with roots in Northern California, as the solution. A group of conservative Republicans in the Illinois General Assembly worked to block his confirmation. Pointing to Fogel's track record of expanding rights to people in prison, they characterized him as "soft-on-crime," an epithet that was then gaining political purchase. The head of the senate commission overseeing prisons, a Republican from a wealthy Chicago suburb, told a story of an eighteen-year-old Minnesotan, released from prison after ten months, who went on to rob a bank and kill a police officer. He presented it as an example of the mayhem that would plague Illinois if Fogel and his brand of "revolving doors" justice was let in. The legislature rejected Fogel's appointment. A Republican, rejoicing, said they had managed to turn back a cult of liberalism and permissiveness.

Governor Walker, undaunted, went ahead and hired Fogel anyway. Not as corrections commissioner, as he had planned, but as a special advisor on criminal justice, a newly created position. Then Fogel was made the executive director of a state commission charged with designing a better prison system. Fogel led a group of legal scholars and criminologists for two years, and, in 1975, they introduced a slate of reforms called *Flat-Time Prison Sentences: A Proposal for Swift, Certain, and Even-Handed Justice*. What Fogel proposed for Illinois was an end to indeterminate sentencing. Under his plan, prison terms would again be established at trial, set with a fixed release date—flat time. Most people serving these determinate sentences would be able to earn "good time" reductions, cutting a day from their sentence for each day served without a disciplinary infraction. But with fixed prison terms, good-time early release would be decided by a formula, not a parole board. It was exactly the change that people organizing inside prisons had demanded. The Department of Corrections would still offer educational and therapeutic programming, and incarcerated people would have opportunities to learn a trade or seek counseling and rehabilitate themselves. But the services would be optional, and participation would no longer be a prerequisite for release. Someone's freedom would not be contingent on a parole board's assessment. In fact, there wouldn't be any parole. Parole in Illinois would be eliminated. "Justice as fairness," Fogel called it.

Fogel believed that sentencing reforms were the key to making prisons fairer and more humane—and to placating prison activists. His "justice model" was premised on ending discretionary parole as we know it. But at the same time, parole was also under attack from those demanding more severe punishments. After the civil rights movement, after prisoner rights and a decade of social and political upheaval, the United States was simultaneously experiencing a punitive backlash. The potential in that moment for transformational change had mobilized other Americans concerned primarily with preserving the existing social order. A Gallup poll from 1968 found that 81 percent of the Americans it surveyed agreed with the statement that "law and order has broken down in this country." The two groups identified by the poll as the main perpetrators of this disorder: "Negroes who start riots" and "Communists."

When Lyndon Johnson campaigned for president in 1964, he called for a domestic "War on Poverty," a way to combat economic and racial inequality and create what he called a "great society." Universally, the same conditions are known to cause increases in violent crime: an overabundance of young men and a lack of work or other opportunities for advancement. The Great Society programs, as they became known, were meant to target the root causes of crime by creating less need in poverty-stricken areas and providing young people with more opportunities. With an emphasis on "maximum feasible participation" by residents of low-income areas, federal block grants funded neighborhood councils, youth groups, job training, and numerous other social welfare programs. The Kerner Commission, the advisory group Johnson created to investigate the decade's civil disorders, recommended that the government go much further in investing in under-resourced communities; the report called for the creation of millions of jobs, significant outlays to inner-city schools, and a significant expansion of welfare assistance for housing, food, and childcare.

But President Johnson and lawmakers ignored the Kerner Commission's findings. In Johnson's last year in office, in 1968, his administration redirected funding from the "root causes" of crime to its policing. "Our protection rests essentially with local and State police officers," Johnson said. It was a turning point for criminal justice in America. "A new and historically distinct phenomenon in the post–civil rights era: the criminalization of urban social programs," the historian Elizabeth Hinton explained in *From the War on Poverty to the War on Crime*. The nation withdrew its resources from the War on Poverty, sending them instead to a new front—the country's police forces, courts, and prisons. There was a renewed reliance on punishment as social control. It was Johnson who first declared a "War on Crime." That rallying call would be taken up and acted upon far more aggressively by Johnson's Republican successors. On his path to the White House, in 1968, Richard Nixon offered white Americans, galvanized by real and perceived threats to the social hierarchy, the promise of "freedom from fear." In place of civil rights, Nixon offered up the racial dog whistle of law and order. "If the conviction rate were doubled in this country, it would do more to eliminate crime in the future than a quadrupling of the funds for any governmental war on poverty," Nixon announced.

In 1974, a sociologist named Robert Martinson reviewed hundreds of records from prison treatment programs and their rates of recidivism. At the time, about two-thirds of people released from prison were later arrested for another crime. Martinson called his report "What Works? Questions and Answers about Prison Reform." The headline-grabbing simplified answer he gave: nothing. Drug and alcohol programs, therapy, basic and higher education, cognitive behavior interventions for those convicted of sex offenses—all of these do lower recidivism. Martinson's own research showed that. Yet tough-on-crime conservatives seized on a narrow reading of the report to argue that indeterminate sentencing and parole should be abandoned. They were in agreement, at least about that, with prisoner rights advocates and many legal scholars.

But they argued that rehabilitation failed because people in prison could not change. The term "career criminal" was then coming into vogue. The designation suggested that some people—coded to mean types of people—were predisposed to crime and undeserving of a second chance. Parole, as prison rights groups showed, had not been overly lenient. California had done more than any other state to develop a system of therapeutic punishment, promoting reform and rehabilitation through education, vocational training, and group therapy. The result: the length of time served under California's parole model jumped by an average of twelve months. In Washington State, the introduction of indeterminate sentencing had doubled prison stays. But in an increasingly popular law-and-order formulation, parole was branded as a form of revolving-door justice. Parole was seen as a way for liberals to coddle violent offenders—to release these inveterates back onto the streets to endanger us all.

In Illinois, by the time Fogel's flat-time proposal was under review, the governor was a professed "War on Crime" Republican. Big Jim Thompson, a former Nixon-appointed U.S. attorney, ran for Illinois governor in 1976 on a tough-on-crime platform and won two-thirds of the vote. In his first year in office, Thompson introduced an alternative to Fogel's sentencing reform bill. The governor's proposal also did away with parole. But Thompson thought the fixed determinate sentences Fogel suggested would prove too lenient. The governor's bill invented a new felony class for serious crimes such as aggravated arson, kidnapping, rape, and sales of large drug quantities. Class X felonies, as Thompson named them, would result in a mandatory minimum sentence of six years in prison and up to thirty years in most cases, extending to natural life without the possibility of parole for habitual offenders. For murder, the governor's proposed mandatory range was initially twenty to forty years, but that range was quickly amended up to thirty to sixty years. Judges, when setting sentences, would be forced to follow these automatic guidelines no matter the circumstances of a case; neither a parole board nor good-time credits could free someone before the minimum date.

In debating the competing bills, Democrats in the state legislature and other criminal justice reformers called the governor's proposal a gimmick, the "Class X" name a ploy meant to scare white suburban and rural voters about inner-city crime. And they were right. Thompson admitted that he made up the name because he knew it would trigger visceral reactions. "You know, movies can be X-rated, the 'X' symbol was a powerful symbol in the American culture. You X'd something out," he said. "It basically was an attempt to say, 'Three strikes you're out.'" The offenders he was conjuring weren't people who deserved justice or clarity on their release dates, or even adequate food and health care during their incarcerations. In many ways they weren't people at all. They were an unknown variable that stood in for the worst possible crime anyone could imagine happening to them or their loved ones. X = Fear.

The tactic worked. In 1978, a version of Governor Thompson's bill became law. Parole in Illinois was done. The Cook County Circuit Court judge who had previously sentenced Johnnie Veal to an indeterminate sentence of 100 to 199 years explained the rule changes to other judges, writing in delighted all-caps, "BIG NUMBERS NOW MEAN SOME-THING." Anyone sent to prison in Illinois after the bill's passage served a flat-time sentence and no longer was eligible for parole. Some would have the chance to reduce their time in prison through a good-time formula. But anyone with a more serious felony would have to serve all of his or her mandatory term.

Illinois was not alone in getting rid of parole. With enemies on all sides, parole as it existed was doomed. In 1976, Maine became the first state to do away with indeterminate sentencing and discretionary parole release. The following year, California, with bipartisan support and the endorsement of prisoner groups, eliminated almost all indeterminate sentences as well. The California penal code was changed to declare that the purpose of incarceration was no longer officially rehabilitation or reform but "punishment." Indiana abolished discretionary parole in 1977. Arizona, Delaware, Oregon, North Carolina, and Washington were among the other states that followed. The end of indeterminate sentencing came even faster than its spread a hundred years before. A total of sixteen states eventually scrapped parole eligibility. Twenty-one other states made many crimes ineligible for parole, dramatically limiting the discretion of their parole boards to decide release dates. During Ronald Reagan's presidency, Congress passed a sentencing reform act that did away with the federal parole system: for anyone sentenced to a federal prison after 1987, parole was no longer an option. In the 1970s, seven in ten people who left a state prison did so after going before a parole board. By 2000, only one in four were released through discretionary parole.

IN PRISON, MICHAEL was C-10609. Johnnie's identification was C-01600. They were known as C-Numbers, for the prefix on their institutional identifications at the time they were admitted. After 1978, people convicted of felonies in Illinois were sentenced to fixed prison terms and couldn't be released by a parole board. But the C-Numbers who predated the law change were exempt and grandfathered into the old system. Michael and Johnnie, sentenced to long, indeterminate sentences prior to 1978, still came up for parole. Neither of them took much notice of the dual-sentencing structure at first. Of the roughly ten thousand people in Illinois prisons in 1978, many were short-termers, serving less than five years. It would take time for the prisons to fill with new admissions, those with Class X mandatory defined terms. Michael came to appreciate being a C-Number. The parole board's decisions might be arbitrary and opaque, but he relished the chance to show that he wasn't just a number. Flat-timers couldn't change their destiny; they were stuck. Michael would rather take his chances with the parole board. He believed in himself. "They're going to recognize me as a good citizen," he'd insist. "I could be their next-door neighbor."

While he was still in segregation for the stabbing, Michael debated how he might do a good bid. "Bid" or "bit" to refer to a prison term likely comes from the Britishism "bird-lime," the lime being a sticky goo used to trap small birds. The "bird" in this sympathetic metaphor of the incarcerated person muddled over time into the word "bid." Michael found there was something about his bid that was impossible to explain to outsiders. Not the dangers or the dramas—he could recount those stories all day. But the way his stay in prison felt outside of time. How he was separated from the rest of the world, kept at a distant remove and forgotten. The unchanging routine thrust upon him. The tedium and the regimented control. Each monotonous day lasted an eternity, and yet weeks and months and years seemed to evaporate and leave nothing behind. It made a difference to no one whether he read a book or stared at his hands. Michael decided he had to make something of his time in prison. He wanted to do more than merely survive. To do a good bid, he needed to figure out a way to live.

Working the gallery in segregation, Michael got in the habit of playing chess with guys in their cells. They set up a board on a stool just outside the bars, and Michael moved a piece, went off to sweep or deliver meals, and on his way back assessed his opponent's turn and took his next move. In that way, he kept multiple games going at once against different opponents. Michael got a chess-for-beginners book from the prison library. He practiced by mirroring the book's sample games, learning to think two or three moves ahead. It was a skill, he said, that helped him "analytically assess" the prison. He also used the games to learn about the men on the segregation wing. *Know everyone before they know you.* One day he was playing against a gang chief from Chicago when the man handed Michael a kite, the notes on small pieces of paper folded over and over into hard pellets that surreptitiously made the rounds of the prison. "I need you to respond back to this for me," the man said. Michael unfolded the paper. The message was from someone in the prison outside the segregation wing, in general population, who wanted direction on a security matter. Michael looked up. The guy whispered, "I'm not too sharp on reading." So Michael read him the note, and then wrote out the reply dictated to him. Michael soon started a small business writing letters. People recognized that he was good with words—he was already a thesaurus-thumping evangelist of *Word Power Made Easy*—and that he didn't abuse whatever private information he learned.

When Michael left segregation after a year and returned to general population, he began tailoring clothes as well. His mother had been a seamstress, and she'd taught him some stitchwork. He made his sewing needles by straightening paper clips. He smashed one end of the metal with the weights on the yard, flattening it before punching a hole through. He sharpened the other end by running it back and forth along the concrete floor. For almost everybody at Menard, the clothes that the prison issued were too large. Michael altered pants and shirts for anyone who wanted a slimmer fit. The cells were freezing the half the year that they weren't ovens, and Michael added insulation to coats. He learned how to take the denim from old jeans and piece together a shirt or jacket.

He started other businesses too. He braided hair and cooked pizza. With his profits, he invested in hard candy from the commissary. He melted down the sweets on a hot plate in his cell, shaping the viscous stew into suckers that he covered in plastic wrap. People in prison traded all kinds of things that they determined were of equal value—cigarettes or a sandwich. But Michael dealt mostly in write-outs, the prestamped envelopes sold at the commissary. A write-out cost the same as a first-class stamp and, Michael calculated, was the price of one sucker. He accumulated stacks of the stamped envelopes. He sent some to his mother to help with his kids. She could turn them into cash at her local post office. He used the currency as well to buy clothes, food, and cigarettes for himself. Sometimes he bought extra candy bars and sold them after hours when the commissary was closed and people were still hungry. He also distilled plums and other fruit into prison wine. "It was *almost* like real wine," he'd say. He could cook down the alcohol into hooch. It might not taste great, but it was strong and could get a person drunk. He could make the equivalent of a dollar off the drinks, or drink them himself.

"Nothing changes because you're behind the wall," Michael would say. "You have to recognize what's in demand, and try to learn it and craft it into a way that you're able to benefit from." He'd been stupid to gamble. He knew that now. The smart thing was to acquire skills that gave him a competitive advantage. "Living off the land," he called it.

Michael courted opportunity wherever he could find it, and he discovered that he could live better off the land if he had a job that put him in close contact with prison employees. Michael worked in the laundry at one facility, and officers brought him their clothes to tailor, since he cost less than anyone they'd pay on the outside. One supervisor gave Michael a book that showed him how to make pockets and build out shoulders. Michael had another job as a sign-out clerk, logging names into a ledger as men traveled from their cellblocks to work details or to school. The staff called Michael "Tab," short for Taboo, and he learned which guards were stealing furniture and food meant for the prison, and which among them might consider a business partnership. About eight years into his bid, Michael worked as a runner for the warden. He filled the warden's pitcher with ice water. He took the warden's shoes to be shined. He tidied up the secretaries' cubicles. "It gave me carte blanche," Michael would say, a freedom of sorts to move about the facility.

After more than a decade in prison, probably as long as he would have served if he'd taken the prosecutor's plea deal, Michael believed he mastered how to do time. It was a skill he'd rather not have acquired, an expertise he wished he could apply elsewhere. But he was a ward of the state. Choosing to live on his own terms didn't help him with the parole board. There was a part of him eager to right the wrong he had done, to demonstrate that he was corrigible and filled with regret. He continued to amass tickets, however. It wasn't always enough to figure out which guards were the good ones and which the assholes. The same officer who brought in clothes for Michael to tailor later confiscated his sewing needles and wrote him a ticket for dangerous contraband. There were a million traps he could fall into. Michael was given a disciplinary infraction for cooking in his cell after lights out. Correctional officers wrote him up for having kitchen matches, for listening to a radio without headphones, for having more belongings than would fit in the gray shoebox allotted him. When Michael had a job in the officers' kitchen, he didn't have time to eat lunch one day, so he put two egg-and-cheese sandwiches in his pocket. He was charged with theft. He had just served the COs their meals.

At one facility, he was selling weed. His mother smuggled it in on her visits, and a guard who looked the other way took a cut of the earnings. Someone in the cell house ratted Michael out, and guards shook down his cell, finding a baggie inside his socks and a couple of joints hidden inside books. Michael was convicted of possession. The drug offense added an additional two years to the one hundred to two hundred years he was already serving, like a ladder propped on top of a mountain. The parole board reviewing Michael's file read that he had highly favorable evaluations from supervisors and psychological exams. Yet the new charge meant he had officially "transgressed institutional discipline." He was not reformed. In its rejection letter to Michael, the parole board wrote, "In view of the grave nature of the crime and your institutional discipline, as evidenced by the fact that while serving a sentence for murder you received a new sentence for possession of drugs, the Board feels that you do not represent a good risk for parole at this time."

Michael was transferred around the state prison system during his bid. From Menard, he went north, to Pontiac—"Thunderdome," people inside called it, because of the violence and the noise. While there, he broke a piece of metal off his bed frame, wrapped the bottom in tape, and sharpened the top; he carried the shiv with him when he showered to make sure he made it back to his cell. From Pontiac, he was sent three hundred miles south, to Shawnee, and from there to Mt. Sterling, in western Illinois. Mt. Sterling was a two-hour drive from East St. Louis, and Michael's oldest daughter came to visit him. Her name was Alicia, but everyone called her Shani. She was a teenager who shouldered the extra responsibility of looking after her younger siblings. When Shani sat across from her father in the prison's visiting room, she asked him why he was constantly getting in trouble. Michael was selling everything from candy and pizzas to weed and harder drugs. He told Shani that he was doing it to send something home for her. How did she think she got money for clothes and class trips? But Shani wasn't buying it. Her father had missed every birthday she remembered. He'd never woken her up in the morning or taken her to school. They'd never even gone on an errand together. She said what he was doing in prison he could be doing on the outside from home.

"Don't you love us?" she asked. "Don't you want to be out there with us?"

Later that night, when Michael was back in his cell, what he called his "house," he reviewed the day's events. Before sleep, he always took time to analyze and inventory his experiences. He replayed conversations. He recalled interactions, considering who looked at him a certain way and why. He made himself see things that others might have missed. Why was shower time changed this week? What was going on with the men moving around at chow? A visitor was out of the ordinary, so he spent extra time reconsidering his talk with Shani.

She had challenged him, and Michael decided she was probably right. As a C-Number, he still had a chance at winning his release through parole. That had become increasingly rare not only in Illinois but also in prisons all over the country. Michael was squandering that opportunity. As long as he kept catching bogus tickets, the parole board would deny him forever.

Michael decided he'd try to go a year, maybe two, without disciplinary infractions. He'd have to make sacrifices. Curb his activities. Be more circumspect. Then he'd see if he could get some rhythm with the parole board.

4

The Stories of the Crime

Donald Shelton, on the Illinois Prisoner Review Board since 2012, threw himself into each parole case as if he were pinning clues to an evidence board and marking the connections with string. He had been a police officer in the downstate college town of Champaign for twenty-three years, reaching the rank of patrol sergeant. He still seemed like a cop. Towering and broad, he wore plain dark suits and a distrustful glare. He was a doer, a solver, a collector of complete sets of technical skills. On the police force, he was the evidentiary expert. He started his department's first crime scene unit. He did fingerprint analysis, tire track and footwear impression identification, photography for both surveillance and investigations. For a time he'd been a drummer in a band called One-Eighty (a belief in radical change?), and in retirement he again picked up both the drumsticks and the camera. The parole board in Illinois, like much of the country, was divided between its conservative and liberal sides, with a small number of critical swing voters in the middle. Chairman Findley was usually in the middle. Virginia Martinez said she started in the middle but moved further to the left. Shelton was among the former police officers and prosecutors who voted less frequently for parole. But everyone on the board, regardless of their political leanings, asked to look at Shelton's detailed notes.

For each parole case he reviewed, Shelton combed through the thick accordion files that the board kept on each candidate. He studied the minutes from previous parole hearings. Delving into prison records, he followed up with contacts inside the state correctional facilities, asking about disciplinary reports, transfers, possible gang activity. "This was interesting enough that I printed it out so everyone could look at it," he'd say during a hearing while passing his colleagues pages he'd highlighted. He reread ancient arrest reports, trial transcripts, appeals, writs of habeas corpus, sworn affidavits. For one case, he read an entire book written about the petitioner's crime. Then he contacted the book's author, asking him to turn over his notes, and Shelton read those too.

At hearings, when there was a silence, Shelton tended to fill it. He talked about old newspaper articles he'd dug up or the idiosyncrasies of a candidate's prior arrest history.

"Yeah, I've got something to say," Shelton announced during one lull.

"Of course you do," a board member next to him muttered.

Shelton tunneled deeper into each case, further into the past, trying to unearth not only the facts of a crime but also something more elusive—a petitioner's character. The two, he believed, were inextricable. Parole boards were supposed to assess remorse, rehabilitation, the likelihood of someone committing a future crime. Board members anticipated that candidates would say anything to go free, so some tried to be human lie detectors. Shelton was quick to point out when applicants appeared to contradict themselves, when the story of a crime repeated over decades altered even slightly. He expected, at the very minimum, that people sentenced to prison take responsibility for their actions. And so he called out expressions of remorse that to him seemed feigned. "He's a liar," Shelton would say. Or "His statements do not comport with the facts of the case. I challenged him on that." Or "I don't believe he's changed." Or "I'm not going to support him. He's marked time." Or "He just can't stop clowning. To be sixty-two and still disobeying orders—for crying out loud, that's silly!" One year when Johnnie was coming up for parole, Shelton interviewed him in prison. Johnnie had previously written a petition for executive clemency, and Shelton placed it on the table between them like it was a winning poker hand. Shelton had compared the document to everything the board had in Johnnie's file—the crime report, the trial verdict, the appeal decisions. He said that Johnnie's petition to the governor for a commutation of his sentence read like an admission of guilt. Hadn't Johnnie written that he understood the pain and suffering he'd caused? Wasn't it true that Johnnie's fingerprints were on the rifles used to kill the two police officers in 1970? Didn't people see Johnnie with a gun? Johnnie tried to tell Shelton that he had it all wrong. "That's not me," he repeated. Johnnie didn't want to sound defensive. But even as he spoke, he felt trapped inside a narrative about him.

Because Shelton's default was to say out loud what he was thinking, he also let it be known at parole hearings when he'd been convinced to free someone. He valued a thorough presentation, and he commended colleagues or lawyers when their arguments for release swayed him. "One of the best presentations I've ever seen" was his highest praise. But many times Shelton simply couldn't get past a crime, no matter how much time the perpetrator had served or what they had accomplished during their incarceration, and he let everyone know that as well. "When I first got the case, I thought, 'Well, jeez, I think I'm finally coming across somebody I'm going to support for parole.' I felt good about that," Shelton said of a man who'd proven remorseful and reformed after forty-three years in prison. "That was before I really actually got into the details of the crime itself."

Chairman Findley would tell his colleagues that their job was to listen to a petitioner in the present and not merely to affirm whatever a court had ruled in the past. The courts dealt with the crime and the sentencing. The board was trying to determine when someone was fit to go free. In practice, though, parole hearings were dominated by the stories of past crimes. The original conviction, something that could never change, tended to overwhelm everything that had happened since. Even crimes a half century old, in their retellings at hearings, remained visceral and present-tense, in the same way that Macbeth is forever plunging the dagger into King Duncan, or Raskolnikov has only just picked up the ax and entered the old moneylender's apartment. Crimes are inherently dramatic, with a perpetrator, a victim, and the most extreme actions and consequences. "Doesn't anyone have an answer to my question why this man walked across the street and beat a fifty-four-year-old woman into a puddle? I want to know *why* it happened," Shelton demanded at a hearing I observed. No one could give a satisfying answer.

A vote for release almost always seemed to hinge on a story told about a parole candidate being somehow powerful enough to overcome the resounding one of the crime. The passage of decades and actuarial tables showing the unlikelihood of a future offense were rarely enough. Members of parole boards across the country needed to hear something new; they required a narrative that transformed the one that was handed down in court with the felony conviction, that branded someone a "criminal" and "convict." Absent a story that made sense of violence that was in many instances senseless, the board members turned back to the original offense, which never stopped being heinous and forever disrespected the law. The present was forever pulled back into the currents of the past.

For parole candidates, learning to tell a story about themselves that was both compelling substantively and delivered in a compelling way took a lot of work. Michelle Lewin runs a nonprofit in New York called Parole Preparation Project, which, since 2016, has helped ready more than five hundred parole applicants for their hearings. Commissioners from the New York State Board of Parole interview about ten thousand parole candidates each year. "The entire process of preparing for parole or preparing someone else for approval is going down a journey of storytelling with them," Lewin said. "It is figuring out what is the narrative about their life and what happened to them they want to tell to the parole board."

The first challenge for many people coming up for parole is figuring out what that story is. They feel shame about the terrible thing they did. They've been separated from society, and years have passed in prison without them talking about their crime to anyone. In California, a group called UnCommon Law starts working with lifers at least eight months before their hearings, using a trauma-informed approach to help them understand the many factors that contributed to why they ended up harming someone else. "It's a process of discovery and introspection," Keith Wattley, UnCommon Law's founder, said.

California prisons hold thirty-four thousand lifers eligible for parole. Wattley's organization prepares candidates through mock interviews and self-reflection and emotional awareness exercises. Wattley said, "Prison takes away someone's name and gives them a number, takes away their clothes and gives them prison blues, takes away their individuality and privacy and family connections. Of course they need help coming to terms with their lives, let alone how to express that."

Once a parole candidate's own story is less a mystery to them, they still have to convince a parole board that they are worthy of release. They have to be good storytellers. A story of personal transformation requires thinking about structure. About which events from one's life to emphasize. About what words to use. They have to get past the parole board's incredulity, standing out as genuine and distinct. "Connect the dots and explain to the parole board what their journey has been in a language the parole board can understand," Wattley said. In *The Shawshank Redemption*, Morgan Freeman's Ellis Boyd "Red" Redding fails to win over the parole board, for decades, because his words sound inauthentic. He repeats the same stock phrases every parole board member has heard a thousand times. Red is paroled only when he breaks free, even if unintentionally, of the tired tropes of redemption and makes the board see him. A parole decision becomes like Jesus's words to his believers: "The truth will set you free." But why should something as consequential as a person's freedom depend on how a few words are spoken and heard? A system as arbitrary and random as that isn't a system at all. It's a contest of phrases. Scheherazade weaving tales to save her life. "Open sesame!" Rather than miraculous, it seems sinister that parole boards require utterances that somehow transubstantiate into their mercy. Red was remorseful and rehabilitated before. He was telling the truth all along! But now, by dropping the veneer of respectability, he somehow tells the same story but better.

Andrew Hundley was one of the first juveniles sentenced to life in prison in Louisiana to be paroled, in 2016. Once free, he started the Louisiana Parole Project, which provides pro bono legal representation at hearings along with reentry support. Hundley's advice for candidates is simple: be as real and honest as possible. "Share the worst details," he said. "Don't whitewash or dress it up."

Board members have an account of the crime in front of them and are looking for discrepancies. Candidates need to be factual. They shouldn't say they made a mistake or talk about excuses. They have to own up to what they did. "It is easier for a guilty man to be granted parole in Louisiana than an innocent man," Hundley said. The Louisiana State Penitentiary is known as Angola, the name of the former slave plantation on which it sits. While there, Hundley had joined the prison's chapter of Toastmasters, the public speaking club. But others needed more practice talking in front of a group. They needed help with voice modulation and inflection. A training manual available to people in Ohio prisons, *The Secret Hints for Winning Parole*, reminds candidates to appear presentable—to brush their hair and teeth, to sit up straight, and to avoid crossing their arms, which might come across as aggressive or defensive. They shouldn't swear, of course, and they should nod to indicate they were listening.

Parole candidates have to show everything that they achieved in prison, and, at the same time, they can't come across as boastful or unaware of the hurt they inflicted. Avoiding passive voice is important. And so is steering clear of yes and no answers. And being specific rather than general. They should say the name of the person they harmed, not refer to them or their relatives as anonymous "victims." They shouldn't come across as angry. They have to sound sincere and vulnerable even though they have spent years—if not decades—in a place that makes them feel bitter and worthless. And when talking about their early lives, about the context of the crime or how they'd suffered harm as well, they have to be careful. If they bring up racism, poverty, misogyny, homophobia, abuse, or any form of victimization they experienced, it can be turned against them as evidence that they aren't taking responsibility for their own actions or thinking enough about the people they hurt.

"It's an impossible tightrope to walk," Lewin said. "It's like, how do I both be proud and share things about myself so that I am not seen as a threat, but also not minimize the harm, and insult the parole board or the victims."

For board members, deciding whom to free and whom to keep in prison is not a science. Were good storytellers more rehabilitated than bad ones? Was someone who had difficulty putting her feelings into words more of a threat to reoffend? There is no evidence that a person who conveyed ideas in a compelling way was any less violent than someone who felt wrecked by their past deeds but could articulate why only in uninspiring clichés. The process remains highly subjective. On the front end of the justice system, police, prosecutors, and juries are more prone to see criminality in people who are not like themselves;

parole, on the back end, reproduces, or even exaggerates, many of the same biases. In 2016, the *New York Times* analyzed thousands of decisions by the New York State Board of Parole and found that Black and Hispanic men were released at a far lower rate at their first hearings than white men. Four years later, after promises of reform, the Albany *Times Union* analyzed nineteen thousand parole decisions in New York from 2018 to 2020 and found that the disparities had not improved—41 percent of white people were granted parole, 34 percent of Black people, and 33 percent of Latinos. After a man in prison in Alabama, in 2019, mistakenly classified as low risk, was paroled and went on a robbery spree that left three people dead, parole rates tumbled in the state, albeit unevenly. From 2019 to 2020, the number of white applicants granted parole in Alabama decreased from 36 percent to 29 percent, while Black applicants fell from 34 percent to 16 percent. In 2021, Alabama paroled just 8 percent of Black applicants.

And what if the parole candidate was someone who didn't speak English? Should they stumble along in a second language or use a translator and risk seeming distant? Or what if the candidate was transgender? Or had cognitive differences, physical impairments, dementia? If someone struggled with mental health, should they even admit it? It could be reason enough to deem them unfit for release. A statute in New Mexico addresses directly the many ways that parole applicants might look, talk, and behave differently from board members, instructing commissioners to be aware of gaps of "culture, language, values, mores, judgments, communicative ability and other unique qualities."

Reginald Dwayne Betts, the acclaimed poet and lawyer who served more than eight years in Virginia prisons for a carjacking he committed at age sixteen, works with incarcerated friends to help them with their parole presentations. He summed up the dilemmas parole candidates faced: "What do you say that amounts to freedom?"

PRIOR TO EACH of Johnnie's parole hearings, the board received a letter from the office of the Cook County state's attorney, which prosecuted Johnnie's case back in 1971. "Under no circumstance should inmate Veal receive any mercy." "It is obvious that the defendant is a cold-hearted murderer with no apparent hope for rehabilitation." State's attorneys regularly oppose parole release for candidates convicted of violent crimes. In Johnnie's case file, there were decades of these protest letters. Each one recycled the same language about the crime, its viciousness and brutality, and reasserted in new ways the need for unrelenting punishment. "This prisoner is a vicious, cold-blooded killer." "The lives of two policemen working to protect the community were extinguished for the sheer and utter amusement of this inmate." "Even in jail, he remains a danger." "To grant such a vile person parole would promote disrespect for the law and would most certainly deprecate the seriousness of his offenses."

Sara Garber wanted Johnnie to write an account of his life. Her plan was to share it with the parole board before his next hearing in 2020. The board already had a picture of Johnnie Veal, the cop killer from Cabrini-Green, this "vile person" and "cold-blooded murderer." In that version of Johnnie, he mattered because he ended the lives of two police officers. In the tragic events at Cabrini-Green on July 17, 1970, he was the villain. He was the irreparable harm he'd caused, the worst thing he ever did—or, he insisted, didn't even do. The parole board might never get past Johnnie's innocence claim. But Garber wanted those on the board to have to contend with Johnnie's own words, with a more complex telling of his experiences. Johnnie needed to be seen as a full human being, the main character of his own story.

Johnnie put off writing about himself for months. Instead of working on the autobiography, he read George Orwell or watched TV in his cell. It was 2019, and like most people in or out of prison, Johnnie followed the news about Donald Trump—the president's first impeachment, Trump's obsession with a border wall, some crazy claim that windmills caused cancer. Darlene had surgery, and Johnnie fixated on her and her spirits. Then a flu bug went around Hill. The men there were packed together like chickens in a processing plant, the air still with their confinement, and the virus spread from cell to cell and person to person. Johnnie stayed in bed with aches and a scratchy throat. Another time he started coughing and wheezing and thought a virus was taking him down again, but he looked around and everyone on the wing was gagging. Not the flu this time; mace.

To inspire his writing, Johnnie collected photographs of his family visiting him in prison, dating back to his teenage years. In many of the shots, Johnnie managed to make a prison jumpsuit look like a style choice, with the collar popped and the front unzipped down his chest. In one, he's embracing Darlene, who is twenty and wearing a polka-dot bikini top. No way a prison would let that in today. There was a photo of Johnnie, with a bountiful Afro, squatting between his children— Peaches, nine, in a pink skirt and bobby socks, and Johnnie Jr., known as Bumpy, eight, in brown slacks and a 1978 abstract-patterned shirt. In another photo, Johnnie strikes the same pose but time has telescoped forward: Peaches is behind him, a grown woman, alongside her mother, Leora, and the children balanced on each of Johnnie's knees are his grandchildren. Johnnie was at Hill, in 2015, when Leora died. They'd stayed close over the years, and he'd been certain that he was going to be the one to go first. Then in 2018, Peaches died. She was forty-nine, born the year before Johnnie was locked up. Johnnie had spoken to Peaches and everything was fine, and when he called her house the next day he was told the news. A heart attack. He had to contain his grief, his impotent sorrow, and tend to his granddaughter, Lawanda Starks, known to the family as Little Peaches. Starks was in her twenties, and Johnnie called her every day, comforting her, helping her get her life back on track.

Eventually, late at night, Johnnie started to write. He brewed tea on a hot plate, and on his typewriter he pecked out what he titled "Abbreviated Biography of Mr. Johnnie Veal." He didn't want his pages to be lost. Anything could happen to his belongings when guards tossed his cell or when he was forced to move every six months. So he made copies in the prison library, ten cents a page, and mailed each section he finished to Garber, eventually sixteen single-spaced pages in all.

Johnnie was born on Chicago's West Side, in 1952, and when he was five his mother, Lillie Mae Veal, moved him and his five siblings into a ten-story high-rise at Cabrini-Green. When Johnnie's aunt died, his mother took in her sister's five children and raised them as well. Johnnie made no distinction between the siblings and cousins; they were his brothers and sisters. "We all lived in a three room bed unit at 1159 N. Cleveland with wall-to-wall bunk beds for eleven kids. We were one big family being raised by a single parent moms," Johnnie wrote. "Cabrini-Green to our family was hope for a better standard of living."

Lillie Veal grew up on her parents' farm in Mississippi and didn't finish high school. In Chicago, she wanted her children to have more opportunities to succeed. "Even though my moms was a single parent on welfare, she gave us a normal childhood and a house full of love," wrote Johnnie. The population at Cabrini-Green was then at its peak, a count of eighteen thousand people, with two-thirds of the residents under the age of eighteen. In nearly every neighborhood in Chicago, the population averaged one child for every two adults; only in the city's large public housing developments was the concentration of children so extremely out of whack. The public schools at Cabrini-Green were the most crowded in the city. Students were taught in trailers and in shifts. Johnnie's mother enrolled her children in the local Catholic parish schools. Darlene recalled seeing Johnnie and his siblings in their school uniforms. She assumed the Veals were rich.

They weren't. Johnnie's parents separated before the family relocated from the West Side. Johnnie's only vivid memory of his father, a veteran of the Korean War who was also named Johnnie Veal, was from a day when Johnnie must have been seven or eight. His father showed up at Cabrini-Green one morning to take Johnnie and his sister on an outing. Johnnie could still see his sister in pigtails. He could see his father's car—a blue 1957 Chevy. But not his father. In a couple of the photographs Johnnie had of his mother visiting him in prison, a man stands alongside her. In a rakish fedora, in his fifties or sixties, about the age Johnnie was now, he is Johnnie's weathered twin—the same rounded cheekbones and pursed lips, the same nose and thick demonstrative eyebrows, the same skin and penetrating dark stare. Johnnie had no memory of his father ever visiting. He erased it. In 1970, when Johnnie's name was plastered all over the news, his father hadn't surfaced. Not during the manhunt or the trial. And he wasn't around when Lillie Veal raised Johnnie and his ten siblings. It was his mom who secured scholarships for her children. "She continued to better her life by studying to be a nurse's aide and enriching our lives with expectation and hope."

On Johnnie's first-grade report card, in 1959, his teacher, Sister Mary Sophia, marked that he practiced self-control and kept "profitably busy," but she gave him unsatisfactory grades in Christian doctrine, phonics, reading, handwriting, numbers work, and art. Johnnie was a leader, however, even at a young age. At St. Joseph's, he prepared mass as an altar boy. He was a crossing guard and Cub Scout. The school's principal, Sister Mary Benet, said he organized the students in games. "Veal's Boys," she called the kids. His athleticism seemed effortless—baseball, softball, karate, boxing, handball. He had coaches at Cabrini-Green who told him he should shoot for the 1972 Olympic games in track and field. He was that fast. "That has always been my dream growing up," Johnnie wrote in his autobiography to the parole board. Many of his friends had acquired nicknames—Slow Down or Baby Frail or Leprechaun. But Johnnie was just Johnnie, a testament to his singular appeal. "When you said 'Johnnie,' it was like saying 'Michael' for Michael Jackson. We knew who you were talking about," a friend whose nickname was Pokey recalled. When they graduated from eighth grade in 1968, Johnnie and some friends celebrated by nabbing a bottle of Seagram's 7 from a parent's cabinet. It was the first time Johnnie tried alcohol, and he gulped the whiskey like he was drinking from a spigot. Before long he was slurring his words and peed himself. The door to Johnnie's apartment, like most units then, was left unlocked. Johnnie's friends carried him inside before running off. Johnnie's mother, thinking he had some terrible illness, called the police. "No, ma'am, he's just drunk," the officers who arrived told her. That was also the last time Johnnie tried alcohol. He had no interest.

Johnnie said that as a teenager, he noticed little else but girls. But he did recognize the neighborhood's decline. "By the time I started to turn fourteen Cabrini-Green had begun to change. I didn't understand what the Civil Rights Movement was nor the politics surrounding Chicago. The youth summer time job programs started to disappear." The Johnson administration's War on Poverty was ending. Federal dollars that had paid for childcare and civil service exam classes and created summer jobs for teenagers were being redirected to policing. The hundreds of factories that surrounded Cabrini-Green, along with their thousands of industrial jobs, were disappearing as well.

The boys in each of Cabrini-Green's towers had always banded together, relatives and neighbors taking on the boys from the nearby high-rises in games or skirmishes. Now they aligned themselves with different street gangs. "A lot of Catholic school kids often was the target during that time because we wore school uniforms," Johnnie wrote. "I had to fight through two gang areas in order to attend St. Joseph's school. The Stones were in 1150 and 1160 and the Black Deuces and Disciples in the 1117 and 1119 buildings." Each morning he ran out of his building, darting down a fire lane and ducking for cover. "It was like walking through a gauntlet every day." Suddenly it wasn't safe to go to the local community center, to the park on the other side of Division Street, to the nearby row houses. His life was ever more circumscribed.

He joined the Cobra Stones at fifteen. The choice was not a difficult one. Johnnie was sensible about it. "When you get beat down enough, you find out early it's best to choose sides to survive." He said that he never harmed those he called "civilians," the residents who weren't gangbanging like him. He wrote in his autobiography, "I was not a saint in my efforts to stay alive in a war zone, but most of all I was not a crazy little teenager without a moral compass in my life either."

Johnnie's mother sent him to a Catholic high school a mile away for ninth grade. The students were mostly white and Latino, and Johnnie was introduced to sports he'd never played. There were kids who bowled and did archery. Johnnie joined the wrestling team. But he didn't last long at the school. Johnnie picked up the Division Street bus outside his high-rise, but on his way to school the bus passed through enemy territory. Returning home one day, Johnnie saw a group of guys waiting for him at the stop before his own; they were armed and ready to board and Johnnie had nowhere to run. He showed the bus driver the handgun he kept in his bag. "If you stop this bus, I'll shoot you," he threatened. He had no intention of harming the driver, but his life depended on the bus skipping the next stop. That was the end of Catholic high school. Johnnie tried a public school closer to his building. But it didn't seem like much of a learning environment, and he stopped going altogether, well short of finishing his freshman year.

Johnnie limited his activities to a two-block radius around his building, or far from Cabrini-Green. He went to dances, always scanning his surroundings. Or he snuck off to Cubs games or the Lincoln Park Zoo. "In the jungle, it's survival mode," Johnnie said of his teen years. "Like in my environment, you see shootouts every day, and you're part of them. But in the jungle, you also play, fish, enjoy the fruits of trees. You live a double life." Once, after roller-skating with friends, he and a buddy walked three girls home. Diane, Nadine and *Wilomena*. "I was crazy about her," Johnnie would recall. The five of them crossed Larrabee, near Division Street, and entered a little corner store to buy Slim Jims and potato chips. He knew being over there was a no-no, that he was venturing beyond a safety zone, but he was sixteen and accompanying three girls and hoping the night wouldn't end. They were on their way out when four boys entered the shop. Johnnie had grown up with all of them. But they were now Black Deuces. Johnnie and his friend ducked their heads and tried to hurry out, but the store was little more than a narrow passage.

"Look who's here, Little Johnnie," one of the teenagers announced. Johnnie leapt the last four or five yards to the door, trying to push his way out. Someone grabbed his coat, and Johnnie twisted and threw a punch. Suddenly six bodies were in motion in the tight space. A boy known as Johnny Camp landed blows to Johnnie's face and neck and arms.

"Pop him! Pop him!" someone shouted. Johnnie and his friend were through the door when they heard the explosion of a shotgun blast. They tumbled into the street and kept running as they ducked behind cars. They made it to the fire station on the corner. Johnnie was struggling to breathe. He touched his neck and came away with a palmful of blood. Johnny Camp had hit him not with a fist but with a knife. Johnnie's throat was slashed. A deep, pulsing gash. Years later in prison, Johnnie Veal and Johnny Camp ended up in the same cell house. They were about to continue their feud when older guys stepped between them, saying what had happened on the streets when they were boys needed to stay on the streets. At sixteen, though, Johnnie was rushed to the hospital. He'd lost a lot of blood. His mother called the parish priest from St. Joseph's, Father Dennis Kendrick, who'd baptized all the Veal children. The priest recited the sacraments over Johnnie's body, anointing his head and hands with oils and giving him the blessing of last rites. The latter turned out to be premature. Johnnie recovered. While he was still in the hospital, one of the Black Deuces figured out how to reach him and called his room, saying, "We're going to finish the job when you come home."

As violence swirled around Johnnie as a teenager, his mother left Cabrini-Green, moving with some of her other children to a neighborhood on the city's distant South Side. Johnnie chose to stay behind. He admitted in his autobiography that he came up hard and reckless, but he had to make the parole board see his full seventeen-year-old self as well as who he was today. "I was not proud of the things I did to other gang members that were trying to harm me," Johnnie wrote. "I learned early on that there were kids like me who was just trying to survive as oppose to the hardcore kids that were perpetrating senseless violence."

IN THE EARLY 1970s, crime in most large U.S. cities was on the rise. There were many reasons for the spike, everything from white flight to the suburbs to the loss of factory jobs, expanding income inequality, and the increase in single-parent households among the least well off. The greatest factor might have been tied to the age distribution of crime, and the huge number of baby boomers, born in the years after World War II, who were then in their late teens to late twenties—the age range most likely to commit a crime. With parole under fire and on the way out, the question was, what should replace it? In considering different sentencing structures, people in and out of prison were also debating the purpose of punishment, and what role incarceration played in crime prevention.

The leading conservative scholar on these issues was then James Q. Wilson, the Harvard political scientist whose "broken windows" theory of crime control would become a blueprint for expanded policing in many American cities. Wilson saw himself as an objective measurer of how cities did and didn't work. He wrote his first book about Black politicians while studying at the University of Chicago, on the city's South Side, and began examining crime because he imagined police officers as "urban ambassadors." For Wilson, the reason crime had shot up was easy to quantify—fewer people were being sent to prison. The U.S. prison population had fallen from 220,000 in 1961 to 196,000 in 1972. Wilson contended that more people in the country needed to be locked up and for longer periods of time. "Wicked people exist," Wilson wrote in his 1975 bestseller, *Thinking About Crime*. "Nothing avails except to set them apart from innocent people."

Wilson agreed with the prevailing view that imprisonment and rehabilitation had proven incompatible. Prisons in America were better at incapacitation, at locking up those deemed dangerous in facilities far from the public. But Wilson argued that prisons served another critical social function, one that was harder to measure—deterrence. He believed that harsh prison sentences delivered a warning to people on the streets: there were grave consequences if they chose to break the law. It was the old model of the stocks and the whipping post, of punishment as public spectacle, although with the punishments administered far away and out of sight. Wilson wrote, "Many people, neither wicked nor innocent, but watchful, dissembling, and calculating of their opportunities, ponder our reaction to wickedness as a cue to what they might profitably do. We have trifled with the wicked, made sport of the innocent, and encouraged the calculators. Justice suffers, and so do we all."

The relationship between punishment and deterrence has always been tenuous. Even Wilson recognized the lack of agreement on the subject. Most crimes are committed by young adults, like Johnnie and Michael and the other baby boomers in the 1970s then entering their late teens and early twenties. People at that age are especially impulsive and less likely to contemplate risks and long-term consequences. Before acting, were they really going to weigh the multiple charges that a prosecutor might stack against them? Were they going to be stopped by thoughts of someone like Johnnie Veal or Michael Henderson languishing in a distant prison? And what about parity under the law? How could it be fair to send one person to prison for twenty years as a warning to others? Justifying an extremely long prison term on some prediction of future crime was flimsy at best. And besides, in the years ahead the country went all in on incarceration. If prisons really worked as a deterrent, then American mass incarceration should have proven it. And yet with two million people locked up in the country's prisons and jails, the present-day United States is nowhere close to being the safest society in all of humankind. The neighborhoods with the highest rates of incarceration are anything but crimeless Edens.

Like David Fogel in Illinois, there were others trying to draw up new sentencing models who were more concerned with using incarceration as sparingly as possible. Norval Morris, a renowned criminologist, envisioned a kind of Hippocratic oath for criminal justice—punishments should first do no harm beyond the most minimal sanction required. "Any punitive suffering beyond societal need is what, in this context, defines cruelty," Morris wrote in a 1974 book, *The Future of Imprisonment.* What were the "societal needs" of a punishment? Morris and others, in rejecting a rehabilitation model for prisons, embraced retribution as a more honest and viable social function. Retribution meant illegal acts had consequences in the form of a sanction. That punishments reasserted the law, teaching the norms of what was right and wrong. It gave victims recourse. Sentencing theorists of this era attached "limited" to "retribution," a hopeful coinage suggesting—wrongly—that imprisonment would be seen as a punishment of last resort and that when used the sentences would be relatively short. In his 1976 book, *Doing Justice*, the legal philosopher Andrew von Hirsch introduced a sentencing theory of proportionality he called "just deserts." "Deserts" because von Hirsch also maintained that people who committed crimes deserved some form of punishment. "Just" because, unlike parole as it had been practiced, the punishments should be fully transparent, clearly defined, and based solely on the seriousness of the crime, and not on the person. All that storytelling Johnnie had to do to humanize himself and make board members see him as more than a felon—that wouldn't be necessary in an objective and impersonal system.

What replaced indeterminate sentences and parole in nearly every criminal justice system in the country were sentencing guidelines. To advance proportionality and fairness, judges at sentencing were required to follow explicit specifications on what punishments they could impose. The predetermined guidelines listed a menu of crimes and then offered up a corresponding sentencing range. That defined range of months or years was based on the severity of the offense and the offender's prior record. In many instances the guidelines were spelled out in two-dimensional grids. The simplicity was part of the appeal. One axis ranked crimes as scores, from least to most serious; the other axis scored the offender, based on previous offenses. The total score was tied to a fixed selection of punishments. So a person with two prior felonies who committed an aggravated assault might equate to a prison term of thirty-eight to forty months, the judge maintaining a little bit of discretion to decide between these upper and lower ranges. Sentencing commissions were formed to hash out notions of just deserts in practice, ranking different crimes by "offense levels." Some of this was common sense. A robbery without a deadly weapon was less severe than a robbery with a gun. A carjacking was worse than shoplifting. Other determinations involved moral and cultural judgments. How bad was drug possession? What did prior arrests reveal about someone if rehabilitation wasn't the point of a sanction?

Unlike release dates as determined by a parole board, published guidelines were meant to be open to public scrutiny, predictable, and consistent. By constraining what judges could decide, the hope was to eliminate the opportunities for subjectivity and bias that troubled the parole system. Whether someone convicted of a crime came before a hanging judge or a bleeding-heart liberal, their sentences would be nearly uniform. Published guidelines functioned as a check on human error and discrimination. Judges could deviate only within the allotted maximums and minimums. It was intended to fix the problem of huge sentencing disparities. A grid or published table looked at a crime as the thing to punish, not at the person.

But sentencing guidelines weren't bias-proof. Far more often, judges, presented with a range of prison time to choose from, gave Black and brown people the longer sentences. A prior criminal history, a determining factor in these guidelines, was not a neutral thing. Blacks and Latinos were more likely than white people to be subjected to a street stop by a police officer, more likely to be detained pretrial, more likely to be pressured into a plea bargain, and more likely to be hit with a parole violation. Black people, too, were less often given alternatives to incarceration, such as fines, suspended sentences, or community service. Sentencing guidelines were also instituted at a time when the very concept of a punishment's legitimate social function was shifting radically. For a brief time after Attica, many politicians in the country felt compelled to address oppressive prison conditions and unjust sentencing laws. Public sentiment demanded it. But that changed. Reports of rising crime, the racial reckoning around civil rights, and the growing awareness of the rights of the incarcerated were met with a "tough-on-crime" retrenchment. Republicans hammered away with a law-and-order platform. Democrats shied from their past efforts to address the root causes of crime. Elected officials from both parties saw that there were enormous political downsides to appearing weak on violent crime.

Sentencing guidelines were products of state politics. They might have been conceived of initially by sentencing commissions, but from there they were voted into law and reshaped by elected officials. Politicians ran regularly for reelection, raised campaign funds, and were more likely than judges or parole board members to be called on to react to each sensational crime that grabbed the public's attention. In Illinois, Fogel's "proposal for swift, certain, and even-handed justice" was supplanted by more punitive Class X felony laws. The same process occurred in other states that curtailed indeterminate sentencing. Legislators, in setting standards, continually one-upped one another in displays of their commitment to public safety by voting for harsher punishments.

In California, for example, the Uniform Determinate Sentencing Act of 1976 abolished parole for all offenses other than murder, a recognition that parole discretion could be as much about keeping people deemed dangerous in prison as letting them out. The new law replaced indeterminate sentences with, depending on the felony type, a mandatory lower, middle, and upper sentence range. Liberals and conservatives worked together for over two years to develop sentencing parameters that they agreed were fair and as limited as possible. People in state prisons and their family members on the outside wrote thousands of letters in support of the bipartisan bill. But in 1977, before the legislation was even signed into law, the sentencing requirements were already being condemned as felon-friendly, as too lenient. In the hands of politicians concerned about these labels, the bill was amended. Several years were added to the mandatory minimums of the middle and upper ranges; the amount of time people released from prison had to spend under state supervision was increased; prosecutors were given the discretion to add enhancements to lengthen sentences beyond the published guidelines. So if a person committed a crime and was in possession of a

gun or drugs or in a gang database or near a school when the crime occurred, prosecutors could stack multiple charges on top of one another
for a single offense, the years in prison increasing exponentially.

The original sentencing guidelines in California were made tougher,
more severe, but the revisions hadn't undone the intent of the new
law. Not yet. But then those amendments were also denounced as too soft.
Just months after the bill and its amendment went into effect, the state
legislature passed a companion bill. More months and more years were
added to the mandatory prison terms and to the length of supervision
after release. The race to escalate punishments was on. The guidelines
bubbled over and grew like some out-of-control laboratory experiment.
The Democratic governor, Jerry Brown, was running for reelection in
1978. One of the Republicans in the race, a Los Angeles police chief,
painted a picture in his attack ads of a tide of violent criminals coming
from prisons and jails, that is, if permissive liberals were left in charge.
One ad intoned ominously, "On one of side of that door are the predators
of society; while on the other side, in the relative quiet of our communities, lie the potential victims. . . . At the center of this turnstile sit
the executive and legislative branch of government." Not to be outdone,
Governor Brown signed the increasingly draconian guidelines into law
at a ceremony inside the offices of the Los Angeles sheriff, flanked by
police and other law enforcement officials.

The end of indeterminate sentencing, beginning in the 1970s, opened
the floodgates to mass incarceration. Changes to parole proved to be the
first sentencing reforms of the get-tough era. How did prison populations reach unprecedented heights? Simply put, more people were sent
to prison, for longer amounts of time, with fewer forms of early release.
In the 1970s and 1980s, nearly every state passed mandatory minimum
sentencing laws like the Class X felony statutes in Illinois. Judges were
legally obligated to sentence from, say, four to fifteen years for a carjacking, or six to thirty years for armed robbery. But the minimums grew
longer. The amount of time in prison required by the mandatory lower
ranges tripled on average over the next two decades.

Most states also enacted truth-in-sentencing laws. Truth in sentencing guaranteed that people in prison for certain serious offenses
serve nearly all of their sentence, usually 85 percent of their time or

higher. No more chance of someone getting out on parole after ten years or shortening a sentence through earned good-time credits. The 1968 Truth in Lending Act protected consumers by forcing lenders and credit card companies to disclose the terms and costs of their finance charges. By applying the term to punishment, "truth in sentencing" implied that a prison sentence was some sacred number that equated to accountability, despite the fact that terms negotiated by prosecutors as part of a plea deal usually diverged dramatically from those handed down by a judge after a guilty verdict. The neologism suggested that leniency was a lie, that parole or good-time credits or any incentive that adjusted a prison term was an underhanded way to swindle the public of its due. The 1994 Violent Crime Control and Law Enforcement Act, written in part by Delaware senator Joseph Biden and signed into law, in celebratory fashion, by Democratic president Bill Clinton, made eight billion dollars available for new prison construction. To qualify for the federal funds, states had to demonstrate that more people convicted of crimes served time in prison, that prison sentences on average increased, and that "truth-in-sentencing" guidelines were enacted so that offenders served at least 85 percent of their terms. The 1994 crime bill incentivized more incarceration. In short order, twenty-eight states and the District of Columbia demonstrated that they met these requirements.

States passed laws to expand their criminal codes, redefining crimes as more severe and giving prosecutors the authority to add enhancements to already-long mandatory minimum terms. In California, for instance, over a four-year stretch in the 1980s, legislators passed eighty different gun measures that added enhancements to sentences. Most of these targeted young Black and Latino men suspected of being members of gangs. In Illinois, a firearm enhancement required judges to add fifteen years to already-long mandatory sentences if someone had a gun on them during a crime but didn't fire it; twenty years if the gun was fired but didn't hurt anyone, and twenty-five to life if the gun resulted in a death. So a twenty-year minimum for someone caught up in a murder, even if they weren't the shooter, became a *minimum* of forty-five years. One of the most common enhancements, a prior record, also disproportionately affected Black people, since African American communities were more heavily policed and Black people were more likely to be charged with a crime. In the 1990s, twenty-four states and the federal government enacted "three strikes" laws directed at repeat offenders—three felonies, even if the third one was relatively minor, triggered a long, mandatory prison sentence, usually of twenty-five years to life. As far as just deserts, a three-strikes law, along with certain statutes that punished "street drugs" such as crack cocaine much more harshly than other narcotics, violated the principle of proportionality. The punishments, of up to life, were often vastly more severe than was dictated by the third offense. Children, too, were increasingly charged as adults—"adult crime, adult time," the rhetoric went. With courts challenging the constitutionality of the death penalty, a new sentence just short of death gained wide use, one that assured a person would never leave prison: life without the possibility of parole.

Parole, for all its failings, has to assess each individual under consideration. Sentencing guidelines, in the name of objectivity and fairness, punish crime in the abstract, thereby opening the way for the public and politicians to transform justice. Everywhere discretionary parole remained, these new sentencing laws also ended up shaping each decision about release. A parole board member like Donald Shelton, like all of us in the United States, is steeped in a culture in which extreme prison sentences have become the norm. What is considered a fair and legitimate punishment today looks as much like 1970 numbers as the costs of a college tuition. Johnnie, trying to tell a story about himself, about why he deserved to leave prison after fifty years, was competing now against an accepted narrative that it wasn't just okay but also somehow necessary for hundreds of thousands of people to be sentenced to death by prison.

CABRINI-GREEN IN THE hours after Sgt. James Severin and Officer Anthony Rizzato were murdered was pandemonium. It seemed like half of the public housing development's thousands of residents came outside to see what happened. Police, too, were everywhere, searching buildings, questioning people, rounding up potential suspects. The officers were a dangerous combination: seething, grieving, fearful. They fired their guns upward at several high-rises, at targets they couldn't see. A police helicopter rattled overhead. Johnnie claimed he was with a group of friends warming up for a baseball game when the shootings occurred. "Me, Slow Down, Baby Frail, and June Faulkner were popping up and waiting on everyone else," Johnnie wrote in the pages sent to the parole board. "When we first heard gun shots behind us coming from the big baseball field on July 17, 1970, we did what we always do, duck and look for a safe exit point. The game hadn't even started yet, then someone said, 'Look over there, two police officers been shot.'"

Johnnie said he joined the onlookers. When he learned that he was wanted for questioning, he thought it unwise to try to plead his case to the officers then marauding the neighborhood. He took a bus 140 blocks to where his mother was living on the South Side. The police were there already. They mistook Johnnie's older brother by a year, Glen, for him, pointing a gun in his face. But they let Glen go when they saw he didn't have the identifying thick scar that stretched across Johnnie's throat. The police left only minutes before Johnnie arrived. He was hidden in an apartment six doors down and, later, in a hotel room. Leora, pregnant with Bumpy, joined him with their daughter, Peaches. On the hotel's television, Johnnie saw his face on every newscast.

They were viciously murdered by an animal, struck down.

His name is Johnnie Veal. He is eighteen, and he is the leader of the Cobra Stones street gang.

Johnnie, in fact, was seventeen, and he telephoned the actual leader of the Cobra Stones, a twenty-five-year-old named Mickey Cogwell, who put Johnnie in touch with a lawyer. Eugene Pincham, a former civil rights activist and later a judge, was then one of Chicago's most prominent Black defense attorneys. Pincham had represented several young men arrested during the riots in Chicago after King's assassination. He represented high-ranking gang members, including Jeff Fort, the leader of the Black P. Stone Nation. Johnnie was now public enemy number one. Apart from being a known gang member at Cabrini-Green, he said he didn't know why he was a suspect. But a citywide manhunt was underway. Johnnie wanted to turn himself in, to prove his innocence. But Pincham feared that while in police custody Johnnie would be beaten or murdered.

James Severin's walk-and-talk community-relations unit was formed because police brutality in Chicago had become an indisputable and recognized fact. In 1967, the Chicago Police Department created a special gang intelligence unit, whose blitzing officers and rough tactics were the opposite of walking and talking. For many Black residents of Chicago, the gang unit represented the "real" police. "To some Negroes police have come to symbolize white power, white racism and white repression," the 1968 presidential commission on civil disorders, led by former Illinois governor Otto Kerner, stated. "And the fact is that many police do reflect and express these white attitudes." Of the fourteen cities studied by the Kerner Commission, Chicago was found to have the most instances of reported police abuse. Chicago even topped the list in the percentage of white residents who thought police brutality rampant. During the 1968 Democratic National Convention held in Chicago, police and state and federal troops essentially rioted. Police arrested more than 650 protestors and sent at least a hundred to local hospitals with injuries.

That same year, Black police officers in Chicago formed an organization to challenge racism and abuse within the department's own ranks. "Black people really need and want good police protection because of the gang terrorism and the crime within the community," Renault Robinson, one of the founders of the Afro-American Patrolmen's League, said. "But there will be a call from the projects and the police won't answer, either because they don't care or they fear for their lives. Then they'll stop some guy who's driving home from work and beat the hell out of him because he doesn't say 'sir.'"

On a morning in 1969, before dawn, the deputy chairman of the national Black Panther Party, twenty-one-year-old Fred Hampton, was asleep in his apartment on Chicago's West Side when fourteen officers charged into his home. The police shot and killed Hampton and another Panther Party member named Mark Clark. Across the country that year, police killed twenty-seven Black Panthers and arrested another seven hundred. The officers in Chicago who shot Hampton reported that they announced themselves at the apartment door and came under fire. They claimed self-defense. But that was shown to be a lie. It was an assassination. Drugged the night before by a fellow Black Panther working for the FBI, Hampton was still asleep in bed when he was killed. Of the nearly hundred shots fired that morning, all but one came from a police officer's gun.

Police oppression in Chicago and the battle against it turned into open warfare. In 1969 and 1970, officers in Chicago shot to death seventy-nine people, three-quarters of them African American. In only one of the seventy-nine uses of fatal force was an officer indicted, and he was later acquitted. During that same time, fifteen Chicago police officers were shot and killed while on duty. Severin and Rizzato were among them.

That was the climate in Chicago as Johnnie awaited his arrest. A group of Black police officials, who understood the dangers, joined up with the Reverend Jesse Jackson, who was then running the Chicago chapter of Operation Breadbasket, which continued King's work by focusing on economic advancement in Black communities. Together, they tried to negotiate Johnnie's safe surrender. A plan for them to meet with Pincham at a Cabrini-Green church fell apart when Jackson was pulled over by other police officers on the way there. The shooting at Cabrini-Green happened on a Friday evening; the following Monday, at lunchtime, Pincham escorted Johnnie to the criminal court building to surrender directly to a judge. "Johnnie Veal Gives Self Up," the news reports announced.

"I was taken into custody and escorted to the Cook County Jail," Johnnie wrote the parole board. "Life as I knew it had ended. The world had just stop and I realized how much I didn't know about life, people and the situation I now found myself in. My faith had always been that the courts would figure this out in due time."

5

Parole Prep

Alone in a cell, in segregation again after another infraction, Michael studied the book on yoga he'd borrowed from the prison library. There were guys inside who found relief from their trapped lives by keeping pet cats or rabbits or playing sports or unending games of Dungeons & Dragons. Others swore by meditation as a source of tranquility. Michael was open to learning new things, and he believed that he'd yet to tap the vast powers of his mind. Sitting cross-legged on his bunk in lotus position, he read and reread the descriptions of each exercise in the manual and studied the illustrations. He closed his eyes and worked to shut out the shouts of guards and the rattle of cell doors. He cleared his thoughts of the rank smell of mold and the bite of his hard bunk. The air was cool as it entered his nostrils, heavy with heat as it left his mouth. Michael relaxed his shoulders, straightened his back, let his tongue lay flat in his mouth. He aimed his thoughts to the parts of his body that pressed into his pancake mattress. He practiced like this several hours a day. One thing Michael had in abundance was time.

In prison, there was so much Michael couldn't control—the other incarcerated men, the guards, his release date. His every movement was restricted, his choices dictated to him. When to wake, eat, shower, walk, turn out the lights. He'd found ways to navigate the prison's authoritarian codes. He'd never been punked, never injured. But it took constant vigilance. Michael was at a medium-security facility downstate. It was safer in many ways than Pontiac, the Thunderdome, but the conditions weren't much improved from the early uprising days of the 1970s. The John Howard Association, a prison watchdog group, went into Michael's prison and surveyed the population. Of the two thousand men locked up with him, a majority of them were Black; a majority, too, were from Chicago, which was four hours away by car. The men at the prison complained about the substandard medical care, the unhealthy food, the lack of personal hygiene supplies. When things broke, they weren't fixed. The temperature fluctuated between dangerously cold and hot. Most of those surveyed said the staff was disrespectful and didn't follow the rules. They said they could get contraband from the outside but not their mail. They wanted more educational opportunities to help with rehabilitation and reentry.

Michael was in his cell one day when guards escorted in a man, muttering to himself. A new cellie. During Michael's time in prison, he'd witnessed the rise of mass incarceration. The population inside flipping from majority white to majority Black. The overcrowding. He'd also seen the growing number of people suffering from serious mental illness. Beginning in the late 1960s and early 1970s, most states stopped treating mental health patients in public hospitals. On the streets, people displaying signs of mental illness weren't given medical or psychological care; they were arrested and locked up. Jails in Chicago, Los Angeles, and New York became the country's largest psychiatric facilities. In prisons in the United States, one of every three people has a diagnosis of a mental disorder. Michael was reading on his bunk, snacking on the dessert he'd saved from chow. His new cellmate jumped up from his bed and snatched one of Michael's cookies. Because it was so far outside the code, because the man gobbled the cookie and returned to his bunk as if nothing had happened, Michael thought for a moment he might have imagined the transgression. Maybe he was the one losing his mind. Michael didn't want to hurt the guy, but he had to do something to reestablish order. He put his elbow into the man's neck, pinning him against the wall. Michael told him never to touch his stuff. The next day, Michael returned to the cell and a brownie he had on a Styrofoam tray was gone. A literal trail of crumbs led to the edge of his cellie's bunk, where the man was still chewing. Michael called for the guards, saying they needed to remove this bug, this crazy person, or Michael might be forced to kill him. He'd never make parole.

"I don't know what to tell you," a correctional officer said. The guard didn't know himself how to manage the SMIs, those with serious mental illness. "They've taken over," he said.

Yoga presented a way for Michael to exist in a world inside his head. He had to control the things that remained his own. The instruction book, a throwback to some earlier transcendental fad, promised an escape into other dimensions. With a pen, as instructed, Michael drew a dot on the cinder block wall. He studied the dot for hours. For days. He broke it down, thinking, *I put that dot there. It's black. The ink has a chemical composition that stains the wall. The wall is made of stone. The stones exist throughout the prison.* He felt a peacefulness as he considered how he was connected to an entire structure that itself was part of the wider world beyond. It was a kind of travel, a freedom. Staring at the wall one day, he saw a corona vibrating around the dot, like heat waves on a highway. Tendrils juddered and jumped, grew and filled Michael's peripheral vision. According to the manual, he was advancing. If Michael stared long enough, he could make the dot become a swirling passageway as large as a manhole cover. He was supposed to imagine himself entering it, going inside. Don't be frightened, the book advised. "Hell no," Michael told himself. He worried he wouldn't be able to come back. He'd never be normal again. Michael licked his thumb and smeared the dot from the wall. He got rid of the manual.

Michael quit yoga, but he was hooked on the idea of self-improvement. He gave up cigarettes, mainly because he was sick of supporting other guys' habits. *Man, can you spare a square?* He replaced nicotine with weed. He'd been doing cocaine and heroin in prison when he could get it. He didn't think he'd formed a habit. But by his midthirties, his body felt filled with wet sand. His muscles rebelled against action. He was weighted down by a lethargy that wouldn't clear.

Michael was transferred to Mt. Sterling in western Illinois, a prison whose population equaled that of the entire surrounding city. The concrete yard was about a quarter mile around. One morning, Michael attempted to jog it. Before he'd made it once around the perimeter, he was doubled over, his arms pinioned to his legs. His lungs convulsed, unable to pull in air. When he recovered enough to contemplate his bodily deterioration, what Michael felt was disgust. He wouldn't make it to fifty at this rate. He decided to make running a part of his daily routine.

He began by walking the yard. Soon he was mixing in short jogs. He built up his stamina, willing himself to continue. Michael liked that he could mark his progress. Once around without stopping. Four laps, a milestone. At Mt. Sterling, the men were allowed a total of two and a half hours of yard a day. Guys gathered around the weight pile, or huddled together in small groups. A few men jogged, and Michael noted the first time he passed each of them. He learned how to steady his breathing. He lengthened his stride. His muscles hardened. The fog in his head lifted. Michael still smoked weed. But the stronger stuff he no longer craved. He ran farther, upping his pace.

Michael could eventually run for ten miles, or even more. When he wore out his shoes, he bought new ones at the commissary. As the prison population grew, the yard was partitioned in half, and Michael was forced to run in ever tighter circles. During the winters, wind and snow barreled in off the Midwestern plains. Michael didn't stop. "I am the rain. I am the snow. I coexist with the universe," he liked to tell himself. If he missed a day or two, he fiended for the exercise. An irritation grew inside him. He craved the control that running provided, the release. A few miles into a run, as fatigue set in, he commanded his body to obey: "Shut up! Do what you're told!" He'd yell out, "The mind is the master!" He'd continue running, passing beyond the pain. He could get to a point where his body felt like it barely existed. And then he could imagine himself elsewhere. He was a passenger in the airplane passing overhead. He was driving in the car speeding along the highway. He was back home.

"Running saved my life," he would say. "I began to see all this power over my own destiny, regardless of what they do at that parole board."

In 1968, Michael was fifteen and working as a welder in an East St. Louis foundry. In California that year, the screen actor Ronald Reagan had recently become governor and the state's prison population reached what was then a historic high—28,400. It was, at that point in American history, an obscenely large number. The two closest states, New York and Texas, each incarcerated less than half that. The Illinois prison population was under seven thousand. The entire federal system held 19,700 people. California locked up almost one of every six people imprisoned in the country. Facing this crisis, Reagan ordered California's Adult Authority, the state parole board, to reduce the prison population by releasing people who were an acceptable risk to go free. During a medical emergency, a hospital with a finite number of beds must distinguish between who needs to be admitted and who can stay home. The Adult Authority did something similar, identifying candidates for parole with a low probability of reoffending. And finding them wasn't hard. In 1971 alone, the California parole board freed ten thousand people, a leap of more than 50 percent from previous years. By 1972, the state's prison population had fallen to seventeen thousand. Reagan was by all means a law-and-order Republican. Doubling down on Nixon's "freedom from fear," Reagan had won the governor's office—and would soon win the presidency—by stirring up anxieties over street crime, drug use, and welfare programs, casting all three as distinctly Black pathologies. But all those people in prison fattened the state budget; for the time being, at least, shrinking the size of government took precedence. Reagan used parole as a release valve to adjust the prison population and avoid overcrowding.

Parole had provided this function for a century. Prison terms, mostly negotiated by prosecutors, weren't sacrosanct; an individual's release and risk could be reassessed. There were also ways to hold people accountable other than prison, through fines or community service. As each of the states and the federal government rejected its parole system in one form or another, there were warnings that without this release mechanism prisons would become jam-packed with people. The think tank the Rand Corporation estimated, in 1977, that the return to determinate sentencing could increase the nation's prison population by 85 percent. It proved a ridiculous underestimate, one that didn't account for the United States going mad on punishment. Mandatory minimums, truth in sentencing, sentencing enhancements, three-strikes laws. By the 1980s, prisons in the United States were being imagined as mysterious black boxes. The constant calls for public safety and crime fighting both increased the inputs and put a stop to many of the outputs. More people arrested for crimes were sent to prison. Prison terms became longer. Opportunities for release were restricted. These were all policy choices. But the public had little interest in the inner workings of these black boxes, apart from the jobs provided by new prisons. "Dangerous criminals" were removed from society and sent away, as if they simply disappeared. The capacity to hold people in these faraway sites was treated as if it were limitless.

For most of the twentieth century, the American incarceration rate remained high relative to other countries but steady at about 100 people for every 100,000 in the general population. What happened beginning in the 1970s was a global as well as a historic aberration. In 1988, when Michael was nearing the end of his second decade of incarceration, the rate of imprisonment in America had more than doubled, to 244 per 100,000 people. Most of the states, the District of Columbia, and many of the country's large city jails were under court order to reduce their incarcerated populations because of extreme overcrowding. Crime was up, peaking during the crack epidemic of the early 1990s. But then crime fell and incarceration continued to balloon. Did locking up many more people actually prevent crime, as James Q. Wilson had contended? Were three-strikes laws and truth in sentencing an iron-fisted deterrent to would-be lawbreakers? It seemed not, based on the unrelated rise and fall of crime numbers. But the country by then had also disinvested in national spending on crime research. As far as entering mass incarceration, the nation forged its policies in the realm of hyperbole and fear, of political campaigns and reports of "super-predators." By 2009, the United States locked up an incomparable 754 per 100,000 people. For Black men in the United States, the incarceration rate rose to 4,347 per 100,000. The United States has fifty state prison systems along with a federal system. They are independent from one another and vary as much as Louisiana, Maine, and New Mexico differ. Yet incarceration rates and prison numbers soared in each of them.

I once interviewed a longtime prosecutor in the Philadelphia district attorney's office who insisted that mass incarceration was a myth, that there was no break with the past. He said prosecutors in the 1980s and '90s and 2000s simply did what they'd always done and put away "bad guys." In a way, the scale of the change was so immense that it did seem unbelievable. But it really happened. In 1973, the U.S. prison population increased by about eight thousand people from the previous year. That was the start of twenty-six consecutive years of rising prison numbers. African Americans were always severely overrepresented in the U.S. prison population. But rates of Black-to-white incarceration in the United States had also remained stable at about three to one. By the 1980s, it was more than five to one, and in 2000 it had reached eight to one. Ronald Reagan thought it an emergency, in 1968, when California's prison population topped 28,000. That figure soon seemed impossibly small. In the 2000s, the number of people in California prisons topped 175,000. Only eleven entire countries locked up more people than the state of California. The number of Black people incarcerated in the Golden State alone exceeded 50,000. Latinos: 66,000.

MICHAEL FINISHED HIS daily run one afternoon when another man approached him on the yard. The guy was big, 250 pounds, with an offensive lineman's girth. His name was Eddie Williams, but everyone called him Big Kane. In the medium-security prison in southern Illinois, people assumed he was Big "Caine," as in cocaine, since he'd been locked up numerous times for different drug cases. The nickname, though, was a nod to the smooth Brooklyn rapper Big Daddy Kane. Williams was someone without an inside voice, who talked at all times as if trying to be heard at a concert. Forty and overweight, he told Michael he wanted to get in shape. He asked if Michael would help him. Michael had generally run alone in prison, enjoying the freedom that the movement provided. But he agreed.

The first thing Michael said when they started was that what they were doing wasn't running. It was training. They were trying always to improve on the day before. Williams made it two times around the yard before he thought he might be dying. Michael smiled. That was Kane letting his body tell his mind what to do. Motioning to the rest of the yard, Michael told him that everybody in the joint was there because their body had told them what to do. "The body masquerades as though it has an intelligence, man. You got to shut that shit down, or it's going to rule you."

In prison, people who were trying to rehabilitate themselves sometimes looked to long-timers for guidance, those who maintained a discipline that allowed them to survive decades of incarceration. For Williams, it seemed this C-Number, Taboo, had taken the discipline to an entirely different level. He wanted that. He was serving an eleven-year bid for theft—stealing from a Save A Lot grocery store—and for aggravated battery of the police officer who tried to stop him. With truth in sentencing requiring he do 85 percent of his time, he could be out in nine years and four months. Williams had children of his own who were now parents themselves, and he thought it pitiful that as a grandfather he was locked up. He was searching for ways to make this bid his last.

Michael and Williams ran. When they rested, they talked. Michael told him there were certain people in prison you had to fraternize with just enough and never more. Those guys weren't responsible, they didn't keep their word, they were heedless. As they rounded the track over weeks and then months, Michael asked Williams to elaborate on what he would do differently when he got out this time. Had he really owned up to his past bad decisions? Had he mastered his addictions? Michael questioned Big Kane the way the parole board members had interviewed him.

MICHAEL CONTINUED TO go to his parole hearings alone. He never tried to get an attorney. He believed the parole board would be offended if he had legal representation; they would think he didn't trust them enough to talk to them directly. It was a prison mentality, internalized chains. He appeared each year for his parole interview, thinking he could show the board that he was compassionate, honest, and far more than the worst thing he did. He believed in his own powers as a storyteller, in his gifts as a salesman and good listener. But it was never enough. A parole board member would ask Michael again to describe the night in 1971 that he shot Richard Schaeffer. Where was he standing? Why did he take out the gun? Why did he run? They'd end up spending a sizable chunk of the interview addressing the small discrepancies in Michael's retelling. He would have done better to relate how he took up running,

how through discipline he made it a part of his daily regimen, how he
now trained others. A story with a beginning, middle, and end that dra-
matized his transformation.

Sixteen states and the federal government abolished parole for most
of their incarcerated populations, yet, like Illinois, they continue to hear
parole cases for those convicted before the law change. Along with the
remaining thirty-four states, each state practices parole in some form.
And each practices it in different ways. But for almost all of them, the
odds are stacked against release. In 2017, the Robina Institute of Criminal Law and Criminal Justice at the University of Minnesota, a leader
nationally on the study of discretionary parole, surveyed chairs of different state parole boards. In nearly every state, the board chairs said
that the most important factor in deciding whether to free someone
was the crime the person committed, not their time in prison, not their
rehabilitation or likelihood to reoffend.

In 2019, Jorge Renaud, an analyst with the decarceration think tank
the Prison Policy Initiative, graded each state's parole release system.
Renaud assigned points to a variety of benchmarks: What percentage
of the prison population was eligible for parole? Were hearings face-to-
face? Did prosecutors and victims of violent crimes get to weigh in? Did
boards base decisions on static things that never changed, such as the
"serious nature of the offense"? Did states help prepare people for their
hearings? Did the boards operate with transparency? Renaud didn't
even bother tallying up a score for Illinois or any of the other fifteen
states that eliminated discretionary parole for everyone incarcerated
after a certain date. Those states got a grade of zero, an F−. But twenty
additional states also received failing grades. Even in those states that
hadn't abolished parole, truth in sentencing, mandatory minimums,
and other more punitive sentencing laws had restricted eligibility to a
small portion of the prison population. According to the Prison Policy
Initiative's research, only four states allowed even half of their incarcerated people to come before a parole board.

Legal representation for eligible candidates was rare. Hawaii (C+)
was among only a few states to provide attorneys to parole candidates
who couldn't afford one. Self-taught jailhouse lawyers were at a severe
disadvantage. The parole board in Utah (C−) penalized candidates if

they'd filed a lawsuit while in prison that was ruled to be without merit. Parole prep volunteers made a huge difference—candidates in California assisted by UnCommon Law won their cases 60 percent of the time; in New York, Parole Preparation Project's success rate was 60 to 70 percent within two years. But these sorts of groups were in short supply.

Renaud had been incarcerated in Texas (F), serving a sixty-year sentence, of which he had to do fifteen before he became eligible for parole. He studied the law. He prepared his own parole packet and figured out a way to present himself to the board. At his first hearing, in 2008, he won his release. But the state required him to remain on parole supervision on the outside for the full length of his sentence—until 2051. A handful of states with passing grades let people know upon their admission to prison when they would first come up for parole, what the process entailed, and what criteria would be used to evaluate them. Wyoming earned the highest mark, a modest B−. Those up for parole in the state didn't have to rely on nonprofits or people locked up with them to figure out how best to craft and present their stories of rehabilitation and readiness for release. Wyoming provided every parole candidate a caseworker to help prepare for his or her hearing.

California earned a grade of F−, since the state got rid of indeterminate sentences in 1977 for most people sentenced to prison. Anyone in California convicted of murder was sentenced for up to life but continued to be eligible for a parole hearing after a specified number of years—eventually some forty thousand people. A woman named Terah Lawyer was one of them. In 2004, after nearly two years in a county jail, Lawyer entered Central California Women's Facility, known as CCWF, the world's largest female prison. She was twenty then and had a sentence of fifteen to life, meaning she could stay in prison until she died but that she'd also have a chance to come before the Adult Authority at her fifteen-year mark. For the first years of her bid, all she could see was the "life" part. She met women at CCWF doing seven to life who'd gone before the parole board and were still locked up after forty years. Her first years at CCWF were full-on depression. She considered suicide. But in 2010, she saw a friend make parole, and the possibility of her own release suddenly became real. The California Supreme Court had ruled, in 2008, that the heinous nature of a crime couldn't be the only reason to deny a person parole; the commissioners had to show that candidates either remained a threat to the public or lacked "insight" into what they'd done. Parole rates in the state more than tripled.

Lawyer launched what she called "Operation Freedom." When other women at the prison came up for parole review, Lawyer barraged them with questions about the process. What were they asked? How were their responses received? If those women had legal representation, Lawyer wanted to know what advice the attorneys had given. She saved documents and copied down instructions. Soon she had binders of information about parole, and she began to share the information with whoever was up next before the Adult Authority. By then, Lawyer had completed two different two-year degrees, one in business management and one in social and behavioral science; she'd earned certificates as a peer health educator and a drug and alcohol counselor. She refashioned herself into a self-taught parole expert, coaching the women at the prison on how to tell the stories of their crime and their insight into it. She learned that you had to go into a parole hearing with no ego, ready to expose the ugliest truths about yourself. That was a challenge, since you most likely weren't that person any longer. Years had passed. So you had to time travel back to when you were an absolute mess and re-create, as authentically as possible, motives that didn't even drive you any longer. You had to pinpoint what compelled your past decisions to cause harm. If you couldn't say all that in front of the parole commissioners, you weren't going to succeed.

Lawyer had advantages in her life that many of the women incarcerated with her at CCWF did not. She'd been one of the few Black students at her suburban Sacramento schools. As a teenager, she had extracurriculars, enrichment, college prep. Yet she nevertheless ended up as part of an exploding population of incarcerated women in the United States. Since 1980, the number of women locked up in America has grown at twice the rate as that of men, reaching two hundred thousand. The number of women in U.S. prisons and jails alone is more than twice the number of *all* people in prison in any European country other than Russia. About 60 percent of the women in prison and 80 percent of the women in U.S. jails were parents, and they struggled logistically and psychologically with their roles as mothers. Mental health problems are far more common for women in prison than for men. In a 2010 survey of women in Illinois prisons, conducted by the Illinois Criminal Justice Information Authority, nearly every respondent said she'd been victimized prior to her incarceration. Past sexual abuse was reported by 75 percent; 98 percent experienced physical abuse.

When Lawyer finally sat down with two members of the Adult Authority, in 2017, she was thirty-four and had spent more than a year doing all she could to put herself together on paper. She'd collected over a hundred letters of support and commendations from staff attesting to her character. Her family was able to afford an attorney, who reminded Lawyer as the hearing got underway to avoid coming across as too proper. Her poise in this venue could work against her. She needed to show raw emotion. The warning was unnecessary. Lawyer could hardly hear the two commissioners over the pounding of her heart. The presiding board member was a middle-aged Black man who had worked his way up through the California prison system, from guard to warden; the other was a middle-aged white woman.

"All right," the head commissioner said. "Tell us, what happened?"

In 2002, when Lawyer was eighteen, she played a part in a murder that was as pointless as it was destructive. She was working as a bank teller in Sacramento, and after her shift one day she called her twenty-year-old cousin through marriage to see if she could hang out with him. His name was Butchie, and he told Lawyer that he'd been outside a Walmart earlier that afternoon, selling pirated CDs (*it was 2002*), and a guy disrespected him. Butchie wanted to "check him," he said, and he needed Lawyer's help. Eager to please and impress her cousin, she agreed immediately. Lawyer approached the young man who disrespected Butchie and, as instructed, feigned interest. She asked him if he'd like to hang out, to hook up. As pretty as Lawyer was, she lured him in no problem.

At first Butchie wanted Lawyer to bring the guy to a public area away from his crew, but then the plan changed. Butchie handed her the keys to a room at a Motel 6. When Lawyer brought the guy there, she sat him on the bed and said, "Take your shirt off." That was the signal. Butchie and his friends sprung from the bathroom. They kicked and hit

the guy with their fists and the butt of a gun. They handcuffed him and
flung him into the bathtub. Then at gunpoint they drove him to North
Sacramento, turning off the highway into a Costco parking lot. Behind
the store was a trail that bordered train tracks. Butchie and his friends
dragged the guy there. They shot him twice in the head. Butchie sent his
girlfriend and Lawyer back to the motel room with bleach to scrub out
any bloodstains.

The two commissioners from the California Adult Authority interrupted Lawyer occasionally, asking for clarification. Did she know her
cousin's friends? How far was she standing from the victim? Why did
she clean the hotel room? Lawyer spoke about the crime for almost an
hour. She didn't think the victim was going to be murdered. But she
said she had taken him to the hotel room knowing he'd be harmed. And
when it seemed like he might be killed, she did nothing to try to stop
it. It wasn't her first crime either. She'd embezzled money from a bank
where she worked, allowing Butchie to withdraw a few thousand dollars
from other people's accounts. And she stole money from her drawer at a
credit union where she also had a job for a time.

"I've come to understand that there are several contributing factors
of why I did this," Lawyer said. At CCWF, Lawyer had taught classes
to other women at the prison on how to set realistic goals, gain self-
awareness, and make sense of past choices—all things needed to tell an
authentic story about one's insight into a "Life Crime." At her own hearing, she explained that her need for approval from others was like a disease. It resulted from her physical abuse at a young age, her rejection by
friends and family, her father's drug use, and her own drinking, which
started around the age of fifteen. "I had no sense of self," she said, beginning to choke up. Growing up, Lawyer had been ostracized at school
for being Black, and at the same time, her relatives dismissed her for
seeming too white. She wanted to be around people like her cousin who
were strong and aggressive. She would do anything to show them that
she wasn't a street-dumb Goody Two-shoes. She stressed to the board
members that she wasn't manipulated to assist with the crime. She said
that she, in fact, was the manipulator. She lied and tried to please everyone to make them accept her. But she'd grown up over her fifteen years

of incarceration. She said it wasn't easy becoming the woman she was now. She wasn't perfect. But she'd come a long way.

"Now I have a sense of self. Now I know who I am. Now I have a backbone. Now I will walk away from unhealthy relationships, especially when I pick up that it's toxic," Lawyer said. "Today, I have a zero tolerance toward rule breaking. I have a zero tolerance toward aggressive acts."

The state's attorney at the hearing said he wasn't buying what he called Lawyer's "shrinking violet" act. "*Golly, I didn't know anything,*" he mocked, in imitation of Lawyer's account. He said Lawyer was manipulative back when she committed the Life Crime, and she was manipulating the parole board now. "It's clear that she's someone who was a very cold-blooded person then, and I would submit that that's what is the same today."

Lawyer admitted that she had told countless lies after her arrest and before she agreed to cooperate with prosecutors. So many lies that she couldn't keep them straight. What she could recall, she said, was the truth, since it was singular and seared in her memory. The female commissioner seemed to think Lawyer sincere. She didn't see any discrepancies between Lawyer's retelling of the Life Crime and the facts from the file. The commissioner wanted to talk more about Lawyer's work inside the prison. She was impressed that Lawyer had facilitated stress and anxiety workshops, that she engaged in laughter therapy, prayer, and a knitting project. Lawyer described the eight-week course she created that focused on personal responsibility, which was about breaking down how people in prison got to that point in their lives—and what they needed to do to move forward.

"I assume you must knit, right?" the commissioner interrupted.

"Crochet," said Lawyer.

"Crochet and other community activities. You've been participating in the Long Termers organization since 2015." She asked if Lawyer had received her bachelor's. The 1994 crime bill made it impossible for incarcerated people to receive federally funded Pell grants for postsecondary education. Other federal educational funding had also been slashed, and the portion of people in state and federal prisons taking part in some form of academic programming had fallen from about half to a quarter. Lawyer did have an acceptance letter to a university in San Francisco, though, and jobs lined up for her on the outside assisting women who were in prison or recently released.

The two commissioners thanked Lawyer for her time and sent her into the hallway as they deliberated. If they rejected her petition, they'd also have to rule whether to grant her a subsequent parole hearing in three, five, seven, ten, or fifteen years. In Illinois, when the Prisoner Review Board rejected Michael or Johnnie or anyone else, it also decided whether to hear the case again in one, three, or five years. In Georgia, with more than seven thousand parole-eligible lifers, the longest someone could go without appearing before the board was eight years. It was a lot for someone to go several years without the hope of release. The possibility of parole at an upcoming hearing at least allowed someone to believe there was a purpose to the daily rituals of a confined life, to the small accomplishments and routine humiliations. Maybe they were adding up to something greater, accruing for the next hearing, preparing them for the life to come after prison.

Lawyer was called back into the room. The two commissioners said they no longer believed she posed a risk to society. She had meaningful insight into her Life Crime. They were granting her parole. Lawyer had stopped listening. She was weeping.

IN 2003, ON his twenty-second consideration for parole, Michael felt things were finally going to break his way. He entered prison when he was twenty; he was now fifty and had spent thirty years behind bars. Those were giant anniversary numbers, end-of-the-race numbers. Any member of the parole board could see that he was no longer a young man, that he had paid a hefty price for his crime. So Michael approached the new parole hearing, in a new century, with his optimism intact. He had his mother, sister, and daughter Shani drive up from East St. Louis for his interview at the prison, and Michael explained himself again to one of the parole board members.

Michael tried to speak at parole interviews as if he were sitting at a kitchen table with a friend, talking openly, emotionally, showing his full self. He had a GED and a degree in business management. He had worked a dozen different jobs while incarcerated and had earned certificates that could help him find employment on the outside in a kitchen or as a tailor or welder. He'd caught the marijuana case in prison way back in 1984, nineteen years earlier, and he last tested positive for drugs in 1995. He hadn't had a serious ticket in years. He conceded that he might have lacked insight into his crime in 1983. Maybe he hadn't fully turned his life around by 1993. But here he was in 2003, a man well into middle age. He cried as he talked about the murder he'd committed and his powerlessness at this point to make it right. He also expressed his frustration. He wanted to know what else the board expected from him. He had complied. He'd rehabilitated himself. If he hadn't done enough time yet to atone for his crime, he wanted to be told what else he had to do to go home. "Tell me," he said. "I'll do it."

As dictated by law, parole boards also heard from victims and their families—those who, even years later, still felt the effects of a crime. And parole boards heard from state's attorneys and from others who were victimized or incensed by a crime. Richard Schaeffer's survivors said it was true that Michael was young at the time of the murder, but so was Ricky, a high school student who had his entire life ahead of him. Schaeffer would never have a second chance at anything, so why should Michael? Michel didn't kill Schaeffer for fifteen years, or twenty, or thirty, they argued. He carried out a death sentence for a few dollars. Michael deserved no less.

A U.S. marshal wrote a letter to the parole board in which he claimed that Michael was a "career criminal" known as "Big Tab" by his fellow gang members in prison. The marshal turned out to be one of Schaeffer's relatives. The mayor of Schaeffer's hometown also sent word to the parole board that Michael was a member of the Metro prison gang. What did the mayor of Belleville, Illinois, know about Michael and his life in prison? Nothing in Michael's prison file suggested he had ever been in a gang. In the 1970s, when Michael appealed his lengthy sentence as excessive, an appellate judge told him not to think of the hundred to two hundred years as real; an indeterminate term meant he could get paroled whenever he demonstrated his rehabilitation and remorse. But now a current member of the judiciary wrote the parole board saying that the intentions of the late trial judge were clear: "This subject was not a likely candidate for parole." He said the trial judge had wanted to keep Michael in prison for life. It was a logical fallacy, one that imposed the terms and codes of new laws onto old ones, but it was nevertheless persuasive. A county sheriff who strongly opposed Michael's release wrote, "Any deviation from the trial court process and/ or dramatic deviation from the imposed sentence would then make this matter a travesty of justice."

The state's attorney from the county where Michael was convicted four decades earlier sent a protest letter to the parole board. "The defendant," he wrote, "poses a major threat to the general public and the citizens of St. Clair County if released on parole." State's attorneys rarely had insight into a person's time in prison and whether that person had reformed. Parole board members knew much more about a candidate's present life; before each hearing, they spoke to a petitioner and studied his or her prison records. "There is nothing in this inmate's file that suggests rehabilitation," wrote a different state's attorney from the same county. Nothing? Really? Michael had his many hustles, but he'd taken advantage of nearly every class and vocational opportunity offered by the state's prison system. A lawyer now in private practice informed the board that he had served as board chair, circuit judge, chief judge, and top prosecutor in St. Clair County. "That public perspective gives a view of this case that few have," he insisted, and he offered his expert opinion on Michael's criminal mind. "Though he has learned how to stay out of trouble in prison, he is not without anger." The retired judge/ prosecutor/board chairman had never visited Michael in prison. He'd never spoken to Michael. He knew nothing about the good or bad or inexplicable of Michael's decades in the state's correctional institutions. "He only wants out," his diagnosis continued, "out to revenge his time locked up."

The board member who interviewed Michael in 2003 seemed sympathetic. Michael said he hadn't intended to fire the gun. But she was less interested in interrogating the intentions of an eighteen-year-old who'd been drinking than learning about Michael's understanding as a fifty-year-old of all the suffering he'd caused. At the full parole hearing in Springfield, the board member pointed out to her colleagues that

Michael had just one minor disciplinary ticket since they last considered his release, and that a counselor at the prison praised his "great turnaround." During the deliberation that followed, many of the board members who'd voted against Michael in previous years also noted his positive adjustment. He'd never received more than a couple of votes at any hearing. The roll was taken and as many parole board members wanted to free Michael as didn't. The final tally: seven to seven. The rule was the tie did not go to the runner. He needed a majority of votes to leave prison.

Michael, however, was elated. His parole seemed imminent. He needed to convince only one additional board member, and time was now on his side. Another year served without incident should tip the scales in his favor. The crime would have receded further into the past, and by all actuarial tables he would, in twelve months, pose even less of a risk. Michael doubled down on preparations for his release. He studied television programs to develop social skills. Watching the news or talk shows, he observed how people in the free world expressed themselves. He took note in commercials or sitcoms when fathers conversed with their children. As his next hearing approached, in 2004, he started to give away his belongings to friends at the prison.

At that hearing, a board member described Michael's crime as well as the two-year consecutive sentence he'd received in prison back in 1984 for drug possession. None of that was new information. Michael was at a maximum-security facility, but he had an A-rating for behavior and was trusted with choice work assignments. The board deadlocked again, seven to seven. Michael remained hopeful. Another additional year could only help. The following year, a board member characterized Michael's institutional adjustment as "marginal." Michael's last major ticket was a decade old. The only tickets he'd received of late were for minor offenses. He was given a month in segregation and a month commissary restriction for passing cookies to someone in a neighboring cell. He was verbally reprimanded for pretending to use the phone; Michael had only wanted to give his cellmate privacy as he used the toilet. His vote total fell to four. The next year, a board member reminded everyone that Michael was at large for two years after his crime. He got three votes. The next year, two. The year after that, a board member wondered out loud whether Michael's being in a maximum-security prison didn't indicate that he was dangerous. Was it due to "bad behavior"? He was denied again.

A woman Michael grew up with in East St. Louis, someone he knew from the neighborhood but hadn't spoken to since childhood, collected hundreds of signatures for his release without even informing him, sending them to the governor and the parole board. "Can you please look into this matter and free Michael and allow him a chance in society?" she wrote. She included poems she wrote in Michael's voice, saying she was inspired by the Lord.

> God knows I'm sorry, and yes I beg each of you for my freedom,
> Without a doubt
> Can you finally find it in your hearts to let me Out?

Michael had come to see himself as a humanist. He believed in people, but not in God, since he couldn't accept that a God in heaven would allow those made in his image to suffer in prison interminably. "A God like that is a monster," he'd say. Michael wanted to make amends for the life he'd ended. He thought how he would feel about someone who murdered one of his children. He would want that person punished. But he wasn't sure what punishment would suffice. He considered the plea deal he'd been too foolish to accept at trial. A maximum of twenty years. He'd have been home already for more than a decade. But if twenty years or thirty years wasn't enough time, then how much? As he ran laps around the prison yard, he came up with a calculation. Richard Schaeffer was seventeen when Michael shot him to death. Michael would double that. He deserved thirty-four years. The formula didn't make sense. Did murdering a younger person warrant fewer years in prison? Why two of his victim's lifetimes? But other calculations were no more sound. There was no science of just deserts, no equation to solve for retribution. Sentencing commissions and prosecutors came up with numbers to express what was required by society to believe justice had been served, and then those numbers changed, and then changed again. At his next interview with a parole board member, Michael explained his math: seventeen times two. That year he got two votes for parole.

In 2006, Illinois passed the Child Murderer and Violent Offender Against Youth Registration Act. The law was a way to toughen already stiff forms of punishment, restricting the movements of anyone convicted of harming a child long after their release from prison. Michael, at eighteen, had killed a seventeen-year-old. He had to register. But he was put mistakenly on a different registry, one for sex offenders. Most halfway houses wouldn't accept registered sex offenders. Without a housing plan for after prison, Michael couldn't be paroled. He wrote the unit of the state police that handled the sex offender registry. Eventually he heard back: "It is your responsibility to contact the state's attorney for the county in which you were convicted." His victim's family was still well known in St. Clair County. Someone from the office had to sign the form verifying that Michael's crime wasn't sexually motivated. No one would. Michael wrote a letter to Craig Findley, the chairman of the parole board, seeking help. "First and foremost permit me to extend my courtesy and respect," Michael began. "Secondly, I'll be brief. My issue is with the integrity of the State's Attorney's Office." It took three years simply to have his name moved off a sex offender registry and onto one for child murderers.

One year as Michael prepared for his next parole hearing, he again read through his prison file. He noticed a document that wasn't supposed to be there. It included the name and address of his victim's brother. Michael knew he was strictly forbidden from contacting Richard Schaeffer's family. Victims and their relatives were supposed to be insulated from any additional anguish or possible menace. A dozen states, including New York, had letter banks for people in prison to send apologies. If victims or their families were interested, they registered and learned whether a letter was stored there for them, and the writer was never informed that it was received. Of the nearly four thousand apologies written by people in Pennsylvania state prisons, 250 had been picked up. Victims or their families in Colorado claimed fifteen such letters. Nothing like that existed in Illinois. Michael copied down the information and hid it. Later, at the small table in his cell, he wrote out a letter by hand on a single sheet of lined paper.

"I have been giving many apologies and have demonstrated my remorsefulness toward others but not to the family who truly deserves it."

In prison for four decades, Michael talked about the harm he'd caused, but it was as if he was speaking into the wind. By law, he couldn't tell the actual people he hurt that he recognized the endless grief he'd caused them. Prison, in a way, insulated him from taking responsibility for his crime. He was never required to do anything for the Schaeffers that might help them heal. But given the chance now, he struggled to find words that weren't hollowed of meaning from overuse. "I am so very sorry!!" "My deepest apology." Michael knew the Schaeffers conceived of him only as this malevolent force that killed their beloved brother and son. He was desperate to show them that he was more than that. "I am so, so very sorry for causing the death of Mr. Richard Schaeffer."

For writing the letter, Michael got into further trouble. He didn't regret sending it. The Department of Corrections' internal affairs division told him never to reach out to the family again. He understood. The parole board again denied his release, unanimously this time. In addition to his denial, the board agreed that Michael would not be permitted to come up for parole consideration the following year. He would have to wait three years for his next hearing.

6

Stateville

Johnnie was in Stateville's law library one day, early in his bid, when two men started battering him with questions. Did Johnnie know about Kahlil Gibran? Had he read Machiavelli's *The Prince*? One of them was the younger brother of Eugene "Bull" Hairston, a founder along with Jeff Fort of the Black P. Stone Nation. Johnnie understood that he was being singled out. He said he read Stan Lee—comic books. And sometimes westerns and sci-fi. The most political book he'd read was one that had been passed around the prison: *The Spook Who Sat by the Door*. The novel follows a man from Chicago who is recruited to be the first Black agent in the CIA, but he returns home after he feels used as a racial token. He ends up training a gang called the Cobras—like Johnnie's Cobra Stones—to lead a revolution.

The two guys in the law library said they'd been watching Johnnie. They noticed how he took charge at the prison, how he soldiered even when the odds were against him. They liked that about him. Johnnie had been fighting and organizing from the moment he arrived at Stateville. He noted right away at the prison that there were Aryan gangs, biker gangs, and Black gangs. But at that time, Italian mobsters still had the run of the place. In the autobiography Johnnie sent the parole board, he said he and other teenagers at the prison felt "like a bunch of rabbits being toss into a den of hungry wolves. The first thing I learned was just being elusive and fast did not guarantee your survival or safety."

The apex predators picked off the animals that strayed from the herd. Johnnie talked a few other teenagers into joining forces with him. Black kids out of Chicago and Puerto Ricans straight from juvie and white boys from the country. If you were alone, you became dinner. So they moved in groups of two or four. If they took a shower or played checkers, they made sure they were with others who had their backs. Johnnie kept friends around him as lookouts as he learned to fix brakes and reassemble engines in a vocational auto mechanics class. If one of them was attacked, the group responded.

The younger brother of Bull Hairston and his friend told Johnnie that they were going to give him a new name. They were going to call him Khalif, a variant of the Arabic for "leader." Johnnie said he was a Catholic school boy. The two men laughed. They weren't talking about embracing a religion. They were talking about a name.

Johnnie understood that it didn't matter what your mother named you. The community could name you something else. Mongoose or Honey Boy. T-Baby or Pot Hound or Gangster Al. But he'd never had a nickname that stuck. He was Little Johnnie, and when he got a mustache people started calling him Johnnie or JV. But after he caught his case, "Johnnie Veal" had become its own epithet, and Johnnie felt that whatever horror it summoned didn't belong to him. The utterer of that name was sure to see everything and anything except him. Johnnie liked to think of himself as a leader. As someone who was noble and just. Pretty soon everyone in Stateville knew him as Khalif.

Stateville Correctional Center opened in the 1920s, on the banks of the Des Plaines River, an hour outside of Chicago. The new facility was meant to replace the aging state penitentiary on the other side of the river, Joliet Prison, which predated the Civil War. Joliet then housed two thousand men. Each of them was assessed by the Illinois Board of Pardons and Paroles, and the best behaved among them "merited graduation" to the state-of-the-art prison a few miles away. At Stateville, each cell included its own window and was backlit with natural light; the doors were made not of bars but of a special see-through glass that was touted as unbreakable. From the outside, Stateville looked like a medieval castle with thirty-three-foot concrete walls topped with battlements. But inside there were acres of fields and an honor farm where men could harvest cabbage and milk cows. Stateville had factories that made soap, furniture, and mattresses. Joliet was not shuttered as planned. This was the era of prohibition, the century's misguided war on alcohol, and then of the Great Depression with its desperate poverty and homelessness. The Illinois prison population more than doubled during that stretch, to nearly twelve thousand people by 1938, overflowing both Stateville and Joliet. That peak wouldn't be reached again—and then rapidly surpassed—until the 1980s, amid the century's misguided War on Drugs.

During the 1950s, men at Stateville were put to work printing Dick Tracy booklets for Chicago public schools and half a million comic books warning youth about the dangers of child molesters. "Don't take candy or money or presents from a stranger." "Don't let anyone fuss with your clothes." The main hallway leading from the cell houses to the workshops was known as State and Madison, after the downtown intersection in Chicago that was the X/Y origin point of the city's street grid. Nathan Leopold and Richard Loeb were incarcerated at Stateville. The wealthy University of Chicago students had killed a fourteen-year-old, in 1924, as an intellectual experiment. Loeb was stabbed to death in the showers at Stateville in 1936; Leopold made parole in 1958 and spent the remaining thirteen years of his life doing hospital work in Puerto Rico. John Wayne Gacy, the serial-killing clown, was executed by lethal injection at Stateville in 1994. It was around then that a videotape emerged that showed another mass murderer, Richard Speck, snorting cocaine at the prison, performing oral sex on another man, and somehow already on his way to transitioning hormonally from a man to a woman. Speck died of a heart attack in prison before the video surfaced, but the scene outraged state politicians and led to a crackdown on Stateville's anarchy. Stateville had once been a prison of enforced silence. It again became more orderly, although Johnnie had been transferred by then.

The giant rectangular cell house Johnnie entered on his first day at Stateville, in 1972, was said to be the longest in the world. Johnnie was first put in a one-man cell that was being used to house three people. Then he went to a cell built for two that held six. He could hardly breathe let alone move. At one point he was transferred into a larger cell lined with bunk beds where twelve men used a single toilet. The other housing units at Stateville were panopticon-style roundhouses that looked like roofed coliseums. Four stories of cells encircled the inner walls of the structures and faced an interior courtyard. In the middle of that courtyard sat a guard tower, shaped like a lantern, with 360-degree views of the surrounding cells. The cells, backlit, and with their glass doors, made it so each imprisoned person could be observed and monitored at all times from the guard tower with minimal labor. The French philosopher Michel Foucault wrote about the panopticon in his history of the prison system, *Discipline and Punish*, that the all-seeing facility was a "marvelous machine" of social control. Prisoners were always visible, so they never knew when they were being watched. "Surveillance is permanent in its effects, even if it is discontinuous in its action," Foucault wrote. The prison's grand industrial design came from factories, which took their surveillance cues from prisons. But the sound amassing inside the roundhouses was deafening. Those trapped in their cells knew they were visible not just to guards but also to everyone else. The COs in their central tower were at a distant remove. Whatever happened on the cellblocks, the guards wouldn't get there in time to stop it.

A parole board member once tried to add up all of Johnnie's disciplinary tickets in prison and counted 360. "The Board continues to be troubled both by the nature of this brutal crime perpetrated against law enforcement officers and with the history of infractions during Inmate Veal's incarceration." But the bulk of those tickets came during Johnnie's early years at Stateville, and Johnnie guessed the actual number was probably much more than that. In the 1970s, Jeff Fort broke up the Black P. Stone Nation, renaming his organization the El Rukns. Part of the original gang went with Fort, and another part went with Bull Hairston. A war broke out among the factions that was especially deadly in the confines of prison. "Who you with?" was uttered throughout Stateville as a prelude to an attack. Johnnie didn't know anything about the beliefs the El Rukns were now professing, about the Moorish Science Temple or the Circle Seven. He also hadn't come up under the ranks of Jeff Fort. Bull Hairston was the older brother of the man who renamed him Khalif. Mickey Cogwell, who Johnnie followed on the streets, didn't become an El Rukn. "The law of the land," Johnnie would say. "You go with your leadership."

Johnnie worried at Stateville that he was being used by older guys. That he was like a child soldier sent into battle. He went from survival mode at Cabrini-Green to survival mode in Stateville. A messenger would yell that a guy had a visitor, and when he stepped into the hallway he found himself in a kill zone. Johnnie had close encounters in the gym, on his walk to the commissary, and in the school building. He would notice guys in general population falling in behind him for an attack. Or a group in the yard waiting for an opportunity to get him alone. Or some lackey would cut him off on the way to his cell to separate him from his friends. Or he was warned that a hitter was waiting for him around the next corner. He had to stay attuned to any signs of danger. If people in the chow hall fell silent, that was a warning something was about to jump off. If people around him cleared out, it meant violence was coming.

Johnnie started wearing a stab-proof vest. He assembled it out of old magazines and strips of plywood that he taped around his abdomen. *Life* and *Ebony*, because of their thickness, were the best. In a knife attack, the makeshift vest might protect his vital organs, keep him from being killed or paralyzed. He was onstage once during a musical performance, playing the saxophone, and something felt off. Johnnie walked out midperformance. Another time he was an extra in a biopic about a baseball player named Ron LeFlore, who did a prison bid before making the major leagues. The movie's prison scenes were filmed at Stateville. Johnnie laughed that LeVar Burton, who played the athlete, hardly knew how to throw a baseball or hold a bat. But even as Johnnie stood on the pitcher's mound during the shoot, with the cameras rolling, he kept a shank in his pants nestled in a sheath that he'd made from a laundry bag and a strip of leather. Growing up in Chicago, Johnnie could always get away from Cabrini-Green, walk the North Side or head to his mother's on the South Side or visit his grandparents on the farm in Mississippi. At Stateville, he had nowhere to go.

One day in 1975, two El Rukns approached Johnnie as he was coming in from playing football. They used their greeting, "All is well," saying word had come down from Jeff Fort, whom they now called Malik. They were supposed to let the war with Johnnie die. Mickey Cogwell had been shot to death outside his Chicago home. It was over. No more hits. Johnnie was dubious, but the guys asked him to break bread with them and hear them out. "Let us holler at you." It was around five in the evening, and they headed to the chow hall. Johnnie sat across a table from them at a safe distance. They told him bygones were bygones. Malik had said they were all one family again. The mess hall was crowded, and when a guy passing behind Johnnie bumped into him, Johnnie apologized, assuming he'd caused the contact. He didn't realize until later that he'd been stabbed.

Johnnie was transported to Silver Cross Hospital. His mother arrived, and so did Darlene, who at that point had been living on and off with Johnnie's family. Johnnie was lucky. The knife missed the artery in Johnnie's neck and the nerves in his back. He told Darlene not to worry. He would be sent back to Stateville in a little more than a week. He said he'd been duped by a Trojan horse tactic. That was on him. It wouldn't happen again. He promised to be as ruthless as his enemies.

MORE THAN FORTY years later at Stateville, in March 2018, thirteen men gathered on a stage in the prison's theater. They were the members of the Stateville debate team. Their coach, Katrina Burlet, who also led a team at an evangelical liberal arts college, had sent invitations to attend the live debate to all 177 members of the Illinois General Assembly. About twenty of the lawmakers actually showed up, sitting in the front rows of chairs in a building that was as big and cavernous as an airplane hangar. Craig Findley came, too, as did a couple of others from the parole board. Guards were stationed around the auditorium and stood with rifles on a catwalk overhead. The debaters, split into two teams, began to argue the merits of reinstating discretionary parole in Illinois. Johnnie and Michael and any other aging C-Numbers still came up for parole review. But the men on the debate team were making the case that the law from 1978 that ended the chance of parole for them and everyone else should be overturned. They argued parole eligibility for all.

Raul Dorado, who was twenty years into a life sentence, stepped to the lectern and told the visitors that he and his teammates had all been between the ages of sixteen and twenty-six when they were sentenced to prison. The same was true for many of the 1,200 people incarcerated with them at Stateville—and for the majority of the two million locked up in prisons and jails across the country. "There's a reason for this," Dorado said. "People simply age out of crime."

Dorado was right about the age distribution of crime. Yet extreme sentences treated people in prison as if they were incapable of change as they got older. As if they were the same at thirty-five or sixty-five as they were at eighteen. Dorado said that parole eligibility would at least give them a chance to prove their readiness for release. Without the re-instatement of parole for everyone in prison in the state, Dorado said, he and his teammates would likely die in prison. Half of them had been sentenced to life. Among the other half, the shortest sentence was thirty-eight years.

Another debater, Oscar Parham, asked the audience to think about the death penalty, which Illinois had abolished in 2011 after decades of advocacy and after revelations that several of the men on death row had been tortured into false confessions. Parham was forty-eight and radi-ated geniality, punctuating most of his sentences with a staccato laugh. He was known to everyone as Smiley, an apt nickname. He now told the legislators and other visitors that the death penalty, as the most se-vere of punishments, had been reserved for the most horrific crimes, for the most exceptional cases—the rare serial killer like John Wayne Gacy or for a mass-murdering terrorist like the Oklahoma City bomber, Timothy McVeigh. These people were considered irredeemable, their crimes so transgressive that they were put to death. According to the Death Penalty Information Center, the United States had executed 1,550 people since the 1970s. But more recently, the death penalty had fallen out of use. Twenty-three states and the District of Columbia no longer sentenced people to die, and a dozen other states had not carried out an execution in more than a decade. Without the sentence of death by execution, the most extreme punishment available became life without the possibility of parole, known as LWOP. People sentenced to live out the remainder of their lives in prison, no matter how long, until their death. Parham said this was where the logic broke down.

Life without parole sentences weren't restricted to the worst of the worst. They became commonplace. In prisons across the country, more than two hundred thousand people were serving life or virtual life sentences of fifty or more years. Parham asked if two hundred thousand people were so irredeemable that they deserved to grow old and die in prison. Were that many human beings so abominable that they never deserved even a chance to prove otherwise?

"Was I a monster who threatened the very fabric of society like the natural-life sentence suggests?" Parham asked the audience.

Parham explained his own case. Thirty years earlier, in 1988, he was a teenager in a gang when a friend killed two people during a drug deal. Parham wasn't present when the crime occurred. He hadn't plotted the murder. He wasn't even the lookout. At eighteen, he was offered a plea deal of eleven years, of which he would have had to serve at minimum half. He decided to fight his case in court and was convicted under the legal theory of "accountability," which allowed prosecutors to charge accomplices or associates as if they committed the offense. Smiley was sentenced to life without parole. "What changed?" Parham asked rhetorically. "How was this leap from five and a half years to forever justified and rationalized?" The crime hadn't changed. Yet in one moment he was deemed safe to return to society after less than six years and then in the next he was beyond redemption. In 2022, Canada's Supreme Court ruled that life without parole sentences were, because of their cruelty, unconstitutional. Of the 193 countries that are members of the United Nations, 155 don't allow life sentences without the chance of parole. Did the lawmakers present at the debate support a system in Illinois that was so irrational and merciless? If parole eligibility were expanded, then a board could reassess the illogic and injustice of cases like his.

"Just as prisoners must change and reform," Parham said, "so must the system."

The debate program at Stateville was less than a year old. In 2017, Burlet approached the chaplain at the prison and asked if she could start a team there. Burlet, who had grown up in a mostly white and well-to-do Chicago suburb, was in her early twenties, with the fresh-faced eagerness of a burnished apple. As a college debater, she'd constructed persuasive speeches about mass incarceration. She'd formulated reasoned arguments about sex trafficking laws. But she'd never personally known a single person affected by these issues. Many debaters who trained in winning arguments in this detached way went on to lucrative careers as lawyers. Burlet, though, was motivated by her Christian faith. After college she used the professional self-help book *What Color Is Your Parachute?* to figure out what to do with her life. According to the exercises in the book, she should be a debate coach among marginalized people.

The debate team met for three hours each Tuesday in Stateville's academic building. During one of their first sessions, Burlet asked the men to pick a topic they'd like to debate. These were guys who signed up for every educational opportunity, even though they had little chance of ever leaving prison. What was one thing they wanted to change about the prison system?

By then Stateville was twenty-five years older than Joliet had been when the "new" prison was built as a replacement. Stateville itself looked like a relic from the premodern past. The stone floors and walls held in the cold and heat, leading to extreme temperatures. There was no air-conditioning and little ventilation. Five years earlier, the prison population in Illinois had peaked at forty-nine thousand; it was down to just under forty thousand and would soon drop below thirty thousand. No prisons in the state were closed, and with underuse Stateville became even more derelict. There were leaks and power outages. Sewage backed up from the toilets and sinks. Lead paint crumbled from the walls. Cockroaches scuttled from invisible openings. Mold blackened the walls. For years, guards and staff were told not to drink the water, that it wasn't potable. But what were the people locked up there supposed to do? They had to shower in the contaminated water, and they ate food cooked in the water. They bought bottled water from the commissary when they could; when they couldn't, they went back to drinking sink water, boiling it in baggies, and used plastic containers on hot plates in their cells, exposing themselves to other leached toxic chemicals. Three of the four roundhouses had been torn down. People realized that the panopticon model was neither safe nor humane. The noise alone, like being inside a jet engine, was both sensory overload and deprivation. The glass doors on the cells became cloudy over time, the men inside appearing as spectral silhouettes. A staffer of many years at Stateville tried to pinpoint what was wrong with the panopticon design: "It felt evil. It did something to you psychologically." The fourth roundhouse was also emptied but remained. It was sometimes used as a set for film and television productions interested in conveying the horrors of prison. Michael Henderson was transferred to Stateville at one point. There was an odor there he couldn't stomach. He said, "It smelled of death." At a recent parole hearing in Springfield, a member of the Prisoner Review Board remarked that a candidate had an exceptionally low number of disciplinary tickets. "At *Stateville*," she repeated in shock, the name equivalent in her estimation to danger and dysfunction. For the men on the Stateville debate team, there was a lot they wished to change.

A guy named Eugene Ross, who went by Al Ameen and led Islamic prayer services at the prison, was the one to suggest that they debate parole eligibility. His proposal was met with echoes of assent. Fifty years earlier, those in U.S. prisons fought for the elimination of parole. At Attica, Folsom, and elsewhere, incarcerated people put themselves in danger to demand an end to indeterminate sentences. They believed fixed prison terms would be fairer and shorter. History had proven them wrong. Parole remained problematic in most of the same ways as in the 1970s. The guys on the debate team could argue that the entire prison system be abolished. But they and hundreds of thousands of others in the country serving extremely long prison sentences still needed a mechanism to get out during their lifetimes. Executive clemency—a pardon or commutation—was a near impossibility. None of them was eligible for discretionary parole. Parole, if it was reinstated, could at least be improved. What could be more relevant to debate than a chance to demonstrate their own worthiness to go home?

At the public event, the men debated one another in a variation of what's known in competitions as British parliamentary rules. One side presented a case in a formal speech, and the opposing team responded. But the guys in Stateville didn't debate the pros and cons of bringing back parole. None of them was going to argue against it. They came up with a clever solution—not *whether* to expand parole consideration for the entire prison population, but *how*. One side contended that the parole board in Illinois should clinically assess each individual, in the same way that the board currently reviewed C-Number cases. In 2018, there were only 111 C-Numbers left in Illinois prisons. Everyone else, about thirty thousand people, wasn't parole eligible. The other side argued that an actuarial risk-assessment tool was necessary to take bias and racism out of the equation and, moreover, to deal with what would become a much greater caseload.

For months the debate team practiced methods of argumentation and refutation. They read and researched and critiqued one another's speeches. By the time the legislators arrived, the debaters knew the material so well they were able to have fun picking apart one another's positions.

"At the end of the day, you have a choice between the opposition team's proposal of idealism and our proposal of practicality," Richard Morris, known as Raheem, said. He had entered prison at twenty-one and was now forty-three. Raheem said that the actuarial system was the only practical solution. "And what does the opposition team propose to ensure public safety? An antiquated system that has proven to be inefficient."

"Boy, oh boy, do we disagree," Luigi Adamo responded. Adamo had earned more than three hundred certificates and diplomas during his incarceration. He said that the complexities of individual human beings caught up in the criminal system couldn't be captured by a set of statistics, and that it was also a fallacy to think that these algorithms were impartial. The data on which they were built—number of arrests, prior felonies—were also caked inside a prejudicial system. Parole boards evaluated someone's rehabilitation and risk to reoffend based on their ability to avoid rule violations in prison. But the rules in prisons were mostly arbitrary, often trivial, and unrelated to any crime that occurred decades earlier. In a place like Stateville that was thick with danger, breaking a rule might mean survival. And a prison record itself was racially skewed. Studies showed that for the same rule violations in prison, Black inmates were more likely to be disciplined than white ones.

"Where does the homeless Mexican national fall on their actuarial tables?" Adamo demanded. "Or the undereducated, single Black male? I'd bet that those same scientific tables would ensure bias instead of prevent it."

Michael Simmons, whose release date was 2052, dismissed this reasoning. "Numbers tend not to lie, despite the witty and empty remarks my opponents may have about statistics." Simmons pointed to several

studies that showed statistical models outperforming humans on pre-
dicting whether someone would reoffend.

Both sides cited practices in other states to bolster their arguments.
In Hawaii, for instance, all incarcerated people were given a parole plan
in the first six months of their incarceration; they knew when they would
be eligible for parole and were given a list, years in advance, outlining
what they needed to accomplish to earn their release. Because actuarial
tables demonstrated that older people were extremely unlikely to reoffend, Virginia gave parole consideration to anyone over sixty who had
served at least ten years in prison. The debaters also mentioned Georgia, a state in which the parole board heard cases of all people in prison
over sixty-two, regardless of their crime.

The members of the debate team weren't saying that anyone in
prison in Illinois would be automatically released. Not at all. Only that
a parole board, in some form, would evaluate everyone, assessing the
risks and benefits of restoring their freedom. Studies showed that those
released from prison by a parole board did better with reentry than
those released through a good-time formula, completing their supervision terms successfully more than half the time compared to a third for
the mandatory releases.

"We believe that granting parole consideration is in itself an act of
justice," Al Ameen said. In 1973, the U.S. Supreme Court ruled that parole was a privilege and not a right, meaning a parole applicant was not
entitled to the due process safeguards of a trial. "An act of grace," as the
courts defined it, bestowed by a parole board. But Al Ameen was citing
language of the parole commission in neighboring Wisconsin about the
need just to have a hearing. "Being released on parole is not an entitlement," he said. "But being considered for parole is."

IN JOHNNIE'S FIFTEENTH year of incarceration, in 1986, the Illinois Department of Corrections deemed him too dangerous and incorrigible
for the general population. Johnnie, at thirty-three, became what was
known as a "circuit rider." The name came from the itinerant preachers
who had traveled on horseback between settlements along the American
frontier. In the corrections system, in the 1980s, to be sent on the circuit

meant Johnnie was moved repeatedly from prison to prison across Illinois. He was shipped to Centralia for five weeks, then on to Shawnee for eight weeks. He was sent to Dixon for ten weeks, Sheridan for four, Danville for two, Graham for a single day, then Shawnee again for nine days, and on and on like that. At each facility, he and the other circuit riders were kept in segregation units, away from the general population, and separated from one another. The frequent transfers, as a tactic, were borrowed from the military. It kept gang leaders, political organizers, and others thought to be inveterate troublemakers disoriented and disconnected. In 1987, Johnnie was transferred twelve times; in 1988, eight; in 1989, seven.

Years passed this way. Johnnie was let out of his cell by himself one hour a day, sometimes less. He could go out on the yard alone, take a shower, and then it was back to isolation in his cell. Visits with his mother or children were made nearly impossible by the constant movement. Mail trailed him and was frequently lost. Christmas cards reached him in July. Each time Johnnie was transferred, guards ordered him to stick his arms through a slot in the door. They handcuffed him and then made him step back and kneel. The guards entered the cell and shackled his ankles and girdled him with a waist chain that they held like a leash as Johnnie shuffled in front of them. The shuttling from prison to prison meant he held on to few personal belongings. He wasn't able to watch television or listen to a radio. He requested newspapers from the libraries in whatever prison he found himself, and if the papers arrived at all they were days or weeks old. That was much of his contact with the outside world. "You're by yourself behind a steel door, in a box," Johnnie said of his years on the circuit. "It takes a toll on a person, locked up like that, isolated, no contact."

In 2015, the United Nations adopted international rules for the minimum treatment of imprisoned people, naming the requirements after Nelson Mandela, who spent twenty-seven years in prison in apartheid South Africa before becoming the country's first democratically elected president in 1994. The Mandela Rules dictated that solitary confinement be used only as a last resort, for exceptional cases, and that it should never extend for more than twenty-two hours on any given day or for more than fifteen straight days. Anything exceeding those limits was torture. Johnnie was in solitary for twenty-three hours a day, for years on end. In U.S. prisons today, tens of thousands of people continue to be held in solitary.

During Johnnie's time on the circuit, he rebelled against his daily treatment. Handled as if he were less than human, he acted in kind, which prompted in return spectacles of brutal inhumanity from the guards. The cycle kept going. Officers hurled racial epithets at him, and Johnnie cursed them. He threw food, plastic cutlery, shoes. He saved mustard packets to clog up his toilet and flood his cell. He took his food tray and other belongings and lit them on fire, the choking fumes from the Styrofoam harming him more than anyone else. Other men on the circuit did worse—they collected urine or feces in cups and flung it at the most reviled guards. Sometimes Johnnie was just mad and needed to perform his rage. Other times he had specific complaints he wanted addressed: edible food to eat, access to the phones to call home during a family crisis, a notary so he could file a legal brief. Once while on the yard at a prison near St. Louis, Johnnie climbed on top of the basketball rim and refused to get down. He hated being incarcerated hundreds of miles from his family in Chicago, and his mother wanted him closer to home so she could visit. Johnnie demanded a transfer. The guards got ladders and pulled him to the ground, where they beat him and sprayed mace into his eyes and mouth.

On the circuit, Johnnie was strip-searched each time he entered and exited a prison. When correctional officers told him to bend over and spread his cheeks, he refused. The entire thing felt to Johnnie like a violation. The guards didn't really care about contraband; they wanted to humiliate and degrade him. Guards, decked in tactical gear, with shields and mace and oak batons, occasionally negotiated a compromise. He could strip down and cough but didn't have to show them the inside of his anus. Johnnie could agree to that. But compromises were rare. "Do your best," Johnnie would say defiantly. And they usually did, unleashing on him with the oak batons.

In 1991, Johnnie had been doing this for five continuous years. He was at a prison four hours south of Chicago, and he was taken into an office and handed a phone. On the other end of the line was one of his brothers. Their mother was dead. Lillie Mae Veal was sixty-two.

The service was held at a funeral home in a suburb south of Chicago, the Reverend William Jenkins officiating. But Johnnie wasn't allowed to go. A reading was given on his behalf, the funeral program explaining that Johnnie "will not be able to attend, not that he doesn't want to but life permits him not to." Those weeks after his mother's death were the closest he came on the circuit to going berserk. The prison put him on suicide watch. "I was crushed and my world was turned upside down," he later wrote the parole board. "Finding a purpose in life to continue my pursuit of rehabilitation programs after losing her was not easy."

THE LAST STATE to abolish discretionary parole for all future offenders was Wisconsin, in 2000. Since then, many states had revised their parole policies, expanding eligibility and increasing the chances of release. In 2014, Mississippi, long a leader in extreme punishment, extended the possibility of parole to all state prisoners serving long and enhanced sentences for nonviolent drug crimes. Louisiana, a state with one of the highest rates of incarceration in the nation, revamped truth-in-sentencing laws that required repeat offenders to serve at least half of their sentence before a parole hearing, cutting that time to a third. Alaska opened up parole eligibility to everyone serving time in prison except those convicted of first-degree murder or certain sex crimes. Oklahoma had the highest female incarceration rate in the country, and therefore the world, and the second-highest rate for men. Like Ronald Reagan in 1968, Oklahoma's Republican governor used parole as a correction, appointing board members who recognized that they weren't a punishment body; they were there to determine someone's suitability for release. It was how parole was supposed to work. In 2018, the state adopted a system of administrative parole, which released candidates without a hearing so long as their crimes weren't violent and they'd served a sizable chunk of their sentence without a serious infraction. The following year, Oklahoma's five-member parole board voted for the mass release of nearly five hundred people convicted of low-level drug crimes. The board also started giving rejected candidates an explanation for their denials, something it had never done in its entire history. That led to a shift in mindset: the board accepted that anyone eligible for parole had earned the right to be released regardless of his or her crime, and so the board members began to ask why candidates should stay in prison rather than why they should be released. It all helped the state leap ahead of Louisiana and Mississippi and nestle into third place on the list of prison capitals of the world.

Like most criminal justice reforms of this century, recent changes to parole largely skipped over people convicted of violent offenses. Taking their cues from the abuses highlighted in Michelle Alexander's *The New Jim Crow*, published in 2010, Democrats as well as Republicans voted to reduce punishments for low-level drug and nonviolent offenses, in an effort to answer for the unjust and racist drug policies of the 1980s and 1990s. At the same time, however, they increased consequences for violent offenses, as if to fend off accusations of being soft on crime. Most politicians still used the same law-and-order rhetoric that had shaped responses to crime for two generations, promising that freeing nonviolent offenders would enable the justice system to focus more squarely on the truly dangerous and undeserving—that is, people like Johnnie Veal or the members of the Stateville debate team. In 2015, Congress passed bipartisan federal sentencing reforms that cut mandatory minimums for "low-level drug offenders" "while ensuring that serious violent felons do not get out early." President Barack Obama said that every dollar spent on locking up nonviolent drug offenders was a dollar that couldn't be used to lock up the *real* criminals: "There are people who need to be in prison, and I don't have tolerance for violent criminals." Obama said of those who committed serious felonies, "Many of them may have made mistakes, but we need to keep our communities safe."

To transform the prison system—and even to keep our communities safe long-term—the United States needs to rethink the severe sentences given to those convicted of violent crimes. Fewer than a fifth of the people in state and federal prisons are convicted of nonviolent drug offenses. The majority of people in prison are there for violent offenses. Stories of innocence and wrongful conviction, a staple of true crime, are vital and compelling. But as far as the prison system, those cases remain relatively rare. What about the vast majority of the people locked up in the country who are guilty? Their stories need to be heard as well. They also have to be treated humanely. "Violent criminals" need a shot at a second chance. When parole boards consider these cases, they at least take another look at the real people behind these convictions. Parole provides an audience to those in prison who otherwise don't have one.

That's what the Stateville debate team demonstrated at their public event in 2018. Joseph Dole, who opened the live debate with a speech about improving parole by keeping ex-prosecutors off boards, was twenty years into a natural-life sentence. Dole believed that the substance of what the debaters said was less significant than what they showed. The legislators and other visitors at the event had to contend with them not as ideas but as real people. These "violent offenders" were human beings with intelligence, ambitions, and valid concerns. It was impossible to be there and not recognize that. It was exactly what Dole and his teammates hoped a hearing before a parole board would also provide. "That did more than anything else to dispel the societal narrative that 'prisoners' are all 'evil' irredeemable monsters that should be incarcerated unto death," Dole said of the debate.

Dole had spent nearly a decade of his prison sentence in the state's super-maximum correctional facility. Opened in 1998, Tamms was designed especially for long-term, single-cell confinement. No longer was it necessary to send the incorrigibles on the circuit; they stayed put in the "supermax" in Tamms, Illinois, a village of a few hundred people at the very southern tip of the state. Most U.S. states and the federal government opened supermax prisons in the 1980s and 1990s, facilities with near total isolation and high-tech forms of surveillance and control. The supermax was not merely an invention of the mass incarceration era; it was in many ways its apotheosis. These prisons envisioned a class of people whose inhumanity warranted the harshest forms of incapacitation, who were undeserving not only of rehabilitation but also of most sensory stimulation. The isolation and lack of human contact, the silence, and the absence of colors also proved to be torture. The supermax caused hallucinations, paranoia, uncontrollable anger, depression, suicidal ideation, and other destructive emotional and psychological effects. At Tamms, Dole worked with advocates on the outside to publicize the abusive forms of isolation and deprivation there. While in his cell at least twenty-three hours a day, he wrote a book, *Control Units and Supermaxes: A National Security Threat.* The assistant warden told him he was going to die in there and that he would deserve it. In 2013, though, Illinois closed Tamms for good, and Dole ended up at Stateville.

Dole and his teammates decided to use the debate as an opportunity to draft an actual bill to overturn the 1978 Illinois law that abolished parole. They were arguing not for sport, but for real change, for everyone in prison in the state to be entitled to a parole review. In structuring the proposed legislation, they pulled from practices in other states. Delaware and Georgia required people to serve a third of their sentence before becoming eligible for parole. Montana, on the other hand, required that someone serve only a quarter of a prison sentence before parole consideration. In Maryland, people convicted of violent crimes had to serve half of their sentence before they could come before a parole board. In Alabama, anyone fifty-five or older could qualify for geriatric parole consideration. In Virginia and Wisconsin, the age limit was sixty-five, so long as the person had already served five years, and sixty if they'd been locked up at least ten years. Massachusetts made pregnant women parole eligible, so long as a physician certified that release was in "the best interest of the mother or her unborn child."

The debaters told the lawmakers in the audience that Illinois shouldn't be a laggard. In Illinois, most people in prison convicted of a serious felony had to serve 85 or 100 percent of their court-mandated sentence. There was no chance of early release. Why not strive for a middle ground? They suggested that anyone fifty or older who had served at least a decade should be eligible for consideration right away. The team members argued that in Illinois, as in California, release consideration should be based primarily on a person's risk to reoffend, and not solely on the severity of the crime. It was a way to make sure that a new parole system would work better than it had in the past. Al Ameen said that Illinois spent about two billion dollars a year on incarceration. He asked the lawmakers to imagine how much money the state could save by releasing people who no longer posed a threat. The state could pay down pension costs. Fund the Department of Veterans Affairs. House the homeless. Parole consideration, the debaters said, also meant keeping in prison those who were still dangerous. Parole was a way, as Zebulon Brockway once put it, of returning to rightful citizenship *only* those for whom the "cure is wrought and reformation reached." But, the debaters said, so many of the people in prison would prove an asset to society if given another chance.

"We are representative of progress, as we advance our minds for a gradual betterment of society," a thirty-eight-year-old named Lester Dobbey, who had been incarcerated since nineteen, said. "We are representative of renewed character."

Immediately after the event, the lawmakers in attendance gathered around the men and asked them questions. Many of the politicians admitted that they had no idea there wasn't parole in the state. They'd assumed the possibility of a second chance was an integral part of any justice system. Of any society, for that matter. Of any religion. Several legislators came over to Oscar Parham—Smiley. They couldn't believe he was still in prison after almost thirty years. If it was true about his plea deal of eleven years, his conviction as a passive associate, they'd look into helping him get out. Some wanted to visit the class. They wanted to learn more about the bill the debate team had drafted. They said they'd been persuaded by the mock debate. It seemed to make sense that people like the guys on the team should at least have the opportunity to demonstrate their worthiness for release. Several of the visiting lawmakers said they might be willing to bring a version of the proposed legislation up for a vote in Springfield.

At the next Tuesday class, the men on the debate team were jubilant. Their class that day was a celebration. They laughed as they reenacted each highlight of the public event. They repeated what politicians had told them. They had come to call Burlet "Hurricane." She was small and always cheery, but when she wanted something she came on like gale-force winds. They joked that only someone with her faith and crusading spirit could have gotten so many visitors into the maximum-security prison.

Three weeks later, however, the prison disbanded the Stateville debate team. Burlet was barred from entering any state prison in Illinois. An assistant director of the Illinois Department of Corrections told Burlet that the men on the team had used reasoning during the debate that wasn't "evidence-based." Another explanation came from the head of the state corrections system, who said the coach hadn't followed "safety and security practices."

Burlet filed a lawsuit against the state. Al Ameen wrote in an affidavit that he and the other members of the debate team had been "able to articulate themselves in a way that prompted legislators to want to consider the issue." They were being punished because their voices had threatened an existing system that controlled them. They were being silenced. Shortly after a press conference that Burlet and others held about the debate program's cancellation, Al Ameen was taken to segregation.

THERE WAS AN irony to Johnnie's years on the circuit. He'd been fighting nonstop since he was a teenager. At Cabrini-Green, he traded gunfire with other boys. A momentary lapse meant he might get his throat slashed or his friends killed. He went from there to the life-or-death struggle of Stateville. In prison, he was always watching out for an attack or plotting one himself. Two decades of constant warfare had left him battle-fatigued, shell-shocked. "It seemed that I was locked in a life cycle of constant danger and trauma from the age of 15," Johnnie wrote in his autobiography. "Some older convicts that were ex-veterans use to always tell me I was suffering from PTSD. I did not even know what the word meant at the time. They would tell me the best therapy for that is finding you something to do like a hobby." Riding the circuit, Johnnie sat in isolation, at least when he wasn't being moved. No one could get to him. The infinite variables of life had been reduced to just a few. Which also meant that for the first time in twenty years he wasn't anticipating an assault. His head wasn't on a swivel. He wasn't listening for the signs of a strike. On the circuit, the noises subsided. The hours alone in silence were relentless and maddening. But they also afforded him the unfamiliar opportunity to turn his attention elsewhere. For the first time in his life, he became a reader.

Circuit riders were not permitted to go to the prison library. But they could order books, and a chaplain on his rounds through the segregation unit delivered them on a cart. Johnnie knew little about the history that engulfed him. Now, however, he read about the Soledad Brothers, about Eldridge Cleaver and Assata Shakur. He schooled himself, making his way through every book in the prison library on Malcolm X and

Martin Luther King Jr. He read about the Black Power movement, the Weather Underground, the Puerto Rican separatist group the FALN. He read about Gandhi and Nelson Mandela. Years of solitary turned into years of study.

His favorite writer of them all—Angela Davis. He fell in love with her. He learned that she was arrested in the fall of 1970, just weeks after he turned himself in to a judge. Their struggles were kindred. During her trial, Davis called herself a political prisoner. Johnnie now understood what she meant. With the zealotry of a recent convert, he wanted to tell everyone about the Marxist critique of capitalism. He was ready to explain why Black people were overrepresented in prisons. How groups struggling for Black uplift were targeted by law enforcement. How neighborhoods like Cabrini-Green were neglected and criminalized, simultaneously under-and over-policed. The pipeline from public housing to the penitentiary. How conditions in prison made rehabilitation a near impossibility. "The structures of oppression," as Davis called them. Johnnie realized that he lived in a country that would rather focus on locking people up than keeping them from turning to crime in the first place. It was what the prison abolitionist Ruth Wilson Gilmore called the state solving a problem by killing it.

Johnnie had witnessed all of this firsthand—the prisons filling up with Black men, the violence that consumed them. Now he possessed an *analysis* to understand it. He began to think of himself differently. He'd never paid attention to electoral politics. His incarceration meant he wasn't allowed to vote. But he started insisting that his family and friends on the outside vote for certain candidates. He wanted to change society. He decided he was a *revolutionary*. He could work toward something bigger than himself.

"I could have easily gone to the left and become a wild man, done something stupid and had made me a terrorist, an anarchist," Johnnie would say. "I chose to take the right path to try to make a difference because I saw how Nelson Mandela prevailed. I read him, and I read Eldridge Cleaver, Malcolm X and Martin Luther King."

7

Rationales

September 26, 1983

Mr. Henderson is a 30-year-old offender who is serving his tenth year of incarceration on the instant offense. The psychological summary states that given "the nature of offense and his past record," that a degree of caution is still warranted. He still has not secured marketable skills to enhance free community integration.

Each time the members of the Prisoner Review Board voted to reject Michael's parole, they sent him a letter explaining the rationale behind the decision. Parole candidates didn't attend their hearings in Springfield. The rationale letters were how they found out why they were denied, and what, if anything, they could work on for next time.

February 26, 1986

The record reflects that you are serving 100 to 200 years for the murder of Ricky Schaeffer, which occurred during an armed robbery in East St. Louis in 1973.

After a careful review of all the material presented, the Board feels due to the violent nature of the offense and your complete disregard for human life, to parole you at this time would deprecate the seriousness of the offense.

October 24, 1989

Parole plans were noted, as was Mr. Henderson's institutional adjustment which has shown considerable improvement in recent years. Since transferred to Shawnee, you have incurred no disciplinary reports, and currently you are in A grade.

December 11, 1992

In 1974 Mr. Henderson was sentenced to a term of 100–200 years for the murder of an innocent man whom he shot without provocation during an armed robbery. Mr. Henderson then robbed the body and vandalized the victim's car.

The rationales contained errors at times. (Michael's crime occurred in 1971, and he didn't rob Schaeffer's body or vandalize his car.) The letters varied from addressing the parole candidate directly to speaking about the person in an administrative third-person. At the actual hearings, board members may have disagreed, even debated vigorously, but the rationales were written in a collective voice. The board's reasoning was spoken as one.

April 18, 1997

After deliberation, the Board denies parole due to the brutal and senseless killing of an innocent victim and the inmate's inconsistent disciplinary reports, many of which are for substance abuse, which the inmate has not been successful at addressing.

As official documents, the rationales also captured the passage of time. All that changed over decades, and how much remained the same.

May 2, 2002

The sentence imposed indicates the feeling of the community that Mr. Henderson should remain incarcerated for an extremely long period.

April 10, 2003

Although, the Board recognized his positive institutional adjustment, it is felt that parole at this time would deprecate the serious nature of the offense and promote disrespect for the law.

May 12, 2005

His institutional adjustment has been marginal. He received a minor ticket since his last hearing.

What was the punishment supposed to accomplish? And when was it enough?

May 11, 2006

Mr. Henderson is 53 years old and has served almost 32 years. . . . Mr. Henderson stated that he did not intend to shoot the victim and was just trying to scare him and the weapon discharged after the car moved.

May 27, 2010

Mr. Henderson expressed remorse and is capable of complying with the conditions of parole.

May 26, 2011

During the course of his 38 years of incarceration, he has acquired 35 major and 46 minor tickets. Since 2000, he has received 12 tickets and the most recent one in 2007.

October 31, 2013

He has served 40 years and his maximum release date is 1/13/2067.

February 23, 2017

Inmate Michael Jerome Henderson C10609 is a 63-year-old African American male, who was born on March 16, 1953 to Ida Lee Henderson and David Henderson. Inmate Henderson's mother died in 2010 and he claims to have never met his father. . . . Inmate Henderson has four children . . . 13 grandchildren and 4 great-grandchildren.

Inmate Henderson has maintained a positive relationship with his sister, Patricia Palmer, and his three daughters through visits, letters, and phone calls. . . . Attorney/Social Worker Moss will serve as a case manager to ensure that Inmate Henderson receives the necessary support through every phase of his re-entry into society.

In regards to Inmate Henderson's health . . . he runs 10 miles per day and credits his love for running as a mechanism to cope and work through stress.

Inmate Henderson has admitted to shooting Richard Schaeffer . . . and says that his mistake haunts his own life, the lives of the victim's family and the lives of his own family. Inmate Henderson understands that nothing can remove the pain from the Schaeffer family. Inmate Henderson tried to explain his feelings of remorse to the victim's family and realizes that action speaks louder than words. He channeled his remorse into self-improvement.

After a complete discussion by the Board and a review of all the facts, the Board voted to deny parole at this time. The Board felt that to grant parole would show complete disrespect for the law.

DURING A PAROLE hearing I saw in Springfield, the board was considering the case of a man who, in 1960, was dubbed the "Starved Rock Killer." Donald Shelton said he didn't want to fall into the trap of looking backward on a long-ago crime, since it wasn't the job of a parole board to "retry a case." He then spoke for ten solid minutes about the evidence used to win a conviction at trial sixty years earlier. Shelton talked without notes or pauses, having committed the details to memory. "This case in particular seems to be one of the ones that we always end up retrying," he said.

In 1960, three middle-aged women from a tony Chicago suburb were hiking at Starved Rock, a state park of deep sandstone canyons along the Illinois River. Their bodies were later discovered; they'd been bludgeoned to death with a frozen tree limb. A twenty-one-year-old named Chester Weger, who worked as a dishwasher at the park's lodge, was interrogated for hours over multiple days. Weger denied having anything to do with the crime. A month later he was given a lie detector test and then another. Over several more months, he was questioned repeatedly, and, after one marathon session, finally admitted guilt, although he recanted before trial and said his confession was coerced. He was found guilty and sentenced to life with the possibility of parole. Weger entered prison a decade before Johnnie and Michael. No one in Illinois had served longer.

Shelton told his colleagues that detectives had offered Weger "truth serum," drugs that might induce babbling but not necessarily the truth. He explained that back then the state's crime lab wasn't even as good as what you'd find in a typical high school chemistry class. According to Shelton, state police botched the investigation. Weger, ultimately, was convicted of killing only one of the three women, which, Shelton pointed out, made no sense. If Weger killed one of them, then he killed all three. But Shelton wasn't arguing that Weger was innocent. All his research, in fact, led him to the opposite conclusion. Shelton said Weger was guilty and had been lying for the past sixty years. He described how Weger at one point told police that he'd dragged the women off a canyon trail and left their bodies in a shallow cave. Shelton had gone to Starved Rock more than once to examine the crime scene. "It's really not much more than an incropping from the rock," Shelton explained. Weger told investigators that he'd been startled by a plane, red and cream-colored, flying low overhead. Shelton said the investigators followed up at the local airport and checked flight logs—they found that a plane matching the description had flown over the state park at that exact time. Weger had been there.

"The deeper you look into this, the more evidence you find," Shelton said.

A board member finally interjected, saying they really should be focusing on whether this man, at eighty, was a risk to re-offend. Their job wasn't relitigating a case from 1960.

"It's hard not to," Shelton said, especially since Weger still insisted on his innocence. "It's very difficult to talk about this case and not look back into the evidence again."

"Not for all of us," Lisa Daniels said. Daniels, on the parole board since 2018, had tattoos on each of her forearms, what she called her "statements of belief." "Love Never Fails," from 1 Corinthians, on one, and on the other, "I Am Forgiveness." In hearings, she tended to repeat a maxim popularized by the wrongful-conviction lawyer Bryan Stevenson: "Each of us is more than the worst thing we've ever done."

Shelton continued. "Because it's such a convoluted—"

"Not for all of us," Daniels cut him off again. "He says it's hard not to retry the case. It's hard not to go back into the evidence. And my response is not for all of us, because I've heard the evidence." Daniels was on the board the previous year as well when Weger came up for parole and was denied. She understood that they had to consider the crime and trial as part of their decision. But those were static, unchanging. "Our role here, I think, is also to make a decision based on . . . where the inmate is today."

Daniels was from Chicago's southern suburbs. Her own son, Darren Easterling, was murdered in 2012 by a man he was trying to rob during a drug deal gone bad. Both Darren and the person who shot him were young Black men. Daniels had read a news report at the time about the incident with the headline, "Man Shot to Death in Park Forest Had Drug, Weapon Convictions." Although factual about the crime and Darren's past record, the article didn't mention Darren's name for several paragraphs. He was both victim and offender but little else. There was nothing there about the hundreds of football games Darren had played, starting at ten in Pop Warner. Nothing about the time, at twelve, when he tried to throw a surprise birthday party for Daniels, and he got a hold of his mother's phone book and called all her friends, asking them to bring pizza, cake, paper plates, essentially everything. The article didn't include a word about Darren's love for his own son and daughter. Not a mention either of the unfillable void left in Daniels's life with Darren gone. There were facts, and there was his truth. Daniels understood that her son could have easily been the shooter and not the one shot; she knew, too, that under those circumstances he would have been reduced to "murderer." "I took it upon myself to speak out on Darren's behalf, simply refusing to allow society to judge him and me for the worst day of our lives," she would explain.

After Darren's shooter was convicted, Daniels realized that she had

been talking about her own son, wanting him to be recognized for his
full humanity. But if she truly believed in second chances, then she
had to believe in second chances for everyone. "It went on like a light
switch," she would say. Daniels gave a victim impact statement at the
young man's sentencing—she forgave him and asked for leniency. She
told the court, "I believe that we are all connected by our humanity. And
I cannot speak for my son's humanity, without speaking for the same
humanity of the man who by only one bad decision took his life."

The act of forgiveness set Daniels on a new path. For months after
her son's death, she was too depressed to leave her couch. But she started
working as an executive assistant to a museum vice president. In her
spare time, she immersed herself in restorative justice, an alternative
form of accountability to incarceration that brought together the person
victimized by a crime with the person who committed the crime. The
person responsible for the harm listened, acknowledged, and tried to
repair what they'd done. For Daniels, Darren couldn't just be dead. His
life had to mean something. So she created an organization named for
him—the Darren B. Easterling Center for Restorative Practices—that
focused on providing therapeutic and intervention services to women
of color who'd lost relatives to violent crime or incarceration.

When Daniels was appointed to the Prisoner Review Board, she decided that she would try to challenge the assumptions of her colleagues
and influence change simply by speaking her truth. That was how she
would honor Darren's memory. She believed in second chances, and
she was going to give less weight to a crime than to what a person had
done in the years since. Some people seemed to be a danger to society
even after decades of incarceration, and she voted against their release.
Prison was criminogenic, and it sometimes made them more of a threat.

Her first case was a clemency hearing, whether to commute a prison
sentence from life to what could amount to time served and freedom.
Daniels listened as another board member said she wasn't going to support clemency. Daniels asked why. The other board members said, "I'm
just not feeling it." The person they were considering for clemency was
Oscar Parham. Smiley, from the Stateville debate team. Daniels started
to list everything she'd heard that made Parham seem like a suitable
candidate for release. His stellar record in prison. The job waiting for

him. His vast network of support on the outside. Was the other board member saying she'd rather Parham remained a burden on the state, that he die in prison, because she wasn't *feeling it*? Daniels said that in her opinion the state's objectives had been met—the person had been punished and was now corrected. What else could he do to show himself worthy of release? There was a silence, and then the other board member said maybe she needed to make a different recommendation. Smiley would soon go free.

Johnnie Veal would often say that grace was something he and other parole candidates had to earn. But this authority to bestow grace belonged to the assortment of ordinary people who made up a parole board. "It must come from the opposite end and not you," Johnnie said. "It has to come from the powers that be in order to grant this grace." At Chester Weger's hearing in Springfield, Daniels and Shelton were illustrating their reasoning, their rationales, for granting or withholding mercy. Neither of them put much stock in Weger's innocence. Shelton thought Weger a liar. Daniels believed other factors more important. But Daniels was confident that Weger, now an elderly man displaying no concerning signs of antisocial behavior, was not a threat to society. For her, justice, whatever it meant, had been served. Shelton believed it was critical to burrow into a person's ongoing relationship to the worst thing they'd done. He wanted to decipher the authenticity of remorse and rehabilitation. There would never be definitive proof of a person's character, but an investigation could still turn up a lot of evidence. Shelton had interviewed Weger in prison. For him, if Weger couldn't be trusted to tell the truth about his crime, if he couldn't take responsibility for what he'd done even after sixty years, then he owed something not only to the victims of the crime but also to all of us—to society. The debt had not been paid.

At Weger's hearing, I was sitting behind Shelton, amazed again at the scope of each of these cases, how every parole review put the entire criminal justice system on display. The disagreements between Shelton and Daniels were both factual and philosophical, concerned not only with what happened, but also with why we punish. Usually, at these hearings, a backwater of the criminal system, I was among the only reporters. But the Starved Rock Killer was a sensation in 1960, and all these years later the crime remained a news hook. In addition to beat reporters from different news outlets, a camera crew had wedged itself into the crevices in the Prisoner Review Board's little conference room. They were filming a true-crime series that would air on HBO in 2021, *The Murders at Starved Rock*. I watched it. The documentary focused solely on the question of Weger's guilt or innocence. Did he or didn't he commit the horrifying crime in 1960? Over three one-hour episodes, there wasn't a second given to exploring the purpose of long prison sentences or anything other than innocence as a reason to end them. It didn't matter that Weger had been in a *correctional* facility all those years. The true-crime series never entertained the idea that someone guilty of a violent crime could return to free society. Nothing of Shelton's and Daniels's exchange made the final cut.

At parole hearings, an incarcerated person's freedom can hinge on the mood in the room, a swing in momentum, the skill with which one board member crafts a narrative, or, more arbitrarily, how hungry or tired people are. When board members spend forty-five minutes debating a difficult decision, they might have less in the tank for other cases on the docket that day. Maybe after back-to-back votes to release people, the board members instinctively tightened the taps, or maybe they leaned into the freeing mood. Weger had been appearing before the parole board for a half century. Now three other board members agreed with Shelton that Weger still needed to display contrition to offset the crime and somehow right the moral balance. They voted against Weger's parole. Nine voted with Daniels.

Weger's younger sister, at seventy-eight, had been following each turn in the deliberations. When she realized her brother would be freed, she went limp and sobbed. A woman in her sixties sitting a few feet away on the opposite end of the small room was the granddaughter of one of the women murdered sixty years earlier. She berated the board for their decision, shouting that if Weger didn't succeed, if he committed another crime, the board members were to blame. They would be held responsible. Then before she left, she crossed the room to Weger's sister and two of his middle-aged nieces. The families had come to know one another from the dozens of parole hearings over the years.

"Take care of each other," she said.

* * *

ON THE MORNING of December 13, 2018, someone assaulted a guard, and the entire prison was on lockdown. Two thousand men confined to their cells. A few of the guys on Michael's wing asked him about his parole hearing taking place right then in Springfield. They knew he was one of the old-timers, a C-Number, among the few imprisoned in the state still eligible for parole. But Michael deflected their questions. He didn't want to appear too concerned. This was his thirty-sixth attempt at parole. It wasn't that Michael didn't believe in his chances. He did. He was incapable of thinking otherwise. As congenitally self-assured at sixty-five as he had been at half that age, Michael had faith that the board members reviewing his case were bound to see him, at some point, the way he saw himself. Yet he'd felt the same inevitability before, for decades even. So he hadn't made any farewell plans this time.

After Michael's vote totals started to plummet in 2005, he did finally get legal assistance. A lawyer from Northwestern University's Center on Wrongful Convictions reached out to him. Michael was represented at another hearing by pro bono attorneys from Chicago's Uptown People's Law Center. Then, in 2016, Marjorie Moss, a lawyer and social work supervisor at a legal clinic at Northwestern's law school, took over Michael's case. She drove 250 miles south to his prison, and they spoke for hours. Michael talked about his crime and life and past parole considerations. He was charming, as witty and sagacious as ever. Moss was trying to get two other people out on parole as well, but meeting Michael energized her.

"Oh my God, this guy has to come out," she said upon her return to Chicago. Michael's crime—a Black-on-white homicide—was committed when he was a teenager. Richard Nixon had been president. Gas had cost thirty-six cents a gallon. Nearly fifty years later, Michael was an old man. The recidivism rate for people his age, especially those whose crime was murder, was miniscule. In a study of 860 people convicted of murder who were paroled in California between 1995 and 2011, only five were sent back to prison for committing a new felony. Zero committed another murder or a felony serious enough to warrant a term of life. Of the seventy-six C-Numbers paroled in Illinois since 2005, eight had ended up back in the custody of the Department of Corrections. Five of them for a technical violation of the terms of their release. Only three had committed another crime—two aggravated domestic batteries and a forgery. Moss sent Michael a book on training for marathons. She said they could run the Chicago Marathon together, if and when he was set free.

Moss was in Springfield that morning at Michael's hearing. Little had changed in the year since Michael's previous review, in 2017, and none of the arguments were new. Several of the current members of the parole board had voted for Michael's release at prior hearings. Most of them had changed their votes as well. A retired circuit judge, the board member who interviewed Michael in prison weeks earlier, detailed the facts of the crime and Michael's record in prison. He said he counted 111 tickets during Michael's forty-six years of incarceration, including one violation for dangerous contraband in 2013. Pete Fisher, a thirty-year veteran of the police force in his hometown of East Peoria, had ended his law enforcement career as the chief of police in a Peoria suburb before joining the parole board in 2015. Fisher wanted to know if Michael had officially renounced his gang affiliation. Shelton asked what Michael's sentence would be if he was convicted of the same crime today, meaning under a totally different set of rules. Another board member questioned whether Michael could even find employment at his present age. Wouldn't most jobs be too physically demanding for him? No one asked whether Michael's ability to do manual labor should have any bearing on his freedom. Someone else said he believed that substance abuse remained an issue for Michael. Chairman Findley added that the state's attorney from St. Clair County continued to oppose release.

Michael, of course, was in his cell 150 miles away. Later that morning, a female correctional officer came over and said Michael had an attorney call. She escorted him to the phones.

"Michael," a voice, barely audible, said on the line. It was Moss. "Michael, Michael, Michael," his lawyer repeated six times, her voice trailing off into silence.

"What?" he asked. But Moss didn't answer. Michael thought he heard crying. He started to hyperventilate. He couldn't breathe. Moss finally managed a reedy reply.

"I think Christmas came early for you."

She said the board members debated for a long time. But they decided finally that Michael, after forty-six years, could go free.

December 13, 2018

The basis for the Board's decision at this time is explained as follows: Reviewing all factors available at this time, it is the Board's conclusion that the subject is a good risk for Parole.

The vote, in fact, had been unanimous, fourteen to zero. Even Fisher, the ex–police chief who'd voted for parole only once before, agreed to grant Michael's release. Moss said one of Richard Schaeffer's brothers, who was now an old man himself, came up to her after the decision and said he understood that enough time had passed. He said his family was going to be okay.

"I'm dreaming," Michael said. "This is not true."

It was true, Moss assured him. He was leaving prison. He was being paroled.

8

Victims

In 1993, Johnnie was transferred for the thirty-third time during his seven years on the circuit. He was moved a few miles from Stateville, into Old Joliet. The nineteenth-century correctional facility would eventually close in 2002, and in the years ahead it would be opened for tours, and around Halloween each fall it would be turned into what was billed as "Chicago's best haunted house," an immersive experience inside an abandoned prison that included the added feature of escape rooms. In 1993, though, Joliet was still a working prison. Johnnie's cell was like a tomb. Concrete block for a toilet. Concrete slab for a bed. A narrow slot for a window. A tiny opening in the metal door to speak to the guards. A low concrete ceiling pressing down on him like the lid of a coffin. Johnnie had recently turned forty, and he was told he was being returned to the general population. His circuit-riding years were over.

First Johnnie needed deprogramming. Apart from the COs on the circuit who treated him like a caged tiger, he hadn't been around other people in years. He was now back on a crowded cellblock. Guards yelling orders, radios squawking, men talking over one another to be heard. It was too much. People who spent years in isolation required some kind of resocialization. It was common for them to feel overcome with anxiety. To jump when their name was called. Eating in the chow hall could feel like being onstage in a crowded theater. They had to re-learn when to interject in conversations, when to smile. They had trouble looking people in the eye, or they recoiled from touch. Johnnie had trouble sleeping. He was in need of counseling. But he was on his own.

Johnnie hurried to reacclimate himself. As soon as he could, he got busy on his education. "How can I sit up here and tell anybody anything, or teach anybody anything, and I don't even have a college course under my belt?" he'd say. His new heroes were college-educated. Angela Davis had a doctorate in philosophy. Johnnie started a two-year associate's degree in general studies. When he finished that, he earned another degree in computer science and worked toward his bachelor's. He chased down all available programs. He attended lectures and seminars. Margaret Burroughs, the poet who founded the DuSable Museum of African American History, on Chicago's South Side, had been volunteering as a teacher in Illinois prisons since the 1970s. Burroughs heard Johnnie playing a Grover Washington Jr. song on the saxophone. She took a shine to him, impressed by his studiousness and leadership, and she encouraged him to explore Black history through writing and music. Another teacher he worked closely with, a prison chaplain named Helen Sinclair, remembered Johnnie as a boy from a class she'd taught at a Chicago church in the 1960s—because Johnnie had carved his name into the piano.

Sara Garber, in preparing for Johnnie's 2020 parole hearing, documented his record from this point on in his incarceration. She wrote in a petition she sent the board: "Johnnie asks to be judged as the person who has taken advantage of every opportunity to better himself, who went beyond that and made more opportunities to help other inmates, who has led Black History Month musical concerts, who teaches and tutors, who was selected by Warden Stephanie Dorethy at Hill Correctional Center to help mentally ill inmates prepare for reentry, who intervened to save a staffer, who stood up to bullies and rapists in the prison, who has the support of numerous individuals and organizations, and who has proven time and again how much he has to contribute."

Neither Johnnie nor Garber believed these achievements alone would be enough to set him free. At Johnnie's previous parole hearing, in 2018, the board members had agreed that his last quarter century in prison was remarkable. Yet not a single one of them voted for his release. Johnnie continued to insist he was innocent. But there were two gunned-down policemen. James Severin and Anthony Rizzato and their families were the victims of this grievous crime.

The concept of victimhood can be complicated. There's a truism about violent crimes, one that's more often cited by defense attorneys and criminal justice reformers: hurt people hurt people. In many instances, the perpetrators of crimes were previously the target of crimes themselves. Very often the same person had, at different times, been both the one harmed and the one causing harm. In a 2022 survey conducted by the nonprofit Impact Justice, 91 percent of men incarcerated for violent crimes said they'd experienced violence in their homes as children. Johnnie, as a teenager at Cabrini-Green, had been beaten up, shot at; his throat was slit nearly ear to ear. He'd victimized other teenagers there as well. He'd been hurt and violent and also claimed not to be guilty of the crime that had imprisoned him for fifty years. Was it possible that the parole board didn't have to believe in Johnnie's innocence to recognize that he was also a victim? Raising the suggestion at a parole hearing could be counterproductive. It could come across as not only presumptuous but offensive. *How dare Johnnie be called a victim when he was convicted of the double homicide of two innocent police officers?*

When Johnnie was still a teenager, his older sister took the bus back to Cabrini-Green. She was eighteen, and she'd moved to the far South Side with their mother. Like her siblings who'd also left, she returned often to the community she'd known most of her life. It was the night of January 30, 1970, and she got off the bus on Division Street and started walking to a friend's building. A group of teenagers surrounded her. "You're Johnnie Veal's sister, aren't you?" a girl, blocking her path, said. What happened next was recorded in a police report. Someone, maybe the girl, pulled a knife. A young man, described as nineteen or twenty, heavy build, wearing a black beret and a long, fur-collared coat, then took over. "Offender put a gun into the victim's back and forced her into an abandoned building." The young man said, "I am going to fuck you all night." Johnnie's sister tried to fend him off. "When victim first refused, he said he would shoot her, victim then consented." "After the offender finished the 2nd time," he told her to tell Johnnie that this was payback.

In the autobiography Johnnie sent to the parole board, he described how he responded to the attack on his sister. "When my sister was raped . . . by some rival gang members I became the person that I had truly despised in other gang members. I went on a revenge craze of pay back with everyone from that gang I thought was involved or was bragging about the rape. I often felt it was my responsibility to protect my sisters and brothers."

BEGINNING IN THE late 1970s and early 1980s, groups of grieving families, people whose loved ones were the victims of horrible crimes, began to band together in their shock and outrage. For these people, the worst thing imaginable had happened to them—an abduction, rape, murder. It was as if the earth had been rent open—there was only before and after. Whatever sense of order and safety they enjoyed was gone. They gathered at meetings and conferences, offering one another the support they needed. They talked through their shared trauma and loss as they tried to function again and heal. They also court watched, making sure that the people who harmed them or their loved ones weren't set free; they lobbied for laws that took into account their experiences.

Coalitions of mourning families proved formidable as far as raising awareness and influencing laws. As victims, the criminal system had needed them for their testimony. Beyond that, even families of great privilege felt ignored by court rulings, plea deals, and sentencing decisions. Crime victims had no constitutional or statutory rights. In terms of the law, their suffering felt beside the point. They complained that they were victimized a second time by a bureaucratic process that protected the rights of those accused of crimes but did little to support or safeguard the people harmed. Because almost all criminal convictions ended in a plea deal, victims of crimes rarely had the chance even to give statements in court. It was like their suffering didn't matter. Grassroots groups of ordinary citizens grew into powerful organizations with chapters across the nation. Families and Friends of Violent Crime Victims. Mothers Against Drunk Driving. Parents of Murdered Children. A victims' rights movement formed and ushered in changes to the criminal justice system. Victims received media training and promoted their cause. Their advocacy led to critical protections for vulnerable people. It was only after these groups demanded it that police departments and state's attorneys' offices created their own victims' services charged with keeping witnesses safe and preventing retaliatory crimes. Victims' rights introduced into the lexicon such terms as "child abuse," "domestic violence," and "stalking."

One of the leading figures in the early victim rights movement was Doris Tate, the mother of Sharon Tate, the actress who was murdered in 1969 by the followers of the cult leader Charles Manson. The murders of Severin and Rizzato at Cabrini-Green caused a local sensation in Chicago; the Manson family murders were among the most sensationalized crimes in the nation's history. This "crime of the century" is related to the story of parole, though, as well as to how cases like Johnnie's and Michael's are understood. Sharon Tate, a rising Hollywood star at twenty-six, was married to the director Roman Polanski and eight months pregnant when three of Manson's young acolytes entered her home near Beverly Hills and stabbed her to death. They also killed Tate's three houseguests and a teenage passerby; the next night, Manson followers murdered a married couple asleep in their bed.

Doris Tate had moved to Los Angeles from Houston during her daughter's pregnancy. The entire family had gathered at Sharon and Polanski's home just weeks before the murders to watch on television as Neil Armstrong and Buzz Aldrin took their first steps on the Moon. After Sharon was killed, Doris was in a stupor for years. She couldn't come to terms with a world in which her daughter and unborn grandchild were gone. One that was so monstrously cruel. Her agony was compounded by the endless fascination with Manson, the salacious speculations of the tabloids. There were wild theories about Sharon Tate's killing that involved drugs, orgies, satanic rites. Then in the early 1980s, Doris learned that her daughter's killers were eligible for parole. They'd been in prison for only a dozen years. Yet here they were with a chance to prove they should go free.

Manson and his disciples had each been sentenced to die by lethal gas. But a couple of years into their sentences, in 1972, the California Supreme Court followed a U.S. Supreme Court ruling and deemed the death penalty unconstitutional: "It is unnecessary to any legitimate goal of the state and is incompatible with the dignity of man and the judicial process." There were then 105 people on California's "death row," including Manson, his followers, and Sirhan Sirhan, who assassinated Robert F. Kennedy in 1968. They each were given new terms of life in prison with the possibility of parole. A parole hearing does not mean release, and it was extremely unlikely that Manson and his acolytes would get out of prison any time soon, if ever. For such gruesome and society-altering crimes, even the potential of parole might seem shocking. It did for Doris Tate. She was rattled into action. She began organizing. She traveled the state collecting thousands of signatures on a petition asking the California Adult Authority to deny parole for her daughter's murderers.

The work gave Tate a sense of purpose, even of power over Manson and his "family." She showed up at each of their parole hearings to persuade the board to vote against freedom. "I will do this the rest of my life," she declared. The case's notoriety now helped her cause: Tate used the obsession with Manson to her advantage. With each new "helter skelter" book, movie, and television show about the horrendous murders, she made the circuit of talk shows. On the game show *To Tell the Truth*, celebrity contestants had to identify the real Doris Tate from among a panel of three middle-aged women; Alex Trebek, of *Jeopardy!* fame, was the show's host, and he recited Tate's personal statement in his melodious enunciations: "I was immobilized by grief. But when the parole hearings began for Sharon's killers, I realized my destiny was to speak out for those who couldn't—the victims."

Tate, white and jowly, with large round glasses and a Texas twang, alternated between folksy and fierce. She was, as they say in politics, relatable. She was relentless as well. Featured in the *National Enquirer*, she implored readers to send letters supporting her work. At the next parole hearing she attended, Tate arrived with over two hundred thousand requests to oppose release. One of Sharon's murderers, Tex Watson, became a born-again Christian in prison. He had been in his twenties and hitchhiking when he was led to Manson; twenty-five years had passed. Watson had married while incarcerated, and, to Doris Tate's fury, fathered four children during conjugal visits—one of the entitlements secured in the state's Inmates Bill of Rights. Tate was disgusted that

Watson had been allowed to make a life for himself in prison. The loss of liberty as a punishment was not enough; she believed he should be denied in prison many other forms of comfort and fulfillment. She also doubted the sincerity of his conversion, and anyway thought it irrelevant. Tate demanded the permanence of his imprisonment for the permanence of her daughter's death. There was no room in that equivalency for rehabilitation or a second chance. At a parole hearing, Tate said that Sharon would never have the opportunity to come up for review or have any future plans. "Mr. Watson, what you're asking for is the very thing you denied my daughter."

In American criminal courtrooms, a crime is considered an offense against the state, not against an individual. Justice is supposed to be blind, the decisions to punish, incarcerate, or release based, in principle, on the benefits to the common good. A victim of a crime has no right to a conviction. As harsh as that might sound to crime victims, it's why, in the service of fairness, those who have a personal stake in a case or connections to the actors can't serve on juries; it's why judges are supposed to recuse themselves. But the growing movement that Doris Tate and others spearheaded argued that the balance had shifted too far in the opposite direction. They saw their own rights in inverse proportion to the rights afforded defendants, a zero-sum system, and they felt voiceless in the business of justice.

Victim rights in the United States had its origins in feminist organizing around violence against women and in anti-rape activism. The nation's first shelters for battered women were opened in the early 1970s; the first rape crisis center, with a telephone hotline for victims, was started in Washington, D.C., in 1972. California's first rape crisis center, instead of relying on the police, put up flyers in the Bay Area detailing the patterns and practices of suspected serial rapists. Other centers "outed" specific men identified by victims as their attackers. For too long, women who reported sexual assault or spousal abuse weren't taken seriously, in large part because, in the majority of cases, they knew or were in a relationship with the men who hurt them. The victims of sexual assault were ignored, disbelieved, or even blamed for what befell them; women who sought redress or protection often felt harmed again by the callousness and judgment of police, hospitals, and courts.

For these reasons, many women chose not to report that they'd been harmed. None of those problems have gone away. But by the 1980s, a decade of organizing and awareness had led to the opening of hundreds of shelters for battered women and thousands of rape crisis centers. Legal and social services were made widely available for abused women. The National Organization for Women formed a task force on rape in 1973 and two years later began to focus on domestic violence. Police departments rewrote policies on sexual assault, and municipalities established various legal protection for victims. The number of reported attacks increased, and so did prosecutions. For the first time, a spouse could be charged with raping his or her partner.

As the victims' rights movement evolved, though, it became as much about policing and punishing as it was ministering to the needs of those hurt. Victim rights became equated with more certain prison terms and fewer chances for release. During the 1960s, the U.S. Supreme Court, under the leadership of Chief Justice Earl Warren, had ruled on a number of landmark criminal justice cases that protected citizens from the potential abuses of the immense powers afforded police and prosecutors. The Warren Court expanded the rights of defendants to counsel, created the *Miranda* rule that required police to utter the words that would be heard on every cop show informing suspects of their rights, and put limits on the use of evidence obtained illegally or outside specific search warrant requirements. For Republicans aiming to reverse these liberal criminal justice reforms, and to retake power in the country, they found a rousing rallying call in invoking the rights of crime victims. Doris Tate herself went on to found Coalition on Victims' Equal Rights, known as COVER, with Los Angeles Police Department brass and deputy district attorneys on her board. As the president of Parents of Murdered Children, Tate was one of the advocates who helped bring down a liberal member of the California State Supreme Court, Justice Rose Bird, who had voted repeatedly to overturn death penalty cases. In television ads, parents of slain children accused Justice Bird of coddling the very people who killed their children. In a statewide judicial retention election, Bird was removed, and she was replaced with a conservative judge. In 1982, Tate was among the prominent activists who pushed through California's Proposition 8, a Victims' Bill of Rights.

Among several measures, the ballot initiative limited opportunities for bail and made prison terms longer for people with prior felonies. Prop 8 also gave victims of crimes and their survivors the right to attend and express their views at parole hearings. Parole board members in the state, before deciding on a case, were now required by law to hear victim impact statements and consider their obligations to the families of those harmed by a crime. Organizing by victims was why the Severins and Rizzatos were able to protest at Johnnie's parole hearings, the Schaeffers at Michael's. Doris Tate said, "Through Proposition 8, I am allowed to speak for my daughter."

Doris Tate died in 1992, at sixty-eight, a few months after doctors discovered a fast-moving tumor in her brain. A Los Angeles district attorney, praising Tate's legacy, said she shaped criminal justice policy in California and throughout the United States. "She really was the leader of the victims' rights movement," he said. "Before she came along the victims were the forgotten people in the criminal justice system." Doris's two surviving daughters promised to continue their mother's work by attending every Manson member's parole hearing. So when Susan Atkins, another of Sharon's killers, came up for parole in 2009, Debbie Tate was there.

The United States was the first country in the world to allow victims of crimes or their relatives to attend and speak at parole hearings. On the most intimate level, they are able to attest to the annihilating pain and never-ending suffering caused by a violent offense. They've lived with it. Their testimonies are powerful in this way, so much so that a parole board might rule differently in otherwise similar cases because the victims were able to attend and share personal stories at one hearing and not at the other. That is, a parole candidate's freedom might hinge on whether the victim's relatives, years after the crime, were busy or unwilling to travel, or whether they'd received counseling and mental health services that allowed them to move on with their lives, or whether they held strong religious or political beliefs that swayed them one way or the other. The power victims have to shape parole decisions puts a lot of pressure on them or their families to show up for every hearing. That power was also another way that parole was arbitrary and inconsistent. In terms of whether an even longer sentence might help deter crime or keep the public safe, victims, of course, lacked objectivity. And because the system restricted contact between victims and offenders, along with any personal repair that could happen as a result, those harmed by a crime rarely had insight into whether someone in prison had reformed or not.

In 2009, Susan Atkins was sixty-one and California's longest-serving female inmate. Already in the late stages of terminal brain cancer, she was wheeled before the parole board on a gurney. When her husband recited psalms, Atkins was able to utter the last lines. But other than that, she showed few signs of being able to follow the proceedings. Debbie Tate wasn't insensitive to this suffering. She'd been her mother's caretaker until the end of her fight with cancer. But she still opposed Atkins's release. Even if Atkins, in her condition, wasn't going to physically harm anyone herself, Debbie said her release might inspire others to invade homes or commit murder. "I cannot say that she could not influence others even if not by direct contact by the message that goes out. I have to be responsible to society." Debbie said that leniency could have a "ripple effect," which could wreak havoc. "Once you start compromising the law, there's no going back."

The California Adult Authority voted to deny Atkins parole, appraising her an "unreasonable risk," and decided that she required at least three more years of incarceration before coming up again for parole consideration. She was dead within a month.

JAMES SEVERIN, WHO was murdered along with Anthony Rizzato at Cabrini-Green in 1970, was a big, tall, good-looking guy, with dark hair and piercing blue eyes. He'd attended a Catholic high school on Chicago's North Side and, at eighteen, enlisted in the army. He served two years during the Korean War, rising to the rank of corporal. Back in Chicago, after his military service, Severin worked as an insurance investigator. But he wanted more than a job; he was in search of a way to give back in some meaningful way he couldn't name. He thought seriously about joining the priesthood. An uncle of his was in a monastery that supplied the priests for St. Joseph's, the church at Cabrini-Green that Johnnie and his family attended. Severin considered the teaching profession as well, and he began courses at Chicago Teachers College. Most of the men in his family had not only served in the military; many had also gone on to careers in law enforcement. The path was well-trodden, familiar. So in 1957, at twenty-four, Severin joined the Chicago Police Department.

Family members and colleagues said Severin had a calming way about him, a composure he managed to maintain even as a cop during a turbulent time in the city. One of his commanders said he never once heard Severin raise his voice. Severin worked overtime and didn't take days off. He made detective after five years. He was later promoted to sergeant. Although he never married and didn't have children, Severin was from a large family, and his siblings each had five or six kids. Severin would check in on his widowed mother, or he'd show up in his uniform at a sister's house in the suburbs and take a seat at the large dinner table surrounded by the commotion of a family meal, like a stone amid the rapids. "He was always the last person at the dinner table," a niece recalled. "One of those people who savors the food. He was the slowest eater I've ever seen." The children found him approachable. A nephew, after graduating high school and before heading off to a tour in Vietnam, moved in with Severin. At dinners, his uncle read to him from *Bartlett's Familiar Quotations*. "Be kind, for everyone you meet is fighting a hard battle." Severin used the adages as a tool to spark conversations about history, morals, and tolerance. "You can't hold a man down without staying down with him."

In 1966, Severin signed up for the assignment to keep Martin Luther King Jr. safe in Chicago. King took several trips to Cabrini-Green—one of the "Chicago Housing Authority's cement reservations," King declared. The civil rights leader assisted residents there who were protesting their overcrowded and underfunded public schools. Two years later, after King was murdered in Memphis, after fires and rage tore through Chicago's Black neighborhoods, Severin volunteered to lead the walk-and-talk unit at Cabrini-Green. Funding for the community-relations beat came from federal grants under President Johnson's new focus on local law enforcement. In charge of eight officers, Severin organized ball games and socialized with families in the public housing complex. In the aftermath of riots in Chicago and of numerous reports of racist policing, following the murder by police of the young Black Panther leader Fred Hampton, and after intensifying unemployment, poverty, and crime in Chicago's Black communities, Severin and his team of "goodwill" officers were there to demonstrate that the police could be of service to all.

The walk-and-talk unit suffered from many of the same problems that would undercut community-policing efforts in the decades ahead. Nine officers on a force of more than twelve thousand was essentially doing nothing as far as changing the culture and operations of police practices in a big city. Talking to children and playing pool with teenagers weren't things that police departments measured or valued. An extra ten kids in a mentoring program didn't get an officer promoted. Severin's assignment was also an ambiguous one. He and his men weren't social workers or job counselors. They were still armed officers charged with solving crimes. Shootings were occurring daily at Cabrini-Green. Opposing gangs fired on one another from adjacent high-rises. Making his rounds, walking and talking, Severin would try to figure out where the guns were coming from, who was doing the shooting, how he could stop it. A priest who sometimes accompanied him recalled Severin coming upon children and pointing to his service revolver, asking if they knew anyone in their buildings who had a gun like that. Renault Robinson, of the Afro-American Patrolmen's League, had criticized the aims of the Cabrini-Green walk-and-talk unit at the time. "If you're going to develop trust, you have to divorce yourself from being an intelligence agent."

Severin was thirty-eight when he was murdered. He and Rizzato weren't the only victims of the crime. Their families were bereft. For the Severins, they lost their beloved son and brother and uncle. James was the third Chicago police officer in the family to die on the force. The city, too, felt terrorized. Severin and Rizzato were the fifth and sixth police officers in Chicago to be killed in the line of duty that year alone. The mass for Severin's funeral was held at a Catholic church on Chicago's North Side. In attendance were six hundred police officers, including fifty Black cops. Jesse Jackson called Severin a beautiful person. "Severin was a rare man. He was a tragic, tragic victim of circumstances," Jackson declared. Officers from as far as Cleveland and Boston showed up. A procession of cars stretched for blocks. The priest delivering the eulogy said Severin had lived a life according to the principles of Christian charity. "He decided he could best achieve his mission through enrollment in the Chicago police force."

Lillie Veal, Johnnie's mother, attended James Severin's funeral mass as well. She arrived with Johnnie's sister. They'd been invited by Catherine Severin, James's mother. Fred Hampton's mother came, too, in the company of Jesse Jackson. Many of the people at the funeral looked at Lillie Veal with pure hatred. Her son, according to all reports, had ambushed and murdered the two unsuspecting officers. But Catherine Severin greeted Johnnie's mother and held her hand. Mrs. Severin insisted that prayers were needed not only for her child but also for Johnnie and the other man accused of the murders, George Clifford Knights. "They're the ones who really need your prayers," she said.

The philosopher Hannah Arendt wrote about the transformative power in forgiveness, calling it "the exact opposite of vengeance." Unlike vengeance, Arendt believed, "forgiving can never be predicted; it is the only reaction that acts in an unexpected way and thus retains . . . something of the original character of action. Forgiving, in other words, is the only reaction which does not merely re-act but acts anew and unexpectedly, unconditioned by the act which provoked it and thereby freeing from its consequences both the one who forgives and the one who is forgiven." Catherine Severin's embrace of Johnnie's mother was surprising, and seemed to be liberating for her. Mrs. Severin cried, praising her own son's peaceful nature. "My Jim is in heaven." But she said she worried now about Mrs. Veal and Knights's mother, since their sons faced what might be a lifetime of suffering. "My hurt is so deep, but their hurt must be deeper. I don't want any more misery for any more families."

IN HIS 1975 book, *The Victims*, Frank Carrington, an attorney and a former federal law enforcement officer, called for a new "victim consciousness" in the justice system. "The victims of crime in the United States occupy, as a class, the same position that the racial minorities did years ago," Carrington wrote. "Today each victim is largely regarded as an individual statistic, if he is regarded at all. We must recognize that crime's victims are a class of people with rights that must be protected." The book's cover conveyed this message as well, with an illustration of a handgun being fired at a target, and the title—"The Victims"—in the bull's-eye. Carrington was then the executive director of Americans for Effective Law Enforcement, a conservative group founded to rival the American Civil Liberties Union in arguing cases before the Supreme Court. Like many conservatives at that time, Carrington blamed what he deemed the permissiveness of the U.S. Supreme Court under Chief Justice Earl Warren, from 1953 to 1968, for undermining law enforcement and causing a spike in crime. Carrington and others decrying liberal criminal justice policies liked to point out that in all the Warren court rulings on policing and prosecutions there wasn't a single reference to the rights of victims.

Not that there necessarily should be. Constitutional law in the United States gives numerous protections to those accused of crimes. It's the foundation of the country's justice system, and a testament to the gravity of taking away a person's liberty, that regardless of a crime's atrocity everyone is considered innocent until proven guilty. That they deserve a fair hearing. Victims' rights changed the balance. Conservatives were able to portray the criminal justice system, and really the entire country, as a binary of victims and offenders. This vision helped dismantle liberal reforms by turning victimizers into abstractions, often racial boogeymen, who were undeserving of protections under the law. California's Victims' Bill of Rights, for instance, allowed certain evidence to be introduced at trial even if it violated a defendant's rights. Carrington drafted a policy paper that laid out a victim-oriented criminal justice strategy for the country, one that would be enacted over the next decades. In addition to ending indeterminate sentencing and reinstating the death penalty, he proposed going after bail reforms, the insanity defense, and protections against illegal searches and seizure; he further proposed increasing drug sentences and juvenile penalties and instituting mandatory minimum fixed prison sentences for all but minor offenses.

When Carrington wrote *The Victims*, there were only a few victim service organizations in the country. That would change. Most of the early victim groups were grassroots, likeminded parents and families joining forces, but increasingly the messaging about law and order, as well as much of the funding, came from on high. Ronald Reagan, in

his first year as president in 1981, created a "Victims' Rights Week" and
signed into law an executive order establishing a task force on "Victims
of Crime." Reagan wrote, "For most of the past thirty years, the administration of justice has been unreasonably tilted in favor of criminals and
against their innocent victims. This tragic era can fairly be described as
a period when victims were forgotten and crimes were ignored." The
task force, to which Carrington was appointed, proposed sixty-eight
specific reforms. Two-thirds of the states soon adopted the measures.
Many of the laws were common-sense and thoughtful protections that
are now staples of the justice system. Victims were notified as cases advanced through sentencing, imprisonment, and release. Victims were
protected from intimidation and reprisals. Other changes undercut
the protections afforded the accused and the guilty and made it harder
for people sentenced to prison to safely reenter free society. Victims,
for instance, were given the right to restitution from offenders through
fines and seized assets; failing to pay this restitution became another
reason to revoke a person's parole or probation and rearrest them. Victims were also granted the right to speak at sentencing and at parole
hearings. An Office for Victims of Crime was soon established within
the Justice Department to fund victim groups. By the 1990s, there were
more than ten thousand victim service groups in the country.

The most dishonest thing about victim rights was how it largely
overlooked those most often victimized by crime. The grassroot groups
advocating for the rights of victims were frequently led by white sub-
urbanites, usually middle-class women. Extreme crimes occurring in
their communities had galvanized them, shocking people into action,
and mostly white Republican leaders had seized on their suffering. No
one should be afflicted by that kind of loss and trauma and disruption.
But as crime victims in America they were also unrepresentative. In the
United States, a Black person is six times more likely to be a victim of
homicide than a white person. Black Americans were also more likely
to be victims of sexual assault, robbery, motor vehicle theft, and nearly
every other type of crime. In Chicago, where Johnnie was from, Black
people were less than a third of the population but made up nearly 75
percent of the murders; Black women in Chicago were two-thirds of the
domestic violence survivors. All victims of crimes need protections and

support. But white, relatively affluent people won rights as victims, and the laws and policies their activism brought about disproportionately affected those who were far more likely to be victims of crimes. Where was the outrage over "compromising the law," as Debbie Tate put it, when the grave injustices were happening regularly to people unlike themselves? The movement thrived on a narrow idea of a victim. It was an us and them. *The victims of crime in the United States occupy, as a class, the same position that the racial minorities did years ago.* In poorer areas, in Black and Latino communities, police and prosecutors arrested, convicted, and sent people to prison at much higher rates. These people remained in prison for longer terms and, if they had exit dates, were stripped of their rights as citizens upon their release. All in the name of justice for victims.

A victim consciousness came to pervade not only the criminal justice system but much of American society. Parables of righteous vengeance suffused popular culture, of heroes meting out bloody vengeance against the villains who committed crimes. Along with victim rights, the country gets iconic movies about renegade police officers, almost always white men, who reclaim extrajudicial killings as noble and just. Clint Eastwood's "Dirty" Harry, Gene Hackman's Detective Jimmy "Popeye" Doyle in *The French Connection*, or any of a thousand of their progenitors or offspring. These vigilantes ignore *Miranda* rights and fair trials and other laws that only prevent them from restoring a form of brutal order. Decades later, Donald Trump as president would repeatedly invoke this myth of making American justice great again, claiming to have spoken to an unnamed mystery Chicago police officer, a "tough guy," or a "strong-looking guy on a motorcycle"—it varied depending on Trump's audience or his mood. But this "cop" allegedly told the president he could fix the "killing problems" in Chicago in a day or in a week if the police were just allowed to do their jobs without the constraints of the liberal legal system, the "crooked media," or the "hate" of Black Lives Matter.

Other movies empowered parents of murdered children or husbands of murdered wives by showing a character exact the revenge they craved. As first personified by Charles Bronson in the 1974 *Death Wish*, and later Liam Neeson in numerous incarnations, the bereaved, usually a father and white, is cheered on through murderous retribution. Seen one way, you could imagine these films as cautionary tales dramatizing why victims shouldn't sit on juries or weigh in on punishments or parole decisions. They're so grief-stricken and enraged they would go on to commit horrible crimes themselves. They illustrate the ongoing danger of the lynch mob. They show the need for something like restorative justice, which offers victims the healing and redress they will never get from a prison sentence. But that's not how these parables were intended, or received. They are ninety-minute advertisements for the death penalty, for unfettered policing and extreme sentencing, for punishment as payback. They make people believe in a Manichaean myth of good and evil—those who do crimes are evil and deserve nothing but annihilation. The ends always justify the means.

Victim rights, as a tool and a way of thinking, supercharged the policies of mass incarceration. The movement helps explain why there wasn't more widespread opposition as the United States embraced a radical expansion of its carceral system. Victim rights focused less on the majority of actual crimes that needed to be solved and the actual hurt people who required protection and support. It conjured up a racialized specter of the country in which everyone, and every white person, was a potential victim of extreme violence. More widely, the movement demanded that police, prosecutors, and politicians respond to this measureless fear of any imaginable *future* crimes. "Within the victims class, the potential victims, can be defined quite simply as everyone; we are *all* potential victims of a criminal act," Carrington summed up in *The Victims*. The idea was a seductive one. The eighteenth-century jurist William Blackstone's principle that "it is better that ten guilty persons escape than that one innocent suffer" had been a cornerstone of Western jurisprudence, setting the standard for proof of guilt "beyond a reasonable doubt." But victim groups and politicians talked about the goal of saving even one innocent person from becoming a victim of a violent crime, dispensing with rational considerations of risk and the residual costs of harsh punishments. Why consider data or our collective well-being if we imagined imminent peril? Questions about why or how or who we imprison were less important than the command for more. "Each new victim personally represents an instance in which our system has failed to prevent crime," President Reagan said.

Who is deemed a victim equates to who is valued and who viewed with sympathy. Those who can't be seen as victims are less human, and they can more easily be punished harshly, permanently. Nearly every law named for a victim of a horrific crime since the 1980s is named for a white crime victim. The Jacob Wetterling Crimes Against Children Act, Megan's Law, AMBER Alert, Jessica's Law, Laura's Law, the Adam Walsh Child Protection and Safety Act, Marsy's Law. In the name of protecting potential future victims, the country implemented punishments so extreme that they reconstituted what was considered normal. New laws dispensed with the notion of just deserts. Supermax prisons were torture chambers. Beginning in the 1980s, a number of states imposed mandatory minimum sentences for the selling of cocaine, with hundred-to-one disparities between those caught with crack, the cheaper version that was proliferating in urban areas, and the more expensive powder version. Although numerous studies have shown that Americans of different races sell and use illicit drugs at equal rates, three-quarters of those sent to prison for drug crimes since the 1980s were Black or Latino. In California, in 1993, a man serving a sentence for kidnapping was paroled and went on to abduct and murder a twelve-year-old girl named Polly Klaas. Klaas's case led California to enact the most punitive three-strikes laws in the country, with other states following suit. These laws, which administered life sentences for even a minor third felony, defied all sense of proportionality. After Klaas's murder, parole approvals granted by the California Adult Authority plummeted. By 1998, the chance of a lifer leaving a California state prison on parole fell to less than one in one hundred.

CATHERINE SEVERIN NEVER attended a parole hearing for Johnnie or Clifford Knights. A year after her son's murder, she was riding in a car on her way to visit her son's grave when another car crashed into hers. Catherine Severin was killed. But her children and their children and eventually the children's children protested release at each hearing. The family showed up at Johnnie's first parole hearing at the start of the 1980s and never missed one after that. "The Severins will never forget. The Severins will always attend the parole hearings until both offenders die in prison," a niece wrote on a message board. "We organize it like a war," another said. Going each year was draining. Emotionally, the family had to hear again about the murder, reliving the devastating events. Logistically, some family members had moved away from the Chicago area and Illinois altogether.

Just as they had for Doris Tate, parole hearings came to define the Severins and give them purpose. In that way, the hearings both united and trapped the family. The indeterminate sentence meant they had to remain vigilant, they could never stop fighting. "Most people say, 'Oh, weddings and funerals,' and our family it's parole hearings," a niece of James Severin, Jean Severin Cabel, said. It was their family tradition. After twenty years, thirty years, forty years of Johnnie and Knights being in prison, the family still felt little of the relief or sense of justice they craved. Nothing could ever undo what occurred. No punishment could change what happened. Hannah Arendt contrasts vengeance to forgiveness in this way: "Vengeance," she wrote, "acts in the form of reacting against an original trespassing, whereby far from putting an end to the consequences of the first misdeed, everybody remains bound to the process."

"I always think of that Japanese tradition where when they break a bowl, they don't throw it away," Jean Severin Cabel would say. "They seal the breaks with gold. And so in Japan they actually relish this broken dish, because now it has gold veins in it. And that's kind of what happened to our family."

There was one member of the Severin family who decided that he no longer wanted to feel imprisoned by the parole process. One of James Severin's nephews had enough. He wanted to break free of this indefinite trap. "I do not feel a sixty-one-year-old man is a threat to society," John Severin wrote in a letter he sent to George Clifford Knights in prison in 2008. An engineer living in a Chicago suburb, John explained to Knights that he was willing to support him in his next parole petition. John Severin didn't question the validity of the conviction. "You were only a few years above a teenager when you committed the murder," he wrote. But he decided that the punishment had gone on long enough. "There is no one else in my family who feels this way of forgiveness."

Like Johnnie, Knights had said at trial that he didn't take part in the shootings. An admission of guilt in the years since would likely have improved his chances with the parole board. But he'd been consistent with his denials over forty years. A defense witness at his trial, in 1971, testified that she saw Knights moments after the shooting outside a high-rise escorting children to safety. How could he be firing a high-powered rifle from one of the high-rises at the same time? Two police officers, witnesses for the prosecution, testified that they saw the same thing. Officer Thomas Wilczenski said in court that gunfire was still coming from the upper floors of 1119 N. Cleveland, so he ducked for cover.

> WILCZENSKI: As I was watching the 1119 Cleveland building, I turned to look north along the eastern edge of the building, and I observed a man coming out of the building.
>
> PROSECUTION: Did you know who that man was?
>
> WILCZENSKI: Yes, I did.
>
> PROSECUTION: What was his name?
>
> WILCZENSKI: Mr. George Knights.

The chief prosecutor asked what Knights was doing, and whether he was alone.

> WILCZENSKI: At that time, Mr. Knight [sic] was with approximately seven or eight youthful children. . . . He was standing with the children on a little sidewalk.

Knights, like Johnnie, insisted that the two of them barely knew each other and had no history together. Johnnie was seventeen and in a gang; Knights was twenty-three, a janitor and livery driver. "Johnnie and I did not conversate. He was on a different plane of life than I was with totally different pursuits and associates. . . . My brother and I would be with others our age and older," Knights would say. "Johnnie was a person that I would see come and go, nothing more and nothing less." With each passing year in prison, Knights's knowledge of the law grew in direct proportion to his anger. "What political prisoner do you know who puts stock in the system that has made them a political prisoner?" he said of his incarceration. He had little faith he might win his freedom at a hearing that he couldn't attend and at which board members faced a roomful of cops.

When Knights heard from John Severin, he was understandably dubious. Both he and Johnnie had received numerous letters from other Severin and Rizzato family members, from police officers and others. Taunts on holidays and notes disguised in greeting cards telling them they were going to die in prison and rot in hell. Nearly forty years into his prison bid, Knights had seen the letters taper off into a trickle. But Knights knew the relatives of the officers still protested his release each year. He typed out a reply to John Severin.

"I must admit that I am skeptical of your intent given the fact that over the years your father sent me harassing mail. If your intent is to inflict mental anguish, don't bother, it would be a futile endeavor." Knights remained gracious, however. "If on the other hand you are sincere, I shall meet you on your terms."

"I am *not* like my father, who played games with you," Severin responded. His father had died in 2006, and John seemed also to be working out some personal family issues that had less to do with his uncle's 1970 murder and with parole. "In order to look them, convincingly, in their eyes, I must look you in your eyes," he wrote Knights. "I think the first Severin voice to the Parole Board to recommend parole is groundbreaking, and I am man enough to stand up to my relatives."

Severin contacted the parole board in 2011, urging them to release Knights. He mischaracterized his correspondences to some extent, saying Knights expressed "extreme regret and anguish about the murder of my uncle." Knights never admitted to the crime in the letters he sent John Severin, although he did acknowledge the tragedy that befell the entire Severin family. John Severin told the board that Knights was "literate, self-schooled," that he "poses no threat to society." He said Knights's term of imprisonment had been sufficient. "I believe it is time to forgive him and allow him and myself to move on with our lives."

James Severin and Anthony Rizzato and their families were the victims of a horrendous crime. Johnnie, as a teenager, had also been a victim, as well as a victimizer. When Johnnie's sister was the victim of a violent rape, Johnnie, like in those vigilante movies, turned to revenge. John Severin didn't write to Johnnie, nor did he mention Johnnie in his correspondence with Knights. In the state's case against Johnnie and Knights, in the "statement of facts" and all the court records, Knights was identified as the shooter; Johnnie, a teenager at the time, was convicted on the theory of accountability, for planning and assisting with the crime. But Severin was not ready to forgive Johnnie after all these years. Johnnie remained somehow the super-predator, a monster akin to Charles Manson and his followers. He was still to be feared. When John Severin appealed to the parole board on behalf of Knights, he added with emphasis, "*I wish to protest parole for Mr. Veal, with no further comments.*"

9

Halfway Back

Michael, now a parolee, sat on the train to Chicago, unsupervised yet feeling watched. It must have been obvious to all, he thought, that he was straight out the penitentiary. He might as well have had a sandwich board hanging from his neck that announced "CONVICT." The release clothes issued to him by the prison were a hodgepodge of different styles and sizes. It was December 2018 and freezing out, yet he didn't have a coat. He didn't have a suitcase either. All his belongings were stuffed into two stretched-thin garbage bags piled at his feet. On his wing at the prison, when word had spread that Michael made parole, men banged a jubilant chorus on the bars of their cells. There were a few haters, there always were; they wanted to know why Michael got to go home and not them. But most people appreciated the magnitude of forty-six years. Michael couldn't process it himself. His leaving was surreal. From the moment he spoke to his lawyer, Michael felt like a different person. He'd been reborn. He tried to organize his belongings, separating what he planned to keep and what to give away. Less than forty-eight hours later, a guard told him to pack his shit. If he wasn't ready by four in the afternoon, they'd leave his ass. Another officer drove him to the train, and that was that. For the first time in a half century, he was on his own.

On the ride to Chicago's Union Station, Michael turned to a conductor to ask permission to leave his seat. He had to use the bathroom. He caught himself and chuckled nervously. It was the penitentiary mindset. Freedom would take some getting used to. Michael studied the passengers around him. It was his first time seeing it—a crowd of people, all of them bowing their heads into cell phones, as if in group prayer. No one was interested in him. A woman bumped into Michael and didn't say excuse me. He choked back the urge to yell, "Hey, I'm here! I just got out! Hello!"

Michael was scheduled to arrive in Chicago in the evening, with his lawyer, Marjorie Moss, meeting him at the downtown station. But the train stopped on the tracks somewhere in central Illinois and sat there for four hours. Michael had no way of reaching Moss. He didn't have a phone. How would she know the schedule change? What would Michael do if she wasn't there? The thought terrified him. He had been to Chicago once before. An aunt who lived in Peoria had taken him. But that was in 1969, when Michael was fifteen. He wouldn't know east from west, up from down. The train finally pulled into Union Station shortly before midnight. Michael edged his way onto the platform, lugging his trash bags as he scanned the crowd. There was Moss, standing beside her husband. Michael and his lawyer embraced. She snapped a photo of him posing in front of the station's giant Christmas tree. Michael hoisted the two garbage bags over his shoulder, like Santa Claus. One of the plastic bags opened like a chute. Forty pounds of books, photos and documents splashed onto the ground.

Michael's new residence, at least for the next several months, was a group home on Chicago's West Side, a transitional halfway house for people reentering society after prison. It was called St. Leonard's House, and Moss planned to drop Michael there. She asked if there was anything he wanted to see first. Was there some food he'd been dreaming of? In the bedlam of emotions since learning of his parole, he hadn't contemplated a first meal. What popped into his head now was a banana. The potassium. When he ran at the prison, he thought constantly about the lack of fresh fruit. They dropped into a newsstand inside Union Station, and Michael picked out four bananas. The first one was gone in three quick bites. Out on the street, Michael paused and took in the world around him. The orderliness of the parked cars one after another as if on a chain. The long shadows of the streetlamps. Everything sparkled with strangeness. That would soon fade with familiarity. But in that instant, Michael imagined he would spend the rest of his days in awe of these everyday delights. The orange winking of a DON'T WALK sign. The wide boulevard gullied by a dark SUV, which seemed as big and fast as a torpedo. Michael was now a part of this world. "They don't know me from the man in the moon! And I don't know them," he sang. "But I love them!"

St. Leonard's was sixteen blocks west of the downtown train station, and two blocks from the United Center, the stadium where the Bulls and Blackhawks played their home games. Michael studied the route. They arrived at the halfway house well past midnight. The two-story brick building was shrouded in darkness—the electricity was out, possibly a blown circuit, Michael would learn. He saw a couple of people out front with flashlights. "Welcome home, brother," someone shouted. They were there to greet him. Two men took turns clasping hands with Michael, pulling him in for a hug. Many of the employees at St. Leonard's were former residents, meaning they'd been incarcerated themselves. Michael looked for a familiar face, anyone he might have done time with. At that hour, he didn't recognize a soul. So he did what he always did—he stayed quiet and observed. *Know everyone before they know you.*

Moss said she'd be back soon to check on him, and Michael thanked her again. He followed a man inside. The building was more than a century old. The carpet was worn to balding, the wood floors chipped. Michael was handed an assortment of toiletries. He'd get new clothes in the morning. He was led up narrow stairs, each creaky step like hitting the keys on a pipe organ. At the end of a hallway, he was shown a room with three single beds. In the dark, Michael could make out the outlines of sleeping men in two of them. Michael shuffled to the third cot and stowed his bags. He returned to the hallway and washed up in the communal bathroom. When he lay down in his corner of the room, he reviewed his day, as he'd done in a cell every night for decades. There was a lot to cover.

*   *   *

So far, I've used the word "parole" to mean the process by which a board decides who should and shouldn't leave prison before the completion of an indeterminate sentence. Discretionary parole. Since 1982, Michael had come up for parole consideration thirty-six times. In 2018, he made parole. But the noun and verb was also a state of being, a precarious liminality between two worlds. Michael was now *on parole*, which meant he was out of prison but still supervised. He had to check in regularly with a parole officer and abide by the conditions of his release. Parole in this sense refers not just to people who were technically freed by a parole board; it also describes everyone released from prison who, as a stipulation of their sentence, had to remain under the custody of the Department of Corrections for a period of time while out in the world. *On parole* is also known as mandatory supervised release, MSR, or community supervision.

Being out on parole, like its cousin, probation, operates as an alternative to physical confinement. Instead of staying behind bars, a person is monitored and controlled in the community. It is significantly cheaper to supervise someone outside of prison or jail than to lock them up, about a tenth of the cost. And for the person supervised, release is almost always preferable to prison. In the outside world, even if wearing an electronic monitor and checking in with a parole officer, a person could, within many limits, try to earn an income, be around friends and family, and begin to feel more like a productive member of society. But it is still considered a period of punishment. While parole is tacked on after a prison term, probation is a form of community supervision given at sentencing as an alternative to incarceration. Someone on parole, or on probation, wasn't yet returned to full citizenship.

Michael met his parole officer and was fitted with an electronic ankle bracelet that relayed his whereabouts. He had to wear it for four months. From seven in the morning to seven in the evening, he was free to leave St. Leonard's; he could visit a grocery store or go on a jog. But every night he needed to be back at the halfway house, near the monitor's base in his room. Otherwise an alert would be triggered and he'd be in violation of his parole. Michael assured Moss that he wouldn't mess up. He would conform to the conditions of his release. He would stay out of trouble. "I'm not coming back to prison," he'd tell people he encountered. "I intend to be successful in whatever I get involved in."

But on parole, Michael faced an array of potential pitfalls. If he missed a seven o'clock curfew or didn't show up for an appointment with his parole officer, that was a parole violation; he would have a "revocation" hearing and might have to serve out the entirety of his remaining term, which meant a release date around 2070, when he would be 114. If he left the state, he was also in breach of his parole restrictions and could be returned to prison. If he tampered with the electronic monitor attached to his ankle, he was similarly in violation. Other states charged back supervision fees to people on parole, and if they didn't pay—or weren't able to—that was also a violation. If Michael failed to report that he'd moved, or failed to find housing or employment, he could be violated as well. If he drank alcohol or smoked marijuana or tested positive for any controlled substance or entered a bar, he could go back to prison.

The list went on. Along with mandatory minimums and truth in sentencing, tough-on-crime legislation over the previous five decades had transformed parole supervision. Terms of supervised release were constantly made longer and the conditions more onerous. In recent years, reforms meant to update harsh mandatory sentencing guidelines hedged by piling on additional restrictions to supervised release. More people were let out of prison, but with more mandatory supervision. According to the American Bar Association, there were forty-five thousand federal and state laws regulating what a person couldn't do once they left prison on supervised release. In his book *Halfway Home: Race, Punishment, and the Afterlife of Mass Incarceration*, sociologist Reuben Jonathan Miller points out that people on parole in Illinois face a thousand collateral consequences of their incarceration dealing merely with restrictions on employment. As a parolee reentering free society, Michael would be sent back to prison if he committed another crime, of course, even a misdemeanor. But the same could happen if he was arrested and never charged with a crime, even if the arrest was for disorderly conduct or loitering or resisting arrest, the sort of vague and questionable public-order charges that could result from a police officer stopping him as he was driving or walking or standing somewhere. Michael was barred from legally owning a gun, and it was a parole violation if he was found in possession of a firearm. It was a violation, too, if he was discovered knowingly associating "with other persons on parole, aftercare release, or mandatory supervised release without prior written permission from his or her parole agent." What was the likelihood that Michael would run into other people on parole? The neighborhoods due west of St. Leonard's, East Garfield Park and West Garfield Park, had the highest incarceration rates in the city, more than six times greater than the national average, and also had the city's highest percentage of residents returning from prison. This happened all over the country. People leaving prison were clustered in a handful of inner-city neighborhoods, areas that already lacked opportunities and resources and that were further destabilized by the high concentration of people cycling in and out of the criminal system. In Brooklyn, a borough of 2.5 million people, half of all those on supervised release reside in just a few city blocks. In Ohio, a vastly disproportionate share of returning citizens are pooled in the same small sections of Cleveland. It was officially a violation of Michael's parole as well if he was caught hanging out with someone believed to be in an organized gang. At the time of Michael's release on parole, the Chicago Police Department's gang database included more than 130,000 names, an absurd number. Since Michael now lived in Chicago, he had a decent chance of interacting with someone on that list.

Michael, by being on parole, joined a population of millions. Along with mass incarceration, the United States had created a symbiotic crisis of mass supervision. In 1975, there were 143,000 people out on parole in the country. From that point on, however, the prison population took off by nearly 700 percent. Hundreds of thousands of people entering prison each year meant that many more people eventually exited, most of them leaving prison and entering some required form of community control. Some 820,000 Americans are now on parole. Another three million people are on probation. The rise of this supervisory state of nearly four million Americans is unprecedented historically and unrivaled globally. In 2020, one in every sixty-six adults in America was on parole or probation. For Black men, it had been as high as one of every twelve.

* * *

ON MICHAEL'S FIRST morning at St. Leonard's, he met his new room-mates, Ray and Robert Jones. Ray was younger than Michael by at least twenty years, but Robert Jones, who went by RJ, at seventy-six, was a decade older, and he was a talker. RJ asked Michael what he thought about breakfast that morning. Michael eyed him warily. A C-Number as well, RJ had spent forty-one years in prison and won parole only a month before Michael. He spoke in a slow, comic delivery, like he was exaggerating lines in a burlesque. RJ asked Michael whether they should buy Christmas gifts online or at a store. Michael remained cagey.

"I don't know, man," he said. "That's something you gotta decide."

"I see you're the silent type," RJ teased.

Michael didn't want to divulge too much about himself. He offered tight hellos to the other men he met over the next few days. He was still figuring out the place. Then later that week, at the halfway house's Christmas party, he was asked by the staff to introduce himself. Michael stood in front of the group in silence. He uttered his name, adding how long he'd been gone. There were shouts of encouragement. Michael scanned the smiling faces in the room. Michael had told himself count-less times in prison that he was getting ready for a moment like this one. He'd recited speeches in his cell, monologues about freedom and human nature, tributes to his perseverance and preparation. But now he was standing at a holiday party, on Chicago's West Side, amid all these cheerful people. The fact of it walloped him. There was nothing in his life to compare it to. It felt like a miracle. Michael started to talk about how he showed up at St. Leonard's at midnight and was met by a welcoming party.

"I never felt so much love and concern about me." He had served time for killing another person, and yet everyone at St. Leonard's ac-cepted him. They put him on a pedestal. Michael's jaw shook, his throat constricted. Heavy tears rolled down his cheeks.

"You can do it," a man shouted.

"Thank you," Michael managed to whisper. Another former C-Number who worked at St. Leonard's put his arms around Michael. Someone else came over and embraced them both. And then others joined them, add-ing to the growing knot of bodies.

Back in their room, RJ couldn't stop talking about Michael's "croco-dile tears," his "performance" at the party.

"This motherfucker must be able to cry on call," RJ shouted. "He had that room fired up."

"I wasn't bullshitting, man," Michael laughed. "That was some real shit. I couldn't stop crying."

For some people coming out of prison, they'd had enough of living in a group setting, and a place like St. Leonard's felt oppressive, with its curfews and requirements and meals at eight in the morning, noon, and five o'clock sharp. They'd already done their time around incarcer-ated or formerly incarcerated people. Michael felt differently. In those first weeks and months, he found comfort in the communal routines. He liked being surrounded by people who had also done time. They understood where he was coming from, like fellow war veterans, and they respected him for the years he'd put in. The halfway house was familiar in ways he needed. For forty-six years, his existence had been regulated for him. When to get up, what to eat, what to wear, when to shower or make a phone call or exercise. Now he had to figure out the rhythm of days that weren't parsed by prison alarms and count times. He learned at St. Leonard's that he'd been "prisonized." At McDonald's, the grocery store, or, even worse, on the internet, there were way too many options. He had to choose from fifteen varieties of toothpaste. He felt paralyzed. He sometimes stood next to the two-lane boulevard outside St. Leonard's and watched the speed of the one-way traffic. He studied how other people crossed casually between the rocketing cars, thinking he wasn't there yet.

Michael's son was living in Massachusetts, working in a glass factory. He sent his father a cell phone, and St. Leonard's helped Michael acti-vate it. Michael's three daughters, along with their children and, in some cases, their children's children, still lived around East St. Louis. The cell phone allowed Michael to reconnect with all of them. He was learning how to be a father, grandfather, and friend. He even reconnected with Joyce, his ex-wife. After decades of no communication, they started talking again. St. Leonard's recommended to its residents that they set-tle in a while before trying to mend ties with family. That they ask their relatives to be patient. "We're selfish for ourselves," the halfway house told its arrivals. "We're going to be selfish so that we can actually look at ourselves and move forward and take advantage of the program." People coming out of prison were fortunate if they still had loved ones who wanted them back in their lives, who needed them. But relatives of the formerly incarcerated could also be demanding, understandably so. They'd spent years raising children on their own, handling every meal, bill, and crisis. Children grew up without a parent, with that daily absence in their life. Parents grew old with their sons or daughters locked away, and the responsibility of their elder care fell to others. For many women making the transition back from prison, the expectations were even higher. They were supposed to be nurturing, maternal, family-oriented; they felt an urgency upon their reentry to prove themselves. The staff at St. Leonard's preached that residents might not be ready to fulfill those expectations—they needed a little time, and space, to figure out the kind of person they wanted to become, so they didn't repeat whatever got them sent to prison in the first place. A former C-Number who worked at the halfway house counseled Michael, "Don't build a house on sand, cause sand always sinks."

Forty men lived at St. Leonard's and eighteen women in its nearby Grace House. They all had to complete a three-month core curriculum, with courses five days a week. Classes on managing anger and building healthy relationships. Classes on substance abuse therapy, relapse prevention, and financial literacy. Michael met with a case manager, a chaplain, and a nurse. He learned how to open a bank account, how to avoid the fees that came with a prepaid debit card. He learned about car loans, identity theft, and the ballooning interest of short-term payday loans. Michael took a mandatory class on human behavior. Michael said he had spent a lifetime in prison studying human behavior. He credited his survival inside to his perspicacity. But prison was no longer his metaphor to comprehend the world. His laboratory was now limitless. In class, they read scenarios of workplace conflict. In the outside world, just like inside, there were established protocols and rules. Michael needed to understand them and then pattern his behavior accordingly.

Michael took lessons on how to navigate the internet. "I'm in that

Facebook," he said. "Either you plug into the 'Matrix,' or you don't exist." Using the satellite images from a map application, he zoomed in on his building. The very spot where he was sitting. That was his space in the world. "Life is so wonderful," he said. In an employment class called Road to Success, Michael studied résumé writing, interview skills, and issues with background checks. St. Leonard's had connections with various local employers, and they offered job training as well. In a construction workshop, residents built a tiny house, the walls and floors and stairs and rafters, putting in wiring and plumbing. Then they took it all apart, gaining demolition experience as well. RJ, Michael's buddy, spent much of his time in a teaching kitchen, chopping basil and defrosting frozen turkey meat. St. Leonard was then trying to start a catering business, with its advanced students as the employees. RJ, a star pupil, was learning to prepare soups and sauces and pastries.

Michael's favorite class at St. Leonard's was Reading Between the Lines. They read and then discussed Shakespeare, the Gettysburg Address, Martin Luther King's "Letter from Birmingham Jail." For someone who liked nothing more than to share his philosophical musings, the class was a joy.

"Michael, why are these different perspectives useful or valuable?" a volunteer teacher asked him. He answered that they taught him empathy. He said understanding how other people felt about certain things helped him develop a "listening ear."

"The key to everything," he said, "you have to listen." One day they were asked to mark up a poem called "To the Foot from Its Child" by the Chilean writer Pablo Neruda. The poem was odd. About a child's foot, and how that foot, being so young and innocent, imagines it can be something other than a foot. That it can be anything. A butterfly. An apple. But the foot goes through life. It steps on the hard ground. It treads on stones and pieces of glass. Everything about the foot's existence drives home the lesson that, no, a foot can't fly. No, you are not going to grow ripe and juicy on a tree. It's into a shoe for you.

Michael wondered what he could have been under different circumstances. Hadn't the stones and glass and rough earth of East St. Louis taught him to hustle, steal, and carry a gun? In Reading Between the

Lines, he was good at analysis and interpretation. What if he'd been able to go to college? He could have studied literature, history, religion. He could have been a teacher. Or was Neruda saying those dreams were silly? That he was doomed to his fate? A foot is a foot and not an apple no matter what it thinks of itself.

St. Leonard's was founded in the 1950s by a chaplain working at the Cook County jail, an Episcopal priest named James Jones. Father Jones saw that men left the jail in Chicago without money, a job, or a place to live. The only thing that had changed during their lockup was that they were worse off, acquiring a record, missing work and their families. Many of them were back in no time. "He had a human responsibility to meet some of these men halfway," a 1963 profile of Father Jones in *Chicago Scene* explained. "In the deepest Christian sense of the word, he is moved by a *loving* anger." Jones started housing released men in his small apartment. Married with children, Jones reached out to the Episcopal Diocese of Chicago, which owned a dilapidated three-story house on the West Side, a building believed to be a former brothel. Jones used it to open St. Leonard's, named for the patron saint of prisoners. The building was surrounded by abandoned properties, and the halfway house acquired one of them and then others. Today, St. Leonard's doesn't charge residents transitioning out of Illinois prisons—their rooms, food, and programming are free. Someone who had been incarcerated for a shorter period of time might leave St. Leonard's immediately after finishing the mandatory supervised release part of a sentence. But someone who'd been gone ten years, or, like Michael, forty-six, had been institutionalized in an entirely different way and might need longer to adapt. Father Jones called the residents coming out of long prison terms "ghosts" or "zombies." "Other human beings are threatening to them because their wills are not strong," he said in the 1963 profile. "Very much as a boxer would be if his arm were put in a cast for six months. When he took the cast off he'd be afraid to go in the ring with another fellow." A program director at St. Leonard's in 2020 named Joni Stahlman said, "Living in prison is traumatic. I don't care if you're in there for one year or if you're in there for forty years. We meet them where their needs are. We try to keep working with them so that they feel comfortable being independent."

St. Leonard's was opened at the same time that halfway houses began to play a larger role in the nation's corrections systems. Beginning in the early nineteenth century, private charities and religious organizations had offered transitional living to those in the country leaving prisons or jails. Only a few of these facilities survived beyond the 1930s. In the 1960s, though, the federal government started to fund group homes for young people reintegrating back into free society. Transitional housing facilities were opened in Chicago, Los Angeles, and New York. The Prisoner Rehabilitation Act of 1965 authorized the use of community residential treatment centers for adults. For centuries, "halfway house" had been used to mean a literal inn or waystation along a journey. In the 1960s, the term started to refer to the waystation on the journey back from prison. In Illinois, St. Leonard's was considered one of the state's best. For members of the Prisoner Review Board, a parole candidate securing a spot at St. Leonard's was tantamount to a "good parole plan." In Louisiana, three of every four parole candidates who worked with Louisiana Parole Project won releasee for much the same reason—the parole board trusted that the organization's residential housing facilities and wraparound services would enable a parolee's successful reentry. At St. Leonard's, more than 80 percent of the residents completed all the programming and weren't incarcerated again.

With mass incarceration, a cottage industry of reentry services built up alongside it. Currently, some 650,000 people leave state and federal prisons each year, and many of them are in need of a transitional residence. Someone can't leave prison on parole unless they have housing secured, and yet there's an extreme shortage of both transitional halfway housing and of homes that are long-term and affordable. There are enough beds in halfway houses across the nation for about 10 percent of the reentry population. Many people leaving prison can't afford rents on the open market, and because of their past felonies they're rejected by landlords and ineligible for public housing and other housing assistance programs. The criminal justice expert Jeremy Travis called these post-prison social exclusions the "invisible punishments" of a felony conviction. Many times people on parole or mandatory supervised release are prohibited from living with relatives, because the family members have felonies themselves or are out of work. The terms of supervision mean they can't live with friends who smoke weed. Homelessness among the formerly incarcerated is ten times higher than it is among the general population, according to a report from the Prison Policy Initiative. And the rate of homelessness is significantly higher for formerly imprisoned women than it is for men, and higher for people of color than it is for white people. Those with past sex offenses can't live near schools or day care centers, and it isn't uncommon for people convicted of sex crimes who have completed their prison terms to remain locked up because there is literally nowhere else for them to live. St. Leonard's stopped taking people convicted of sex offenses after one former resident went on to commit multiple rapes and the facility was sued and lost donors. St. Leonard's didn't take people convicted of arson either. Nor were they set up to handle people with extreme mental health issues, and the buildings weren't Americans with Disabilities Act compliant. If you couldn't climb the rickety stairs, you couldn't stay there. Without a stable home, the formerly incarcerated found it harder to secure jobs, access schools, and reunite with relatives, all of which made it much more likely they'd return to prison.

Grace House, St. Leonard's women's facility, is a short walk away from the building where Michael lived. Some eighty thousand women are released from state prisons across the country each year. But women are far more likely than men to serve out their sentences in county jails rather than being moved to a prison post-conviction. Each year nearly two million women leave jails. The number of women under community supervision has doubled in the past thirty years, to over a million. Just as prisons were designed for men, so were most post-release programs. Yet women returning from prison and jail are desperately in need of places like Grace House. They are more likely than their male counterparts to be unemployed, low-income, and to have dropped out of high school. Many women returning from lockup can't find safe housing away from abusive partners.

The majority of women in jails and prisons are also mothers, and at Grace House they have to grapple with the shame that often accompanies their incarceration. Michael and other men at St. Leonard's are encouraged to take their time tending to their own needs before re-establishing themselves as partners and parents. Women rarely have that luxury. Much more so than men, their crimes are also seen as ones of abandonment. The stigma is they'd chosen drugs or prostitution or theft over their families. Women at Grace House receive help with trauma, substance abuse, childcare, and intimate-partner-related violence. They often need legal help involving custody issues with their children. There are about 2.7 million children in the United States with incarcerated parents. Studies show that they are more likely to do poorly in school, to suffer from depression, and, eventually, to be incarcerated themselves. At Grace House, residents learn trades they might be able to do from home.

Terah Lawyer, who was paroled by the California Adult Authority in 2017, eventually found her calling on the outside. When she left the Central California Women's Facility after fifteen years of incarceration, she had two hundred dollars in gate money and moved into a transitional living facility in the Bay Area. She experienced a whipsaw of emotions. Intoxicated with freedom, she panicked in elevators—a closed door and a cramped space was too much like a prison cell. She wanted to find work, to start a career. She wanted to race to make up for all the years she'd lost to prison. It was impossible. As someone with a felony record, she faced barriers and the circular logic that returning citizens were likely to fail and therefore didn't deserve the full rights of citizenship that would help them succeed. The rules at her transitional facility blocked her from visiting her parents in Sacramento. She was required to take more than twenty hours of treatment classes a week, even though she had already taken thousands of hours of treatment classes over the past fifteen years. The requirements made it nearly impossible to start a full-time job. She lost an opportunity with an organization that worked with incarcerated women, which was exactly what she'd trained to do inside. She'd later diagnose her depression during this time as what she called post-incarceration syndrome.

Lawyer was hired by Impact Justice, an Oakland-based nonprofit that focuses on criminal justice reforms. She designed, developed, and led an innovative housing initiative called the Homecoming Project. The program used the Airbnb sharing-economy model to connect people willing to rent an extra room in their homes to someone in the vast reentry population. Unlike the halfway home Lawyer was sent to, the Homecoming Project was designed to place people inside a neighborhood, to make them feel like part of a community. It made sure hosts and clients were well-matched, sending "community navigators" to the homes to check in on them. In addition to paying the rent for six months, the program also linked clients to relevant workshops and health services. By 2022, Homecoming had placed eighty people in homes. The number was small compared to the demand. California's prison population had fallen by nearly fifty thousand people since 2009. The need for housing and reentry services had exploded. But Lawyer saw the Homecoming Project as both a practical solution and a conceptual one. "Homecoming is much more focused on relationships, on tying people into communities, with regular community members," Lawyer said. "It's changing the narrative. Reevaluating what a home is. And also changing public opinion about who the formerly incarcerated are, and how we treat them."

By 2022, Lawyer had also done much to change the narrative of her own life. Since leaving prison, she'd finished a bachelor's in business administration, graduating with honors. She got married—she was now Terah Lawyer-Harper. She and her partner bought a house north of Oakland, which after fifteen years in prison gave her a different feeling of being part of a community. Her parole supervision ended just in time for her to vote on a California ballot initiative to give people on parole for felony convictions the right to vote. *It passed!* "I feel like a whole person out here," she said. Then Lawyer-Harper was hired as the executive director of a holistic reentry nonprofit called CROP, Creating Restorative Opportunities and Programs. CROP's signature Ready 4 Life reentry initiative is like the wraparound support at St. Leonard's but bigger and more ambitious. It utilizes all the work that Lawyer-Harper had done in prison to ready herself and others for their returns. Housing is provided for a year in Los Angeles or on a campus being built in the San Francisco Bay Area. Beginning in 2023, new cohorts of thirty people will start every four months. The cohorts undergo several months of reconditioning, of healing and personal development, then several more months of training for careers in the tech industry, and then apprenticeships and job placement. Funding comes from state contracts as well as donors and private philanthropies, and people in the program receive a thousand-dollar monthly stipend in addition to having all their basic needs met. They also receive help securing long-term housing.

I first met Lawyer-Harper in 2019 when we'd both traveled to Finland and Norway with Impact Justice as part of a delegation of Americans to see prisons different from the ones in the United States. Incarceration in these Nordic countries was so much more focused on reintegration that it was like we'd entered a bizarro reality. When I asked Lawyer-Harper if there were other reentry programs like CROP's Ready 4 Life, she said proudly that there weren't. She listed all the things that made it unique in the United States. The thousand-dollar stipends. The emergency housing. The financial, professional, and emotional support given to people coming back from prison. It provides a vast safety net at the moment when returning citizens need it most. CROP recognizes that the investment would pay off in both future cost savings and long-term public safety.

"It's Finland!" I shouted. "It's Norway!"

"That's right," she said.

IN APRIL, AFTER four months at St. Leonard's, Michael was offered an opportunity to stay. Next door to Michael's dormitory, St. Leonard's operated a residential building with forty-two single-occupancy kitchenette apartments. Michael moved in to one of these units. He had his own place. His own key. After a half century without it, he now had his own private bathroom. He could take a bath rather than a shower. The apartment wasn't elaborate—just five steps from front door to back window. It was divided down the middle by a wardrobe, the kitchen on one side, his raised bed on the other. But Michael said he had everything there he needed. He had a small table and two chairs. He had a radio tuned to a jazz station. He had a television propped on top of a dresser and a pile of DVDs. He had a row of books next to his bed. He had a leather jacket hanging in his bureau and shoes stacked in boxes. He owned utensils, Tupperware, dishes, a Crock-Pot, and an air fryer.

The apartment was partially subsidized by the Chicago Housing

Authority, and Michael paid the remaining rent out of his Social Security. He could stay there indefinitely, until he felt ready to handle the pressures of what he called a normal life without St. Leonard's. RJ was still in their old room with roommates. He and Michael struck a deal: RJ could keep food in Michael's fridge, as long as he came by and cooked for both of them from time to time. Michael's entrepreneurial mind was already spinning—plans to bake cakes and pies and cookies. He and RJ could sell them to other St. Leonard's residents. One day while they sat in the kitchenette apartment, Michael told RJ that from his prison cell he'd dreamed all of this. He swept his hand to display the bounty of his new life.

Michael said, "The soft music, a fireplace, a woman, a nice glass chess set."

RJ pointed out the obvious: there was no fireplace, no woman, and no chess set. Michael laughed. But everything else, he said, had already come true.

The morning after he moved into his new apartment, Michael packed a knapsack with his ID, birth certificate, and proof of residency and headed east. After the grayness of Chicago's winter, the spring day radiated with promise. Daisies and tulips peaked out of the hard ground along Madison Street. It felt like a beginning. Michael got on a bus heading to the Loop. He was a parolee. And because he had technically moved, albeit only next door, he had to get a new state ID, with his new address, at the secretary of state's office, and then he had to register the change with the Chicago Police Department. Those were the rules. Michael followed them to the letter. The trip was an excuse as well to revel in his fluency with the city. Michael's daughters were pressuring him to move back to East St. Louis, saying he'd already been away so long. But he had developed a bond with Chicago. He met people there who didn't know how to find city hall or the main library. Michael had it all figured out. People started asking him for directions. He'd solved the big city. He belonged there. He no longer inserted his bus card backward. He'd memorized his different pin numbers. He learned that most calls coming in on his cell were going to be telemarketers or robots or scams. He imagined that the people on the bus saw him as just another normal citizen. "When you get to know me," he wanted to say out loud, "you've got a true friend. I am an asset, not a liability. You are dealing with a solid, genuine, and honest person."

At the offices of the secretary of state, Michael dropped off his paperwork. Smooth sailing. He left the building and wandered downtown, a moving part of the city's bustle. He picked up the bus heading south. He had to comply with that 2006 law requiring anyone convicted of murdering a youth to register a change of address with the local authorities. It was just paperwork. In prison, Michael called the guards "police." Now, as he walked into the city's main police headquarters, a building with hundreds of cops, he felt no fear. They no longer controlled him. He dropped his backpack onto the conveyer belt to be scanned. He received a tag and a number to wait his turn. He made all the right moves. He heard his name and went to a desk and handed an officer his papers. The officer greeted him warmly and asked Michael to please wait. Michael waited.

The officer was having trouble finding Michael in the system. When more time passed, Michael began to wonder. Needles of heat pricked his neck. He twisted in his seat. Behind him, in his periphery, two cops hovered. Were they looking at him or just standing there? Did their bodies stiffen? Michael admonished himself. It was the old paranoia. The suspicions he'd needed in prison to survive. He hadn't shaken them yet. But he was getting there. The penitentiary mindset came less frequently. He'd been institutionalized so long that he sometimes couldn't read the signs in the free world. The officer at the computer looked up.

"I'm sorry to inform you, Mr. Henderson, but you're under arrest."

Michael thought the man must be joking. He wasn't. The two officers behind Michael moved in on each side of him.

"I know this isn't real." Michael gasped. The room was suddenly spinning. It had to be a mistake. He'd made no false moves. "Please, please, I'm not the one," he cried. It made no sense. There had to be a mix-up. Why would Michael come to the police station if he'd done something wrong? The officer said he had no explanation. All he knew was the computer said there was a warrant out for Michael's arrest.

Michael told the man that he was sixty-seven years old. That he just got out of prison after forty-six years. That his life now was wonderful. He couldn't go back.

"I just need some help in correcting this error. Someone made a very egregious error."

The officer said his hands were tied. Nothing he could do. He did allow Michael to look up a couple of numbers on his cell phone. Michael called Marjorie Moss and the office at St. Leonard's. No one picked up, and he left messages.

Before Michael was booked, an officer who processed him was surprised that Michael wasn't in the gang database, that he wasn't hooked up and didn't have a long string of arrests.

"You are totally not of this era. You don't even exist in our computers. You don't have any history," the cop said.

Officers confiscated Michael's backpack and wallet. They took his shoelaces and cut out the cinches on his jacket. They locked him in a cell.

10

Retrying the Case

After the abolition of parole in Illinois, Johnnie came to feel trapped by the law change—a catch-22 of being sent to prison under one system of sentencing but then judged by another. "Rehabilitation went out the window. It became retribution and punishment," he would say. As far as winning parole, though, Johnnie wasn't doing himself any favors by insisting on his innocence. For members of the parole board, a story of remorse and regret was easier to swallow. Why, suddenly, after fifty years, should the board believe Johnnie and accept that up to then the entire criminal legal system had gotten it wrong? That there were abusive police officers, unethical prosecutors, credulous or indifferent judges, and previous parole board members just like them who'd reviewed the case numerous times and never saw it? The legal scholar Daniel Medwed found that truly innocent parole applicants faced what he called an "innocent prisoner's dilemma." Medwed wrote that these candidates must choose between, on the one hand, "admitting guilt and improving the chances for parole," and, on the other, "maintaining innocence and essentially ruining any possibility of parole." Johnnie was arrested and convicted well before the forensics revolution of the 1980s; there was no DNA testing that could disprove his guilt. Besides, there wouldn't have been anything to test. The police never found a murder weapon, or any other physical evidence against him.

In representing Johnnie, Sara Garber wasn't interested in the question of guilt or innocence. "Fuck innocence," she liked to say. Equal parts idealistic and profane, Garber recognized that wrongful convictions destroyed both individual lives and the integrity of the entire criminal system. Garber was in her early thirties, nose-ringed, the daughter of an archaeologist and primatologist whose research had taken the family to remote villages in the Amazon when she was a child. In her work as a criminal defense and civil rights attorney, Garber grappled with the daily inequities perpetrated in courtrooms, what she described as "every other fucking eighteen-year-old Black kid getting thirty years for something you couldn't even imagine them getting it for." Garber now had a client who claimed innocence. She told Johnnie about his parole chances improving if he admitted guilt, even if it wasn't true. But Johnnie wouldn't budge. He wasn't going to trade away his dignity for marginally better odds. Garber saw that she would need to perform a sleight of hand at Johnnie's parole hearing in 2020. She would make it clear that he deserved to be freed whether or not board members believed him guilty. It wasn't her job to prove him innocent; a parole hearing wasn't a courtroom, after all. Board members needed to accept only that there were questions about Johnnie's conviction, enough to get them to look beyond their critiques of remorselessness and consider the full weight of his accomplishments and time served. To do this, Garber would first have to dig into Johnnie's fifty-year-old case and find what, if anything, supported his claim.

Garber had her paying clients. She and a law partner had recently opened up a two-person practice, with tiny offices in downtown Chicago. It was constant triage, deciding what had to be done this minute and what could wait until tomorrow. She was representing other parole candidates pro bono as well. Garber had previously known nothing about C-Numbers. Like most people, she had assumed that just about everyone in prison was eligible for parole, a second chance. In 2012, she went to a training session led by a woman named Aviva Futorian, a lawyer in her seventies in leopard-print glasses and a silk neckerchief who talked passionately about the "longtimers" in need of legal help. Futorian said these C-Numbers were going to die in prison if they weren't granted parole. Garber signed up to represent a man who'd been in prison longer than she'd been alive. That client was paroled, and it was the most gratifying experience of Garber's career. A win at trial felt to her like fending off one bad thing amid a flurry of attacks; a client winning parole after decades in prison felt like an overwhelming good. "Like, man, this guy is fucking leaving prison. He is walking out the door. And that is so fucking cool," Garber would say. She told Futorian the good news. Futorian said, "That's fantastic. When are you taking your next case?" Garber began to assist Futorian with the ad hoc parole project in Illinois. She wrote to people in prison, determining who needed a lawyer, enlisting law students or corporate tax attorneys or legal aid clinicians to take a case, and then, invariably, coaching and coaxing them along the way.

For Johnnie's upcoming hearing, Garber tried to track down his original case materials. The Chicago Police Department didn't respond to her requests for the records from the 1970 investigation. Months later, the department sent her 154 heavily redacted pages. It was like reading a Mad Libs, with sentences missing key nouns, verbs, and proper names. The outline of a story without its details wasn't of much use. Luckily, Johnnie could fill in many of the blanks. The court records proved even more elusive. They were missing. Garber had her suspicions that the disappearance was intentional. But a half century of bureaucratic sediment and technological change could have also been the culprits. The boxes were eventually discovered, dozens of them, in the wrong section of Chicago's criminal courthouse. As Garber leafed through the pages, though, she could see that huge chunks of the trial transcript, literally thousands of pages, weren't there. She needed to review the complete court record to uncover any inconsistencies. Court documents were also stored on microfiche, pre-digital miniaturized reproductions on reels of film. It took the city another year to locate the relevant film in a building downtown.

Garber's reward for finally getting the records: she now had to comb through more than fifteen thousand pages of trial transcripts.

JOHNNIE'S TRIAL STARTED in July 1971 and stretched through August. The courtroom, without air-conditioning, was sweltering and packed each day. As soon as the doors opened in the mornings, police rushed in and filled the front rows, making sure they were visible to all. Garber could also see why the transcript was one of the longest in Cook County history. The judge who presided over the trial, Louis Wexler, seemed to have the habit of ruling with whoever spoke last, so there was an unstated contest between the prosecution and the defense to have the final word. "Counsel's unarticulated premise here is that if he keeps pounding away at the court on a given point that your Honor is going to waiver in some way and give in to him," Nicholas Motherway, the lead prosecutor, said, summing up the tactic employed by both sides. The questioning of every witness ground to a halt in endless objections, disparaging cross talk, admonishing sidebars, and lengthy debates on all matters. *Could a witness be called on rebuttal to comment on a matter that was already rebutted? Was the use of the word "gangs" itself prejudicial? Could the record reflect the scowl on the face of the prosecution?* "The history of this case is one of dilatory tactics throughout," the prosecution complained.

Motherway, an assistant state's attorney for less than five years, led Cook County's organized crime unit, which by then was trying many criminal cases involving suspected Black gang members. A year before, he had the distinction of asking that charges be dropped against the seven Black Panthers who survived the police raid that killed Fred Hampton and Mark Clark. The state's attorney's office had the gall to charge the seven with attempted murder, armed violence, aggravated battery, and unlawful use of a weapon. "The methods used to recover and identify the evidence seized by our police in the apartment may prevent our satisfying judicial standards of proof," the state's attorney said in an official statement, failing to mention all the evidence of a police crime and cover-up in the form of a hundred or so bullets that riddled the apartment's walls and furniture.

Johnnie and his codefendant were represented by Eugene Pincham, Chicago's preeminent Black defense attorney. Pincham asked one of his frequent law partners, a young attorney named Sam Adam, to help him with the case. Adam ended up officially representing Johnnie, and Pincham Knights, although the two lawyers worked in tandem throughout the trial. The prosecution asked Knights what he told his lawyers about bullets he legally bought in Indiana the day before the shooting. Adam insisted that Pincham himself take the stand.

ADAM: Did Knights ever tell you that he had purchased any bullets for Johnnie Veal?

PINCHAM: He did not at no time tell me that he purchased bullets for Johnnie Veal.

At one point a flummoxed Judge Wexler simply yelled at Adam, "Shut up!"

Garber found the trial transcripts entertaining but exhausting after hundreds, let alone thousands, of pages. Throughout the trial, Adam and Pincham interrupted the proceedings to complain, quite seriously, about intimidation from police. Officers "rough rode" Johnnie to and from the courthouse, slamming on the brakes of a police van so Johnnie, handcuffed in the back, pinballed off the walls. (Baltimore police were accused of using the same tactic in 2015 when transporting Freddie Gray, breaking Gray's neck and killing him, although a federal investigation did not prove that officers drove "maliciously and sadistically" in a way to cause harm.) At the Cook County jail, a sergeant strip-searching Johnnie reared back and punched him in the mouth. Officers wanted vengeance for the murders of Severin and Rizzato, and at the courthouse cops came close to Johnnie and Knights and muttered: "We're going to fry you." "You're going to die, motherfucker." The defense attorneys pleaded with Wexler to stop officers in the front rows from taking photographs of defense witnesses and scaring them. "Judge, I ask you to reaffirm your order directing the police officers to get out of the front row," Adam said. The judge contended that he'd already done his part by telling one officer to sit elsewhere. "He has got a gun," Adam continued. "I don't want policemen in the front row with guns."

One day during the trial, a fire alarm sounded. Wexler exited through his chambers. The jury was escorted out. The entire courtroom was cleared. Johnnie and Knights remained. They both sensed something was off. A bailiff pointed them to the bullpen. On the way there, Johnnie noticed that an exit door leading to the hallway was left open. It was like an invitation to flee. The bailiff was gone. All they had to do was walk through the door and disappear into the free world. Knights, several years older than Johnnie, placed a hand on his shoulder to hold him back. They peeked through the opening. They each saw it—six or seven police officers lined against the wall in the hallway, forming a gauntlet, with their hands on their revolvers. It looked to Johnnie like an old western. "The saloon door opening and all goes quiet," he recalled. He figured the officers were hoping he and Knights would try to make a run for it, so they could administer a punishment right there. "It didn't take a rocket scientist to see a setup."

DURING THAT 1971 trial, the state's attorney for Cook County, the area encompassing Chicago, was Edward Hanrahan. Motherway's boss, Hanrahan hoped one day to succeed Richard J. Daley, who'd been mayor of Chicago since 1955. When Daley died in office in 1976 and Hanrahan finally had a shot, it was too late. By then, the state's attorney was under investigation for orchestrating the police killings of Hampton and Clark. Demonstrators met him with placards that read, "Put Hanrahan in Jail Not City Hall." Four years later, in 1980, Daley's oldest son, known by the diminutive Richie, was elected Cook County state's attorney. After just two years in that office, to the surprise of no one, Richard M. Daley ran for his father's old job. He lost the mayoral election to Harold Washington, then a U.S. Congressman representing the city's South Side, who managed to galvanize a coalition of Black, Latino, and reform-minded white progressives. In 1983, Washington became Chicago's first Black mayor, and Daley went back to work as district attorney, retraining his ambitions on the future.

District attorneys, more than any other elected officials, contributed to the unprecedented growth of incarceration in the United States over the past fifty years. Top prosecutors controlled the levers that fed the country's prisons. County state's attorneys, or DAs, have always wielded immense authority within the criminal system. After an arrest, they're the ones who decide whether to charge a person with a crime. They decide the number and severity of the charges. Under the tougher sentencing laws that began with the rejection of indeterminate sentencing and parole, district attorneys acquired even more discretion. Prosecutors were able to threaten defendants with enormous mandatory prison terms, with additional charges stacked on top of one another, and with enhancements adding more years to each offense. Because of truth in sentencing, a threat of thirty-five years for someone convicted at trial was really a promise of at least 85 percent of thirty-five years. With district attorneys holding all that bargaining power, the number of criminal convictions ending in a plea deal jumped from about 80 percent, in the 1970s, to an astounding 95 percent in the coming decades. A common joke in criminal justice circles is that you see more criminal trial rulings on TV in any given week than in the nation's courtrooms. State's attorneys came to set the terms of nearly every punishment.

Their influence on the carceral system didn't end there. When police officers make an arrest, it is up to prosecutors to decide what to do with the suspected crimes. No charges. Community service. A fine. A misdemeanor. Drug treatment. A felony. The rates at which district attorneys pursued felony convictions against people arrested by the police also rose dramatically. In a study that examined thirty-four states, the chances that an arrest resulted in a prosecutor filing a felony charge jumped from a third of all cases in 1994 to two-thirds by 2008. In Philadelphia, the district attorney's office, prior to the arrival of Larry Krasner in 2018, filed charges in 97 percent of the cases brought to it by the police. Crime rates ebbed and flowed from the 1970s onward, as they always had. But what made mass incarceration a clear break from the past was how crime was punished. Imprisonment became the go-to response like never before. From the 1990s to the 2000s, crime in the country fell precipitously, but the number of people in state and federal prisons during that time actually doubled, to more than 1.6 million. As crime went down, arrests declined as well, and yet prisons swelled with new admissions. The Fordham law professor John Pfaff wrote in *Locked In: The True Causes of Mass Incarceration*, "Almost all of that increase was due to prosecutors bringing more and more felony cases against a diminishing pool of arrestees."

Like most DAs of this get-tough era, Richard M. Daley brandished his high conviction rates like a credential for higher office, touting his success in sending "dangerous criminals" to prison. Under his leadership,

Daley announced, felony convictions were up, drug convictions up, the average length of prison sentences for armed robbery, rape, and murder all up. He also said his efforts to keep the public safe were being undermined by a system that spat "convicted felons" back into the community to commit more crimes. A weak-on-crime foil made the public feel endangered and more in need of law-enforcement vigilance. District attorneys were not responsible for the ballooning costs of imprisonment. State's attorneys in urban counties, whether in Chicago, Detroit, Memphis, or any big city, won convictions, mostly through plea deals with Black and Latino young men, and then sent these people into a prison system operated and paid for by the state. In Illinois, more people than ever before were being sent to prison, and the state was still in the process of building new facilities to meet the overwhelming demand. To ease the dangerous overcrowding, thousands of incarcerated individuals were selected to leave prison before the completion of their sentences. "We were and still are spending a lot of our time putting repeat offenders back in the system," Daley declared. In his press conferences, he went after another form of early release—parole. The Illinois parole board was busy hearing the cases of the many C-Numbers whose crimes occurred before 1978. Daley said a study conducted by his office found that the parole board, in 1983 alone, had freed thirty "ruthless and cold-blooded killers."

Daley presented Darrell Cannon as Exhibit A. Cannon, who was said to be a hitman for the Black P. Stone Nation, was convicted of murdering a toy store owner in 1970 on Chicago's South Side. At trial, a judge sentenced Cannon to death, although on appeal his sentence was reduced to an indeterminate sentence of one hundred to two hundred years. Cannon, a C-Number, came up for parole in 1983, after serving twelve years of his sentence. He had letters of support from correctional officers and the endorsement of his warden, along with hundreds of petitions for his release. The parole board met and decided to grant Cannon his freedom. Daley pointed out that it took Cannon a mere ten months on the streets to kill again. That was the revolving door of justice Daley vowed to seal shut.

Daley was able to further restrict the state's parole practices. Cannon represented the dangers of leniency, of indulging any form of early release for those convicted of violent crimes. It didn't matter that the far greater problem in prisons involved people remaining locked up long after they no longer posed a risk to reoffend. Up to then, the parole board in Illinois was splitting into groups of three to hear each parole case; to win release, a candidate needed to convince two of the three members of each panel. Now the state modified its rules so that the entire board, of up to fifteen members, was required to hear each case, and a majority was necessary to grant parole. Governor Thompson, responding to the furor whipped up by Daley, got rid of the parole board's most liberal member, a social justice organizer who voted for release at a higher rate than any of her peers. Daley also made it easier for victims' families to attend and speak at hearings, and he began the practice of sending an assistant district attorney to monitor the monthly hearings and reflexively oppose parole for nearly every candidate. Daley repeated critiques from the previous decade that had already stripped parole boards of much of their discretion. "How else can this small group of individuals with such unchecked power be held accountable for their decisions?"

Daley's campaign against the parole board had its desired effect. From 1978 through 1982, the Illinois Prisoner Review Board granted parole in more than half the cases it considered. In 1983, the year Daley publicized Cannon's second homicide conviction, the board was releasing about one of every four candidates. Then, in 1984, that rate crashed to 4 percent, which is roughly where it stayed.

SARA GARBER PLODDED through the thousands of pages of transcription from Johnnie's 1971 trial. Eventually, she was able to piece together the prosecution's case against him. The State called forty witnesses. None of them was an eyewitness to the crime; no one claimed to have seen Johnnie or Knights fire a shot. Most were there to impugn Johnnie's character. Of the forty, Garber counted only seven who offered what she considered substantive evidence about the murders. One was a police officer stationed at Cabrini-Green who testified that Johnnie asked him, a few days before the shootings, where he might get a broken rifle fixed. The prosecution had suggested that the person plotting to kill cops went to a uniformed officer to inquire how he might repair what would be the murder weapon. The scenario also meant that the officer then did nothing. Garber found it as preposterous years later as Johnnie's defense attorneys had at trial.

Prosecutors called a guard from the Cook County jail who testified that he overheard Johnnie in lockup, there for aggravated battery four months before the shootings, say he wanted to build his reputation by killing "some gang leader or a couple of cops." The State didn't demonstrate elsewhere that Johnnie was invested in building his reputation; prosecutors, in fact, argued the opposite, that Johnnie was already a fearsome gang leader. Nor did the State show a direct link from a seventeen-year-old's supposed boast to a double homicide several months later.

There was also a man at Cabrini-Green who couldn't get his car to start who said he saw Johnnie walking with a guitar case, the prosecution's implication being that the case held a rifle. Another man testified that Johnnie approached him, at what Garber figured out was the same time he was seen elsewhere with the guitar case, and asked about empty apartments. Both men changed their statements under cross-examination, and their testimony contradicted each other's as far as Johnnie's whereabouts. He couldn't be in two places at once. The prosecution argued that the rifle shots killing the officers came from a bathroom window in a vacant sixth-floor unit in one of the Cabrini-Green towers. But it wasn't clear how they settled on the bathroom as the sniper's perch. In the police reports, residents told officers the shots came from multiple locations. Witnesses saw someone firing from a window on the seventeenth floor. From the ground floor. From different buildings. When police arrived on the scene, they reported taking fire from multiple high-rises.

The two witnesses for the prosecution who gave the most detailed testimony were buddies of Johnnie's, sixteen-year-old twin brothers named Jake and Jerry Davis. They said Johnnie asked them on the day of the shooting to get him a rifle and ammunition. They corroborated other testimony, affirming they saw Johnnie with a guitar case, and that Johnnie showed them the empty sixth-floor apartment, which Johnnie told them was "where we're going to ice the police from." On the witness stand, the Davis brothers said they observed Knights with another one of their friends, Sidney Bennett, who was also initially a suspect. They testified that after the murders, Knights slapped Jerry five and said, "Congratulate me, I just killed two police. . . . I shot the fuck out of those two."

Just months before the start of Johnnie's trial, the Cook County state's attorney prosecuted another high-profile case involving the murder of a Chicago police officer. In the summer of 1970, James Alfano, a detective with the gang intelligence unit, was riding in an unmarked squad car, behind an abandoned hotel, when he was killed by sniper fire. Officers flooded the area around the shooting, taking twenty men into custody, most of them known to the police department's gang unit as Black P. Stones. The response was nearly identical to the one at Cabrini-Green that same summer. Seven of the men taken into custody for the Alfano shooting were later charged with the terrible crime, based largely on the testimony of one of the suspects. The men were defended, as well, by Pincham and Adam, who argued that the police were desperate to solve the heater case irrespective of the truth. Under cross-examination, the prosecution's star witness admitted that his testimony was a lie; he revealed that he was threatened with life in prison and so repeated what prosecutors and cops told him to say. Pincham told the court, "Without any investigation, the police swooped down on the Black P. Stone Nation fifteen minutes after the crime, and then they wrote a script to prove their already formed conclusion." Pincham pointed to the seven defendants, young Black men, members of a gang, each of whom stood accused of the murder of a policeman. The city wanted a "cop-killer" brought to justice. But Pincham said the law guaranteed everyone a fair trial and the burden of proof beyond a reasonable doubt, regardless of their background. Police abuses left unchecked led to tyranny, Pincham declared, quoting from the book of Matthew: "If ye have done it unto the least of these my brethren, ye have done it unto me." The jury, of whom eight were white and four Black, voted to acquit on all charges.

The outcome in the Alfano case came to bear heavily on Johnnie's trial. It raised the stakes for the prosecution. With two more police officers murdered, the state's attorney couldn't afford another loss. At one point during the trial, Motherway dumped Severin's and Rizzato's bloody uniforms on a table in front of the jury, shouting, "Give them justice!" For Pincham and Adam, the acquittals in the Alfano trial suggested a pattern and practice of police misconduct. They used the same strategy in their defense of Johnnie and Knights. They argued that the police had vacuumed up nearly a hundred people from Cabrini-Green, many of them young men with past criminal records; they said cops threatened and beat them, settled on a few suspects, and then wrote a script that became the testimony needed to pin the murders on Johnnie and his codefendant. Pincham and Adam used Jake and Jerry Davis as proof.

Under cross-examination, Jerry said he was afraid of the police, and Jake stated that his testimony was coerced by police officers and state's attorneys. Then in a post-conviction hearing, the brothers said their testimony was entirely false. They now told an explicit account of police abuse. The Davises said officers charged into their bedroom at Cabrini-Green the morning after the shooting and accused them of the crime. An officer pointed a shotgun at Jake and demanded to know where they hid the rifles. The teenagers were interrogated at the Eighteenth District police station. Jake and Jerry said police shouted that they were liars and beat and slapped them. Officers showed Jake a warrant for his arrest, for a theft from a grocery store, saying he would go to prison for the petty crime if he didn't cooperate. "Who killed the police?" an officer yelled. "Didn't Veal do it?" The Davis brothers said they didn't read the statements they signed. They were driven by police officers to a camp. Then taken by police to a motel. And then put on a train to Mississippi, to stay with their grandmother. They were removed from Cabrini-Green for three months. The prosecution said it was for their own protection, since they were testifying against a gang leader in their neighborhood. They were snitches. But Adam said the police kidnapped the boys. When the Davis brothers returned to Chicago, Jake described how police officers picked him up and took him to a high-rise at Cabrini-Green controlled by a rival gang. The cops told him he better not change his testimony. When the police left him there, Jake ran to safety.

The last witness, and the one that would prove the most damning, was another teenager from Cabrini-Green named Billy Dyson. Dyson was a member of the Black Deuces, a gang that warred with the Cobra Stones; one of its members had slit Johnnie's throat a year earlier. Dyson

testified that Johnnie came up to him in the bedlam after the cop killings and boasted about the crime he'd just committed: "See how the
Stones do it? Let's see if you all can get three." Dyson had also been
taken into custody that night and questioned. At trial, Adam argued
that Dyson had everything to gain by pinning the crime on Johnnie. He
both saved himself from the police and put away a hated rival. "There is
nothing I can say if you believe that kind of testimony from his enemy,"
Adam told the jury. Adam went after the prosecution's case point by
point. There was no confession. No credible motive. "If this were not so
serious, it would be laughed out of court," Adam said. "If it wasn't that
two fine policemen were shot down, if it were something else, stealing a
bicycle, it would be laughed out of court on the same evidence."

Garber found the pairing of Johnnie and Knights also to be un-
convincing. Knights was twenty-three, married, and working as a janitor. When Garber asked Johnnie about Knights, he said they weren't
friends and never associated with each other. To Johnnie and his teenage companions, the six-year difference in age meant Knights was an
adult, someone at a completely different stage of life than them. "We
weren't doing the same stuff as older cats. He wasn't an athlete. Holding
down a job to us was being a paperboy," Johnnie would say. "I couldn't
even think of him at first, couldn't place him," Johnnie said of seeing
the reports in the news that the two of them were the wanted suspects.
"He's the janitor? Brenda's husband? He's not hooked up." Johnnie said
the first time he and Knights exchanged more than a few words was
at the courthouse before their preliminary hearing. "Imagine being
tried as a juvenile alongside an adult that is somewhat a total stranger
to you," Johnnie wrote in the autobiography sent to the parole board
fifty years later. "My codefendant George Knights was not a friend or
someone I knew and associated with on the streets. To us kids he was
a janitor."

The prosecution's assertion seemed to be that Johnnie and Knights
teamed up to kill the police officers as part of a celebration of a gang truce.
But at trial, Knights vehemently denied being in a gang, and the state's
attorneys never proved otherwise. Knights had purchased rifle shells
the day before the murders. It was the strongest evidence against him.
When Knights testified in his own defense, he claimed he had been

working as a livery driver, giving a customer a ride to the gun shop, and the passenger didn't have ID, so Knights made the purchase for him. There was also no evidence showing that those particular shells were used in the shooting the next day. And why would Johnnie be asking the Davis brothers for rifle shells right before the shooting if Knights had already bought ammunition? The more Garber looked over the case, the more it didn't add up. The prosecution contended that Knights was the shooter, Johnnie the accomplice. But even that division of labor was presented as guesswork. Motherway said at trial, "We can show that Knights killed them both and that Veal is responsible, or vice versa."

Adam never put Johnnie on the stand. Looking back on that strategy now, Garber thought it the right call for a defense attorney. Johnnie was a minor. The case against him was circumstantial. "There is no evidence against Veal except that which dripped from the lips of three perjured witnesses," Adam told the jury. After reliving that trial for thousands of pages, Garber agreed with Adam that the prosecution hadn't proven guilt beyond a reasonable doubt.

Adam closed by trying to get the jury to see their vital role amid the firestorms of the last few years, amid the protests and police brutality and the multiple murders of and by police. Adam told the members of the jury that if they could demonstrate that the justice system worked for everyone, even for people like Johnnie Veal, then much of the country would feel less disaffected and would have less cause to take to the streets.

"If you render a conviction in this case, it is another reason for the young men and young women throughout our city to lose faith in the system. This whole city, this whole nation, is going through a mass psychological retrospective. We are all looking at ourselves. We are all trying to decide does our system work, is it worth preserving, should there be a revolution, should there be an evolution, should there be a change within itself. We are all looking for the answer to that."

The murders of Severin and Rizzato were a tragedy. Garber could never know with certainty whether Johnnie had any part in their deaths. But it was clear to her that he was swept up in the hysteria of the time. After assassinations and riots, cops were being killed and the public believed that Black gangs and Black militants were running wild. Johnnie, a Cobra Stone from the infamous Cabrini-Green housing project, became the embodiment of those fears. Maybe his guilt for this particular crime wasn't even what the prosecution had to prove. Johnnie was made to represent the absence of law and order. His was a kind of collective guilt attributed to an entire community, a group of people. He was Black criminality personified. The prosecution exploited that terror to win a conviction.

Motherway said in his closing remarks, "Sooner or later the violence, the anarchy that is represented by the actions of these two defendants—" Pincham objected to this vision of an apocalyptic wave of young Black males coming from the projects, but the judge said to disregard Pincham's statement, and Motherway continued. "The barbarism that is represented by this evidence will eventually, like that ripple, it spreads out, travels that far and has its effect." Motherway warned the jury that the police were the last line of defense. On Chicago's North Side, in the wealthy suburbs, in residential neighborhoods where "good citizens" worked and took their children to the park, people might still be safe enough to leave their homes and let their kids walk to school. But that would come to a disastrous end if monsters who murdered cops went unpunished. The jury had to decide whether they wanted the city to survive.

Throughout the trial, Adam had found Johnnie to be remarkably composed and mature for a teenager. "I never had a client that I considered more of a man," Adam said years later. During breaks in the trial, the two of them chatted about baseball, about Ernie Banks and Willie Mays. They talked about the case and Johnnie's chances. "He was always up," Adam recalled. "He always thought we were going to win the case. And when we didn't, he was trying to comfort me."

The jury deliberated for a couple of hours before coming back with the guilty verdicts. Judge Wexler ordered Johnnie to stand and asked if he had anything to tell the court. Johnnie did. He was brief.

"If this is justice, so be it," Johnnie said. "But as long as you sit on the bench, I want you to know that you are sentencing an innocent man to the penitentiary."

* * *

THE STORY OF Darrell Cannon, Richard M. Daley's Exhibit A of revolving-door justice, revealed much more about parole and the criminal system. When Cannon was arrested, in 1983, just months after he was released by the Prisoner Review Board, he signed a confession admitting to taking part in the killing of a drug dealer who had stolen from his gang. But once he was out of police custody, Cannon said officers had coerced the confession out of him. Awaiting trial, Cannon was painfully specific as he described how three Chicago police officers took him to a remote site on the far South Side. One of the cops forced a shotgun into Cannon's mouth and pulled the trigger. Cannon thought the back of his head had been blown off, he actually felt it, before he realized the gun wasn't loaded. He told the cops he was present when the murder occurred: he'd been driving, and his friend in the back seat shot the man. But Cannon swore he had no idea what his friend was going to do. That wasn't the story the officers wanted. So with Cannon's arms handcuffed behind him, they pulled down his pants and underwear. They took out an electrical device and attached it to his testicles. The cops weren't bluffing this time. Electricity ripped into him. Cannon said the police clipped the device to his penis and fired the electrical charge. They put the contraption inside Cannon's mouth. "They broke me," Cannon would later say. He admitted to whatever they wanted to hear.

Among the many responsibilities of a dangerous and difficult job, police officers wield the immense power to determine what is known and believed to be true. In any encounter and interrogation, cops separate the "bad" guys from the "good," author the reports that become the facts, and corroborate a version of reality that's hard to dispute. *It's not what happened, it's what the police said happened.* Few people believed Cannon's version of events. He detailed his torture at trial. His wife filed an official complaint. Cannon's accusations, in addition to serving his own cause, suggested that sworn officers of the law were committing atrocities. Police operate on the front end of the criminal system. They are the first encounter in nearly every case, and prosecutors build convictions on the work and word of police; parole boards, decades later, still reference the "statement of facts" to help determine who deserves to go free. When the policing is tainted, the entire system is corrupted. The officers who arrested Cannon took the stand and denied the allegations. It was the word of a Black gang member, a convicted murderer, against that of two Chicago police detectives and their commanding officer, all of them white. Cannon was sent back to prison, this time with a sentence of life without the possibility of parole.

Cannon's story might have ended there, with his growing old and eventually dying in prison, invisible to the outside world. But Cannon was locked up among other men who said that Chicago police officers, from the very same unit and same overnight shift, had also electrocuted them. Not that Cannon or these other men knew of one another. Their trauma was a private shame; the unstated rule in prison was that you didn't talk about your case. The slow work of linking together the individual cases of abuse fell initially to a lawyer named Flint Taylor and to other attorneys from the firm he helped found, the People's Law Office. They had previously worked on Fred Hampton's murder, litigating the case for thirteen years to expose the official police narrative as a lie. In 1987, Taylor heard from a man on Illinois's death row named Andrew Wilson who described how he and his brother Jackie confessed to a double murder they didn't do after they were electrocuted and beaten by a Chicago police commander, Jon Burge, and officers under him. Taylor took the case, and a break came two years later when he received a tip from someone inside the Chicago Police Department confirming the assaults. The whistleblower said that what happened to the Wilson brothers wasn't an isolated case; Burge and his "Midnight Crew" at the Area 2 Violent Crimes Unit had used an electroshock "torture machine" on a number of Black suspects. The leaker insisted on remaining anonymous, writing to Taylor that they didn't want to end up "shunned" like Frank Laverty. Laverty was an Area 2 cop who'd disclosed in court a few years earlier that detectives on the force kept a secret "street file" on each investigation—a file containing all the evidence that contradicted the case against whoever the police said did a crime. Police in Chicago were routinely rigging the statement of facts, deciding who was guilty before trial by withholding this evidence from defense attorneys and presenting only their preferred narrative. *They put this case on me.* For breaking the police code of silence, Laverty was relegated to collecting urine samples from police recruits. Burge once demonstrated for other Area 2 cops what to do with an officer who snitched—as Laverty left a room full of police, Burge took out his gun, aimed it at the back of Laverty's head, and said, "Bang." "Deep Badge," as Taylor dubbed his source, offered the name of another imprisoned Burge victim: Melvin Jones.

Taylor found Jones, and from there he and fellow lawyers, along with a relentless reporter named John Conroy, who wrote for the free weekly the *Chicago Reader*, learned of others in prison whom Burge and his crew had tortured. The tools of pain and terror used in each instance were eerily similar. Burge had been an army interrogator at a prisoner of war camp in Vietnam, and it seemed he brought these military tactics back home to his policing in Chicago. Tracking down these cases was an odyssey. It was eventually revealed that from 1972 to 1991 Burge and officers he supervised tortured at least 125 African American men who were taken in for questioning.

Daley, as DA, knew of the torture claims against Burge as early as 1982. A doctor at the jail had examined one of the victims and written the police superintendent, demanding "a thorough investigation of this matter." The police chief forwarded the letter to Daley. Daley declined to investigate. Daley's office had also prosecuted the torture victims, and Daley refused to reopen any of the convictions. Daley later publicly commended Burge, and, in 1988, Burge was promoted. Burge and several of his detectives were suspended in 1991. By then, Daley had finally assumed his father's old office—he was Chicago's mayor. He would end up running the city for twenty-two years, a year longer than his dad. Well into his mayoral tenure, in 2008, Richard M. Daley, when pressed by reporters, offered a halfhearted apology for the Burge scandal. "Whatever happened to them in the city of Chicago in the past, I apologize. I didn't do it, but somebody else did it." Reporters said Daley then laughed "sarcastically." He had long dismissed reports of systemic police torture. "But I was not the mayor. I was not the police chief. I did not promote him. You know that. But you've never written that, and you're afraid to. I understand."

Burge was fired in 1993. The Fraternal Order of Police sponsored a St. Patrick's Day float that year with the theme "Travesties of Justice." It was dedicated to several disciplined officers, including Burge, two of his detectives suspended for failing to report or stop the torture, and two patrol cops who had seized Black teenagers after a White Sox game and dropped them off in a white neighborhood, where they were beaten. After negative coverage in the media, the police union decided to change the float's theme and banner. Burge moved to Florida after being kicked off the police force. He bought a boat he Christened *The Vigilante*. Taylor and other lawyers continued to pursue him, and in 2010 Burge was convicted of obstruction of justice and perjury and sentenced to four and a half years in prison. The City of Chicago ended up paying more than one hundred million dollars in settlements in Burge-related torture cases. But Burge kept his police pension and got out of prison, with good time, a year early.

During all this time, Darrell Cannon remained in prison, serving his life sentence. In 1998, when Illinois opened Tamms, its new supermax prison, Cannon was among the first people transferred to its total-isolation cells. Other lawsuits against the city corroborated his torture claims. At last, Cannon was awarded a new trial, and in 2001, he agreed to a plea deal that would free him in less than three years. But he also had to clear the Prisoner Review Board. Officially, he was in violation of his 1983 parole. When he came up for parole in 2004, board members said they believed he was tortured but that he was also complicit in the second murder. The board voted to deny his parole. Cannon's lawyers had to sue the parole board, and in 2007, after twenty-four years in prison this second time, nine of them in the supermax, Cannon went free. "I loved having my freedom, but by the same token it shouldn't have taken that long," Cannon would say.

Years later, at a parole hearing in Springfield, Craig Findley reminded his colleagues of Cannon's case. They were considering the release of a man named Rudy Bell, a supposed gang "general" convicted of a murder that, forty years into his prison sentence, he still said he didn't do. Findley said Cannon was convicted of two murders and suspected of others. "He was a man that people would say, 'If you got into a car and Mr. Cannon was in the back seat, don't sit in the front seat.'" It was an image vivid from mobster films. Findley described the torture by Burge and other Area 2 detectives, and the board's reticence to parole Cannon. "I've seen Mr. Cannon twice since he was released from prison," Findley added. "He has never been noncompliant with parole."

Indeed, Cannon gave talks about his torture in public schools, as part of a curriculum tied to a 2015 reparations package agreed to by the City of Chicago. It was painful for Cannon to recount his abuse, but even more painful not to. "I will never forgive them. I will never stop hating them," Cannon said of Burge and the three officers who beat and electrocuted him. The anger sometimes consumed him, for the years taken from him and the racism and for some terrible notion of the ends justifying the means. He said of the courts and the parole board and Richard Daley, "Jon Burge was a friend of theirs because Jon Burge was, quote, 'getting rid of the bad guys.'" Cannon took three different medications each day for high blood pressure. While locked up, he contracted hepatitis C, he believed from the razors that the men in the prison were forced to share. Cannon had two little dogs that brought him some peace, a miniature dachshund and a shih tzu–pit bull mix, and he sometimes went to Lake Michigan to stare at the water, or to the Lincoln Park Zoo to see the rhinoceros. "I'll go talk to that one rhino that'll be walking around in its cage all by itself. I can relate to that."

Findley compared the case of Rudy Bell before the parole board to Darrell Cannon's. "I don't know that Mr. Bell is that man, but that's in my mind, just as I think about this case." Findley voted to parole Bell, but all thirteen of the other board members voted against release.

11

Community Corrections

Locked again in a cell, Michael repeated to himself that he'd done nothing wrong. He fought the urge to scream or bash his skull against the concrete floor. After forty-six years as a prisoner, he had been a free man for four months. But now that new life seemed over. Despite his oaths never to return, here he was—he was back in a cage. Michael tried to locate where he could have slipped. He never missed a curfew or a meeting with his parole officer. He aced every requirement. He was even careful what he looked up on the internet, not sure who or what was monitoring him.

There was that one time he caught a ride with a friend from St. Leonard's, and the guy pulled up to a grocery store and parked in a handicapped space. With the car still running, he said he'd be right back. Michael had bristled. The sign said $250 fine. Michael couldn't stand the carelessness. He slid over to the driver's side. He'd operated a tractor a couple of times in prison, but the last time he'd driven a car he'd yet to go to prison and was twenty. His foot was a concrete block, and the car lurched backward; Michael mashed the brake and jolted to a stop. Just then a police car rolled up. Michael clenched the wheel as he eased into a legal parking spot. But the squad car had passed on by.

Michael had also started selling cigarettes to other residents at St. Leonard's. He bought cartons by the bulk and sold a pack for eight dollars and individual loosies two for a dollar. He told guys they didn't need to be smoking, that it was a killer. They should take control of their lives, use their minds to master their bodies. "Heaven or hell isn't up or down. It's within you," he preached. He sold to them nonetheless. He wasn't legally allowed to sell cigarettes. But Michael didn't think anyone outside the halfway house knew about it. That couldn't be it either.

In the holding cell, Michael couldn't sleep. The steel toilet was caked in weeks or maybe months of shit and piss and vomit. The smell alone was suffocating. He sat up and tried to make sense of his predicament. At eighteen, he ran from his crime. But not long into his bid, he realized he deserved to be punished. He broke the social contract. He stepped outside the laws and moral codes of society. He committed a murder. As far as his serving out his punishment, Michael believed he ended up fulfilling his part in the contract. He was ready to be a productive part of society, to love and be loved. It was then the state's duty to uphold its side in the agreement. And the parole board gave him back his liberty. It didn't need to take forty-six years, but he was free. Even after his release, though, he found out he couldn't shed the conviction. He was marked. They were just waiting to get him.

Who was "they"? *Who* got him? Michael ran through every scenario. In the jail cell, Michael kept coming back to the idea that Richard Schaeffer's family had somehow orchestrated this arrest. That's where his mind went. The relatives of the boy he'd killed in 1971 finally got their revenge. As a conspiracy, it was probably irrational. But Michael couldn't think of a better explanation. When the parole board voted to release him, someone from the Schaeffer family told Marjorie Moss that enough time had passed. That could have been a trick. Maybe they wanted Michael to taste freedom before snatching it away.

Michael had called Moss when he was arrested and left a message. She later listened to it in horror. She contacted a public defender, who could get to Michael faster, and that person called a parole officer who showed up at the precinct the next morning. The parole officer told Michael not to panic. He said he'd figure out what was going on. He also admitted that he was kind of excited to get this case. When he was in college, in one of his criminal justice classes, he studied C-Numbers, and in his previous job as a correctional officer at Stateville he'd met a few. So it meant a lot to see one of them who'd made parole and was out in the world. He said he'd do all he could to make sure Michael didn't go back.

By midday, the parole officer discovered the problem. When Michael switched apartments, from the room he shared with RJ to his new studio apartment, no one moved the base to Michael's electronic ankle monitor. After seven o'clock, Michael was in his bed watching the movie *Seven Pounds*, one of his favorites, because it is about Will Smith's character repaying the debt he owes. The base, in his old room, one building away, triggered an alarm. It looked to the system that Michael had skipped curfew, and a warrant was automatically issued for his arrest. The problem was eventually made clear to all, and Michael was again allowed to go free.

Michael counted himself among the lucky. One of the most common violations of parole involves someone moving to a different residence without prior approval. Others involve missing an appointment, or testing positive for alcohol or drugs. With more than a dozen requirements to complete each day, people on mandatory supervised release were bound to miss a couple now and then. Parole supervision was set up as if the goal were to prove someone's criminality by catching them in any of thousands of infractions. The system was not broken. It operated as if failure were by design. For violators, warrants were issued for their arrest. But unlike Michael, the issues were rarely resolved so easily. Many ended up back in prison.

In 1978, twenty thousand Americans had their parole revoked and were re-incarcerated. By 2010, 184,000 people on parole were being sent back to prison annually, and a total of 451,000 under community supervision—on both parole and probation—were incarcerated. Mass incarceration created the collateral epidemic of mass supervision, but the latter now fed the former. A perpetual motion machine of imprisonment. In state prisons across the country, almost half of all new admissions were there for violating the terms of their probation or parole. In thirteen states, a third of the people already in prison were locked up for a supervision violation. In such states as Arizona, Wisconsin, and Utah, it was half. In Idaho, it was two-thirds. Of those out on parole who were sent back to prison, many had their parole revoked for technical reasons, like a missed curfew. They were sent to prison but hadn't actually committed another crime. The legal system wasn't protecting the public from violent offenders—*the truly dangerous.* Prisons in America were filled with people who had failed to abide by a litany of onerous restrictions. One of every four people who entered a state prison in 2017 was sent there for a technical violation of their probation or parole.

The hundreds of thousands of people leaving prison and reentering society each year are in need of support. They are desperate for work, a stable home, counseling, help with alcohol and drug dependency, depression, low self-esteem, and planning for the time ahead. What they get instead in the United States are surveillance and policing. The country created a rigid caste system in which those with a felony conviction continually face barriers to reentry. With a felony, people out on parole struggle to find employers who would hire them. They are frequently denied food stamps, student loans, and public assistance. While on parole, people in most states can't vote and take part in the democratic process. Some states ban those with a felony conviction from ever serving on a jury. Even after they are eligible, people on parole still find it hard to secure health insurance or the right to vote. Denying people the services and protections they need upon their release, saddling them with thousands of restrictions, making them understand that they are considered far less than full citizens, pushes people further to society's margins. It makes it far more likely that they won't be able to succeed in the outside world.

Some states, in trying to reduce prison populations and costs, have begun to address a mass supervision process that cycled people back into detention. California, which still had over half a million people locked up or under supervision, passed a law in 2009 that financially rewarded counties for reducing the rate at which those on probation were violated, thus incentivizing rehabilitation over imprisonment. Eighteen states added ways for people to reduce their supervision times, offering days off for days of compliance. People on parole or probation in Missouri who earned that compliance time cut on average fourteen months from their mandatory supervision. Louisiana put a time limit on how long someone could spend in prison for a first technical violation, meaning people wouldn't have to serve the remainder of their original sentence because they missed an appointment, struggled to find housing, or succumbed again to addiction. New York's 2022 Less Is More Act allowed people to reduce their supervision terms and restricted re-incarceration for technical parole violations. Most of these reforms, however, revealed problems in the system that were structural as well as cultural. States could subject fewer people to community supervision, as well as for less time and with fewer restrictions. But operationally that system still denied vulnerable people the very necessities they needed in order to remain free.

At St. Leonard's, Michael started jogging several mornings a week. Out of lockup, he resumed his routine. He woke up before dawn on Mondays, Wednesdays, and Fridays, stretched, and then at 5:45 in the morning joined volunteers from a group called Back on My Feet. The nonprofit used running to build community around education, employment, and stable housing. Michael's first runs through the neighborhood were a revelation. He wasn't circling a prison yard. He was able to continue straight, block after block. He passed homes and cars and trees and children and shops and dogs. He didn't have to use running to imagine being out in the world. He was free to run anywhere his legs could take him. His group headed east from the halfway house, and Michael could see the downtown skyline a couple of miles away.

Back on My Feet offered awards for participants as they reached certain mileage goals. Michael liked to say they were testing him, to see if he was willing to go to the extreme to get himself together. He was. He got a T-shirt, then a sweat suit and a stopwatch to time his runs. The Chicago Marathon was nine months away, and he was building up his endurance. After thirty days with Back on My Feet, the group provided him with a bus pass. They took Michael to an outing at a Cubs game. He had never been to a baseball game. When Michael was growing up in East St. Louis, his mother, a die-hard St. Louis Cardinals fan, liked to watch broadcasts while sipping on a beer and talking back to the television set. Michael never understood baseball's appeal. And sitting near the top of the upper deck in Wrigley Field, on a windy April night in Chicago, he never felt so cold in his life. "You won't get me like that again," he said.

On the runs, Michael chatted up the volunteers. They were young professionals, mostly white or Asian. They were perfect strangers, their experiences nothing like his own. And yet Michael and a volunteer would talk for the entire jog—about religion and relationships, about career ambitions and finding meaning in their lives. That they connected proved something to Michael. "You meet all types of people running, beautiful people," he would say. "You learn how to network. That's going to help me get a job and be worthy of friendship and love and respect. And that's the way you're supposed to live life."

Michael also volunteered himself at a nonprofit called Working Bikes that shipped old bicycles to countries in Africa and Latin America. He learned to dismantle and clean bikes. He learned to repair gears. He was allotted points for his volunteer hours, and Michael cashed them in for a used red ten speed, a helmet, and a lock. He was determined to get his own car—and a driver's license. But in the meantime, a bike allowed him to explore the city. "A bike gives me even more freedom," he would say. He and another guy from St. Leonard's, a former C-Number with a long pharaoh-like beard, rode past the office buildings in the Loop, to Millennium Park and the lakefront. They snapped pictures of Buckingham Fountain, the giant reflective Bean, and Navy Pier. Along Lake Michigan, Michael walked on a beach. Another first. Michael and the other C-Number had done a bid together in the 1970s. When they thought about it, they realized they'd also crossed paths inside in the 1980s and 1990s, and probably in the 2000s as well. They rattled off the decades in prison, the words unable to covey the meaning of that much time.

Michael wore an "Impeach Trump" button on the rides. It was 2019, and the Democratic presidential primaries were heating up. Michael was excited to vote in the Illinois primary in several months, his first time casting a ballot. He was decided already—Joe Biden. The other Democrats in the primary were hammering Biden for his criminal justice record as a senator. In the 1980s and 1990s, Biden, not to be outdone by Republicans, pressed for mandatory minimums and longer sentences for those convicted of drug crimes. Biden had warned of "predators on our streets" and "violent thugs." As the chairman of the Senate Judiciary Committee in 1990, Biden boasted that "liberal" Democrats were now for more police and prisons. He said, "One of my objectives, quite frankly, is to lock Willie Horton up in jail." Willie Horton was the Massachusetts man who was on a weekend furlough from prison in 1986 when he went AWOL and committed a rape and other crimes. Two years later, in the presidential race between Vice President George H. W. Bush and Massachusetts governor Michael Dukakis, Horton, who is Black, was infamously—and effectively—used in a political ad to instill dread in the electorate; Dukakis, a liberal Democrat, was depicted as weak on crime. Horton was on furlough, not on parole. But rates at which the Massachusetts parole board granted release plunged from about 70 percent to 38 percent. The number of people in state and federal prisons allowed to go on furloughs fell to a few thousand nationally. The Massachusetts furlough program, meant to reacclimate incarcerated people to life after prison, had actually been a massive success, with 99 percent of those allowed on leave returning without incident. That didn't matter. By invoking Willie Horton as an avatar of Black criminality and impending danger, the first President Bush and Senator Biden of the tough-on-crime era were announcing an embrace of a justice system that sacrificed the ninety-nine people out of a hundred.

The Biden campaigning in 2019, however, promised to end mandatory minimum sentences—at least for nonviolent crimes—and to do away with the death penalty and cash bail. Biden had been one of the authors of the 1994 crime bill—in a previous presidential run his campaign touted it as the Biden Crime Bill. Admitting his mistakes, he now vowed to reverse the huge racial sentencing disparities that he had helped create. He would decriminalize marijuana and offer states cash incentives to reduce their prison numbers. "I like Joe Biden," Michael said. "He's been there." After eight years as Obama's vice president, Biden seemed like someone Michael knew. "He won't take no crap. He's his own man. I'd like to see him get another eight years." Michael, eleven years younger than Biden, chuckled. "If he lasts that long."

RJ wanted to join Michael on his bike trips. He kept on insisting that he knew how to ride a bicycle. Michael was skeptical. RJ had survived all those decades in prison. Now that RJ was free, Michael didn't want to get him hit by a car. They went into the alley behind St. Leonard's. "Show me," Michael said. RJ wobbled as he balanced on top of a bike. He whipped the front wheel back and forth to stay upright, his head down in frightened concentration. RJ made it seven feet before crashing into a light pole. They would have to leave RJ behind.

For another outing, though, Michael and RJ were driven downtown. They joined a training session led by Sara Garber, Johnnie's lawyer. Garber had gathered twenty law students and attorneys and was trying to convince them to volunteer to represent C-Numbers at parole hearings. Michael cried as he recounted his parole experience. RJ was more like an emcee at an event, making sure everyone was engaged. The two of them had given a few public talks together, and they'd become a kind of duo, the tears followed by the jokes. "We was like night and day," Michael would say. They'd met only months before, but already people assumed they were longtime friends.

At the training, RJ thanked his lawyers, Susan Ritacca and Courtney Kelledes, friends of Garber's who were helping her lead the session. After earning parole, RJ commissioned a painting of Garber, Kelledes, and Ritacca below the words "The Phenomenal 3." "It was only after I was fortunate enough to obtain these attorneys here, and you guys heard them really brilliantly articulate their position, so there should be no wonder why I'm sitting here today," RJ said with a gracious flourish. Aviva Futorian, who had lured Garber into this work several years earlier, was there as well. "We're also very thankful for you," RJ announced. "You're the matriarch of the C-Number project."

Also in attendance to offer her insider's perspective was Virginia Martinez, one of the members of the Illinois parole board. Martinez described what it was like to dig into these "horrific crimes," revisiting grisly murders and looking at old crime-scene photos. She said, "We have to start with what are the facts of the case, and you can hear sometimes one of our board members gasp." It wasn't just the violence that made the work on the parole board taxing. Martinez also worried about making what she called a "mistake"—recommending release for someone who then went on to commit another crime. And at the same time, she felt the weight of responsibility of giving someone a fair hearing, of being an advocate for applicants she believed should go free. Each decision was laden with the past. When she met the parole candidates in prison, these old men far removed from their crimes, she learned about their backgrounds, the want and lack of opportunity. For board members, figuring out what to do in the present could feel impossible.

For a time while she was on the parole board, Martinez also volunteered at the U.S. southern border in Texas, helping migrants with their asylum cases. She translated for women and children who were escaping gang violence in El Salvador, Guatemala, and Honduras, advising them on how to tell their appeals chronologically and effectively. Martinez's own father had crossed the Mexican border alone when he was fourteen before making his way to Chicago and a job in the city's steel mills. During parole hearings, Martinez sometimes used her own experiences to explain her votes. She told her colleagues once about being in law school in the 1970s, how on her breaks she went into the big department stores in downtown Chicago, Carson Pirie Scott and Marshall Field's, and how security guards followed her because she didn't look like the other shoppers. She said the encounters filled her with the urge to act out, to answer the unfair scrutiny by flouting the conventions and rules that apparently didn't apply to her. In another hearing, she talked about the guys from her neighborhood who fought in Vietnam, how they returned home from their tours full of fury at the racism they experienced both overseas and now back in Chicago.

Martinez had voted to parole Michael. But at Johnnie's previous hearing, in 2018, she had told the other board members that she was conflicted. She was impressed by Johnnie's transformation in prison, but she explained that she remembered the murders in 1970. She was a young woman in Chicago, and she recalled feeling the police killings personally, the threat and sense of chaos in the city. Nearly fifty years later, she had decided that parole would still deprecate the seriousness of the crime.

BETTER SYSTEMS OF prison reentry existed, just not in the United States. In Finland, for instance, people did not face numerous restrictions upon their release from prison. On the contrary, they were inundated with social services at a moment when the support was needed most. They received generous welfare subsidies, job training, housing assistance, and unemployment benefits. It was what Terah Lawyer-Harper was trying to replicate, on a small scale, in California. In many northern European countries, in fact, the entire prison sentence, from its first days, was focused on preparing someone for the transition back to free society. In such countries as Norway, Germany, and the Netherlands, conditions in prisons attempted to mirror life on the outside. "The principle of normality," Tapio Lappi-Seppälä, who as a member of Finland's Ministry of Justice had helped draft the country's penal codes, said. "You should arrange all the conditions and all the practices to correspond to the practices in civil society, because that is where the prisoners go back." Doing so was a matter of public safety as much as human rights. Even in the United States, the million incarcerated people who weren't serving life or virtual life were going to return home. What was the best way to ensure that they wouldn't commit more crime? People locked up in these European countries were also deprived of their liberty. That was the punishment for their offense. But far less so than in the United States, imprisonment didn't mean they were also deprived of their physical safety and well-being, their health, nutrition, privacy, and intellect. "Men come to prison as a punishment, not for punishment," the British prison reformer Alexander Paterson pronounced in the 1920s.

In Finnish prisons, incarcerated people were encouraged to vote, were paid a decent wage for their labor, and were given the same health care as any citizens. All things that made their eventual return more likely to succeed. They were also generally incarcerated near their families, to encourage prison visits and furloughs home. Families on the outside in Finland received counseling and financial support if the head of the household was incarcerated. There were ways as well for people in prison to graduate through a stepped release process, from traditional prisons, with locked doors and high walls, to open prisons, in which people lived in unlocked dorms and could leave the facility during the day to travel to work or school or to care for their children.

Such policies might seem impossible, logistically and culturally, in the United States. The scale of the American carceral system is incomparable, with two million people locked up in prisons and jails and an additional four million on probation or parole. The United States is much larger geographically and more diverse than countries in Europe. Wasn't it possible that racially homogenous nations were simply more willing to look after their own? The United States is also much more violent, with more guns and murders than any developed nation. Plus, the American prison system is inextricable from a history of racial subjugation and oppression. All of that is despairingly true. But the comparison to Finland is an intriguing one. Finland and the United States had the same incarceration rate in the early 1970s. Each equally high. Finland declared independence from Russia in 1917. Unlike its Scandinavian neighbors, Finland created a punitive criminal system that was less focused on treatment and reentry. The country had three to four times more people in prison than other Nordic countries and twice the incarceration rate. As far as prisons, Finland was the America of Europe.

But beginning in the 1960s, political will in Finland coalesced around change. "Good social policy is the best criminal policy," a national slogan proclaimed. The country began to implement a flurry of penal reforms, none of which alone was especially remarkable or untried in the United States. Finland raised the threshold of a felony conviction for such crimes as theft and drunk driving, which meant more people faced fines, suspended sentences, or community service rather than prison time. The country abandoned the practice of detaining people pretrial, except in extreme cases. It shortened fixed prison sentences and implemented a system of early release. The average length of a prison term in Finland was now eleven months, and close to half of all prison sentences were three months or less. Finland also had no plea bargaining—at least until it was introduced in 2015—no trial penalty, no three offenses and you're out. The laws were changed so that first-time offenders left prison after serving half of their sentence; for repeat offenders, no matter the number of repeat offenses, they were required to serve two-thirds of their time and didn't receive enhancements at sentencing.

Mayhem did not ensue. During the 1980s in Finland, amid quickening urbanization and economic instability, crime was on the rise. The public did not panic. Politicians did not reverse course out of fear of being labeled weak on crime. When sensational crimes of violence occurred, as they always will, these terrible incidents did not foment a revolt against the reforms. Finland also stopped incarcerating people for technical violations of their release, avoiding the secondary imprisonment of parole violators that stocked U.S. prisons. Altogether, the reforms transformed incarceration in Finland. The country went from having one of the highest incarceration rates in Western Europe to one of the lowest in the world, at 51 people in prison per 100,000 inhabitants. The United States, which moved dramatically in the opposite direction from the 1970s onward, doubling down on imprisonment and longer sentences, climbed to a rate of more than 750 people per 100,000 in 2009. Since then, the numbers have dropped, but the percentage of Americans in prison remains more than ten times that of Finland's current rate.

Finland's reforms weren't only about prisons and sentencing. They included a much larger embrace by the country of a Nordic social welfare model. The Finnish government began funding programs that ensured a living wage for all residents, that assisted working parents, and that provided free health care and subsidies for housing and higher education. Criminal justice practices and social safety net programs are interconnected. In Finland, closing the income gap reduced incarceration rates by counteracting the root causes of crime.

In the United States, the eightfold growth of mass imprisonment was a statistical anomaly. For a century after the end of slavery, incarceration rates had remained relatively stable. But the country invested in policing and prisons at the same time that it stripped funding for food security, housing subsidies, and job programs. Tough-on-crime rhetoric went hand in hand with attacks on the welfare system. As both California governor and U.S. president, Ronald Reagan stoked racial fears of an undeserving underclass comprised of both dangerous criminals and the criminalized poor, groups that threatened what was coded as a white American way of life. Some forty years before Trump, Reagan ran for president under the banner "Let's make America great again." These ideas entered the mainstream. Bill Clinton signed the law to "end welfare as we know it" two years after enacting the sweeping 1994 crime bill. States followed the lead of the federal government, but the federal government was also responding to the same trends taking place on the state level. In 1970, the United States, from the federal government down to the municipal level, spent about the same on social welfare programs as it did on law enforcement. Today, the country spends twice as much on crime and punishment as it does on social services.

The United States, despite its virtuous democratic ideals and talk of exceptionalism, ranks worst, or near the bottom, among wealthy nations not only in incarceration and gun violence but also in child poverty, infant mortality, medical bankruptcies, single-parent households, mental illness, drug addiction, drug-related deaths, and high school dropouts. The enormous investment in the United States in a massive carceral system reflected a range of distinct policy choices, which were also moral choices. Imprisonment became the default response to crime. Imprisonment also became the de facto response to poverty, lack of social mobility, addiction, joblessness, housing insecurity, mental health issues, and segregation. A sense of justice in the United States was shaped by a profound lack of mutual responsibility and collective identity. The historian Alex Lichtenstein called mass incarceration the country's new and perverse form of welfare, writing, "Yet if two-thirds of parolees return to prison, perhaps it is because the economy offers them no jobs and the welfare state excludes them as ex-felons. Their return to the social services provided by incarceration, from this angle, makes a degree of sense."

In 2019, when I was touring a medium-security prison in Oslo, a Finnish government official praised a new women's prison being built in the country. He described the way the women's facility welcomed in children, taught parenting and life skills, and included programming for substance abuse. He said nothing about its security. Finland spends roughly eighty thousand euros a year to incarcerate a single person in one of its closed prisons, which in 2022 was the equivalent of eighty thousand dollars. In California, the state's Legislative Analyst's Office estimates that it costs on average $106,000 annually to imprison someone, with "security" ($44,918) and "inmate healthcare" ($33,453) being the two largest line items. In Finland, the money spent on prisons led to savings by avoiding the collateral costs of higher rates of crime and recidivism. The official in Oslo added that there was another quality-of-life benefit. He offered that Finland, as a whole, was happier because of its lower incarceration rate. Finland perennially placed near the top of a United Nations "happiness index." The United States, a country that set down the very words "the pursuit of happiness" in its Declaration of Independence, was nowhere close. The official reflected for a moment on the disparities. "In the U.S., having two million people in prison," he said with bewilderment, "you must lose the kind of flood of happiness from the society."

MICHAEL, OUT ONE morning at dawn with his running group, was paired with a Back on My Feet volunteer named Kate. Michael peppered Kate with questions about herself—she was a young lawyer considering a move to California with her boyfriend—and he offered her advice based on his years of contemplating human behavior in prison. He loved the conversation. His running, less so. Michael was getting slower. For several weeks, he had been falling to the back of the pack. He told himself it was easier to hold a conversation if he was following the joggers in front of him. He didn't have to worry about the route or traffic. For stretches, though, he had to stop and walk to catch his breath, something he hadn't done since his first weeks jogging the prison yard. Michael was still planning to run the marathon in the fall. But he worried his age might be catching up with him. Sixty-seven. And most were prison years. One medical study estimated that each year in prison cost a person two years of life expectancy. The stress and processed food and inadequate medical care shaved time off a person's life. American prisons made a body age faster.

Michael listened to Kate talk about the job in Chicago she would give up if she chose her relationship over her career and moved. But he was thinking the entire time how his lungs stung. He asked Kate if they could rest for a second. He sat on the curb. She waited for him, hopping from foot to foot to stay warm. He said he'd be able to finish the run, just give him a few more minutes. The second time he sat down, Kate convinced Michael that heading back to St. Leonard's was for her benefit. She said she was cold and had to get to work. She called an Uber and took him to his apartment.

The next day, Michael packed a bag with his medical records, his state ID, his birth certificate, every bit of documentation he had. He walked the mile south and east to the big county hospital. It took a while, but a doctor saw him in the emergency room. Michael described his increasing fatigue. A nurse took his blood pressure. A technician X-rayed him. He underwent other tests. When the doctor returned, he said five of Michael's heart valves were blocked. He'd had a heart attack. Or, rather, many mini heart attacks.

Michael had once faked a heart attack while running. It was during the second decade of his incarceration, when Michael was in his late thirties. He'd been flirting with a nurse at the prison named Debbie. She'd come by the staff commissary, where Michael worked. She had straight brown hair that fell in a waterfall to her waist, and she ordered popcorn and a Diet Coke. Michael offered her a free sample of frozen yogurt, saying it was their secret, and she smiled in a way that made him think there was something there. When she returned another day, she looked at Michael's ID and said she hadn't seen him in the hospital. "Are you frightened of nurses?" she teased. There was definitely something there. So on the yard after his run, Michael told a guard he was experiencing chest pains. Sent to the infirmary, he was hooked up to an electrocardiogram machine. Debbie walked in. When no one else was around, they hugged. A line was crossed. They met a few times in a small storage room behind the commissary. Debbie told Michael that she and her husband had an open relationship. Michael didn't know what that meant. She eventually mentioned the affair to another nurse at the prison, and not long after that she was gone, either transferred or fired. That was as much as Michael knew about heart attacks.

The likelihood that a formerly incarcerated person dies in the first weeks after their release was thirteen times higher than the mortality rate of the general population. Overdoses and suicides were the most common causes of death. But incarcerated people also experienced heart disease, respiratory illness, and cancer at much higher rates than everyone else. Despite Michael's daily exercise regimen in prison, the ten miles a day around the yard, it turned out he was not insulated from the long-term health consequences.

The doctor told Michael that they could operate right away. They would have to go into his leg, get veins, and use them to replace the bad arteries in his heart. The doctor said Michael would likely recover.

"Come on with it," Michael said. "Whatever it takes. Cure me."

He called his parole officer to say he wouldn't be checking in while in the hospital. He didn't want another warrant out for his arrest. After the operation, his friends from St. Leonard's came to the hospital to see him. Four days after the surgery, he was back in his kitchenette apartment. He walked fine. Within eight weeks, he was riding a bike. He started working his way up to a jog, running, resting, then walking. It was like starting his training all over again. He had to recondition his body. He wanted to get back that feeling of freedom from running. He picked up his pace. He asked his doctor about the marathon. Michael said since the surgery it was like he had more energy, more power, maybe because he was again pumping oxygen through all those valves that had been plugged. The doctor cautioned Michael. He told a story about a friend, a twenty-six-year-old, never incarcerated, who completed a marathon and dropped dead. The doctor said Michael had been in pain for a reason. He should listen to his body, even if his mind told him otherwise.

"What about a half-marathon?" Michael said. The doctor considered it.

"Maybe a 5K."

"I'll never give it up," Michael said. "It's where I solve my problems."

12

Lockdown

It was the start of 2020, and Johnnie was a bottle tossed end over end. His parole hearing was scheduled for the fall. One moment he believed he could win parole—a gut feeling that he would somehow go from zero votes to eight this time. And another moment he dismissed the Prisoner Review Board as a lost cause. He often came back to the same dilemma of his indeterminate sentence. He imagined reaching for the door to leave prison, but it kept receding into the distance, like in the TV show *The Twilight Zone*. The punishment had no end. Johnnie said, "I tell everybody, we are caught in a political time warp. 'I cannot parole you because you got a sensational case,' or, 'I cannot parole you because it was so vicious.' 'I cannot parole you because of getting feedback from the police department.' 'I cannot parole you because of who you are.' What's the purpose of parole?"

Johnnie nevertheless entered what he thought of as battle mode. He needed every moment to plot and plan and prepare for his upcoming hearing. Each morning he hopped out of his bunk by 5:30 a.m. and got dressed. He tuned into MSNBC, to check out what was happening in the world. He did sit-ups and jumping jacks. He walked over to the hospital to get medication for his hypertension, for his enlarged prostate, and for an inflammatory lung disease he had called sarcoidosis, which sometimes made it hard to breathe. And then he worked on his freedom. He met in the dayroom with his think tank, his small crew of trusted confidantes, and they strategized over their different cases. Johnnie watched videos of Les Brown, the former politician turned motivational speaker, and he tried to pick up techniques to speak persuasively for his parole interview. He grabbed a phone when he could, calling Darlene and other friends and family. He had every phone number committed to memory, and he kept a running list in his head of who had stuck with him through the years, and who among the diehards could be relied on as his hearing neared. He wanted someone to take point on transportation to Springfield. His family was now scattered across Illinois, Minnesota, and Wisconsin. Darlene would have to travel all the way from Kansas. Johnnie felt he needed at least as many supporters to show up at the hearing as police officers. He asked someone to make T-shirts, so that his backers looked like a unified team with a message. He called his grandkids, getting them ready to testify in front of the board on his behalf. On other calls he dictated statements to be posted to a "Free Johnnie Veal" Facebook page.

Then, late at night, he lay awake in his bunk trying to anticipate any political twists that might affect his chances. In 2018, a Chicago police officer was murdered right before Johnnie's parole hearing, a commander in charge of the present-day Cabrini-Green. It had sealed Johnnie's fate. What would it be this time? He thought about who else might be coming up for parole, and how their hearings might bear on his. Were there other police cases? Any high-profile gang chiefs? He thought about local political races. And also Donald Trump and the up-coming presidential election. Johnnie tried to figure out what he could do to protect himself from any potential perils.

There were some reasons for hope. The parole board in Illinois had become more merciful. Its release rate was up. In all of 2017, the Prisoner Review Board had paroled only two C-Numbers. In 2018, the total had increased to nine. Those in prison the longest generally were convicted of the most serious crimes, and even in their sixties, or older, they were presented as threats to society. "Scary Willie Hortons," said Aviva Futorian, who regularly monitored the hearings. At a monthly meeting in 2019, though, the board voted for parole in three of the seven cases it heard. Two months later, four people were granted parole. "That might tie a record," Chairman Findley announced as he called the session to a close. Then a couple of months later, the board tied the record again.

There were several explanations for why approvals were up. More of the parole candidates in Illinois had lawyers, which meant they had better parole plans. Attrition, too, had played a part. With each passing year, it became harder to make the case that the C-Number senior citizens remained a risk. "I've reached the point now that I'm sort of grading on a curve," Shelton said during deliberations of one case. But the makeup of the board had shifted as well. Up until 2019, a majority of the board members had previously worked in law enforcement, as police officers or prosecutors, and their voting records reflected that they were the least likely among their colleagues to support parole. A former prison official and a former prosecutor didn't have their terms renewed. Daniels and Martinez were added, as were two other board members with a history of restorative justice work. The former cops and prosecutors suddenly found themselves in the minority. Pete Fisher complained of a lenient groupthink among his more liberal colleagues, an adherence to what he called a "40/70" rule—"you've been incarcerated for forty years, and you're seventy years old, it's time for you to go home." Fisher said, "No it's not. You don't send somebody home because they've been in prison for forty years." He felt other board members were ignoring the original crime. "I don't care if the guy is up to be canonized as a saint, it's still, what did you do? What got you here?"

During a hearing in Springfield, Martinez described a robbery and double murder from 1971, saying the crime gave her nightmares. A cabdriver was struck so hard with a claw hammer that the murder weapon lodged in his skull. In the past, a visceral retelling of a murder like this one would have likely overwhelmed any story of mercy. But Martinez was recommending release. She believed that Henry Dee, one of the two men convicted of the crime, was innocent. Other board members didn't buy it. Dee's codefendant, James Sayles, had also claimed innocence but after decades in prison eventually admitted to the crime. Five years after accepting blame, Sayles was paroled.

"We all know some convictions, even at the appellate level, are bogus," a board member named Salvador Diaz, a former Chicago police officer, said. "I've met Dee before, and I was impressed," Diaz added. "But he had the victim's property on him."

"That's what the police say," Martinez cut in.

"Simply because police chase someone doesn't mean they're lying." Diaz said he might have voted for Dee if he had said "no comment" rather than "I'm innocent."

Chairman Findley sometimes warned that as a group sitting in Springfield the board was ill-equipped to reconsider guilt or innocence. The past was a fog, and what had been handed down to them as the truth was no doubt messier. In some cases, police officers coerced confessions or planted evidence. Prosecutors presented a skewed version of the facts. Parole candidates changed their stories and were either lying decades ago or now as they told the board what it expected to hear. Board members weren't able to call witnesses. They couldn't launch investigations, even if Shelton tried on his own. There weren't the procedural standards or checks of a courtroom. In New York, where Michelle Lewin operated her parole prep nonprofit, she avoided calling what parole commissioners did a "hearing." "There's basically no rules that govern what questions the commissioners can ask and what kind of response time applicants are given. So it's really an 'interview' by the parole board."

Henry Dee, at seventy-three, seemed on the verge of another rejection.

"Can I offer something for consideration?" Lisa Daniels asked. "Mr. Dee was told that if he did not acknowledge committing the crime he would never be paroled. Maybe we take into consideration that Mr. Sayles was given that same advice and took it."

"Yes!" a board member shouted.

"That's exactly what I was going to say," another announced. There was something close to a collective sigh, as if many of them were waiting for a story to snap into focus that allowed them to move beyond the crime. Dee got nine votes and was paroled.

Along with the parole board in Illinois, the country's views on prisons and punishment, its values, had evolved as well. In 2020 the U.S. prison population was down four hundred thousand from its 2009 peak. California's prisons accounted for a big part of that drop, their population having fallen by 43 percent. Illinois's was also down by 40 percent. In Connecticut, with fewer people in prison, the population was down by more than half. John Pfaff, the legal scholar, found that from 2007 to 2013 states had passed three times the number of laws focused on decarceration as opposed to laws geared to making punishments harsher—a complete reversal from the previous three decades. More than half the states enacted legislation to roll back the severity of mandatory sentences. From 2007 to 2017, according to the Pew Charitable Trusts, twenty-one states expanded eligibility to parole hearings or made discretionary parole release more likely. Eleven states made geriatric or medical release more available. In 2018, Donald Trump signed into law the bipartisan First Step Act, a slate of prison reforms that softened some of the crueler edges of federal incarceration. No longer would pregnant women in custody be put in constraints during childbirth. The law also recalibrated good-time credits, leading to the release of seven thousand people. In a country with two million locked up, these changes were a first step on a long, long journey, but they were at least pointing in the right direction, so long as other steps followed.

In Illinois, the members of the parole board sometimes seemed amazed to find themselves inside this cultural flux.

"Boy, I hate to go along with everybody else," Fisher said at a 2019 hearing when the tally was already twelve to zero in favor of release. The former police chief had voted in support of parole only a couple of times during his four-year tenure.

"Uh-oh!" one of his colleagues rejoiced.

"What is happening?" another laughed.

When a longtime friend of Johnnie's, a fellow C-Number at Hill, learned he was being released in 2019, Johnnie was the first person he saw. They were outside the prison library.

"Man, I made parole," he told Johnnie.

"You made it. That's good, brother. That's good." Johnnie couldn't help but think that his friend's news might be good for him as well. His buddy was also represented by Garber, and his vote totals had climbed from one at his previous hearing to nine. Zero to eight didn't seem impossible. Maybe the politics this time would break in Johnnie's favor.

* * *

THE PRISONER REVIEW Board didn't meet in January or February of 2020. When they next convened, in March, it was amid much uncertainty. The day before, a Wednesday, the World Health Organization declared a global pandemic. There were 647 confirmed Covid-19 cases in the United States. President Trump had dismissed the virus as no big deal. "It will go away," he repeated. That Wednesday, though, felt like the start of a very big deal. A basketball player on the Utah Jazz tested positive, and before a game tipped off the teams were rushed off the court, leading the NBA to suspend its season indefinitely. The first universities announced an end to in-person classes. The actor Tom Hanks and his wife posted on Instagram that they were quarantining in Australia after a positive test. Trump spoke from the Oval Office that evening, saying he would ban travel to the United States from twenty-six European countries.

The parole board went ahead with its hearing the next morning. The meeting was moved to a much larger space. The number of visitors was limited, with everyone seated far apart and required to wear a mask. Two people were granted parole. Three were denied. The next day the prisons in Illinois went on lockdown. And then the state issued a stay-at-home order, closing all schools, nonessential businesses, and most governmental offices. Courthouses stopped hearing cases. Prisons barred visitors, including lawyers and parole officials. The Prisoner Review Board cancelled its upcoming meetings. Like nearly everything else, the parole system came to a sudden halt.

Those first months of the pandemic were terrifying. So little was known. Johnnie watched the news from his bunk. The nation's chief medical advisor, Dr. Anthony Fauci, said the spread of the coronavirus couldn't be stopped. Through collective efforts, though, the nation could "flatten the curve," lowering whatever would become the peak number of infections. In that way, lives could be saved. Across the country, Americans were instructed to "shelter in place." To isolate in their homes, to socially distance from anyone outside their household— relatives, friends, work colleagues, people on buses and in stores. Cases quickly jumped borders. By mid-April 2020, 750 people were dying each day in New York City alone, so many that the city deployed dozens of mobile morgues to store the bodies. The virus attacked the lungs. People couldn't breathe. They died as if drowning. In this country of abundance, in which access to everything was treated as a birthright, there weren't enough ventilators. There was a shortage of hospital beds. People couldn't find hand sanitizer, latex gloves, Clorox bleach. They hoarded toilet paper. Unsure how exactly the virus spread, people washed their groceries before putting them away, microwaved mail, scrubbed their hands so many times they cracked and bled. "Stay calm," President Trump told the American public. "We're going to have a great victory." The number of people killed by the virus in the United States soon hit ten thousand, then days later twenty thousand, then in little time sixty thousand, far more deaths than in any other country. Trump called the virus "vicious" and recommended drinking disinfectant or exposing the body to ultraviolet light as cures. Three months into the lockdown, after Covid-19 deaths in the country topped 120,000, Trump tweeted, "The number of ChinaVirus cases goes up, because of GREAT TESTING, while the number of deaths (mortality rate), goes way down. The Fake News doesn't like telling you that!"

For Johnnie and other people in prison or jail, social distance was an impossibility. Johnnie was locked up with 1,600 men at Hill. He was confined on a wing with more than a hundred people. He shared a tiny cell. The country's correctional facilities were perfect breeding grounds for an outbreak. They were overcrowded, with people crammed together in cages or in dormitories of side-by-side beds. They were poorly ventilated, unsanitary, and provided inadequate health care. No one could get up and move to a remote location or choose to be alone.

Every winter, and sometimes in the summer as well, Johnnie caught the flu along with most everyone else at Hill. And from the start of the pandemic, the coronavirus tore through the country's prisons and jails. In Chicago, in the spring of 2020, the Cook County jail had the largest known outbreak in the nation, accounting for one of every six recorded Covid-19 infections in Illinois. Stateville, another super-spreader site, reported its first Covid-19 death in March 2020 and its second days later. By May, at least twelve at the prison were dead and hundreds sick. Stateville had one decrepit roundhouse that had yet to be demolished, and the panopticon was reopened after sitting dormant for four years to serve as a sick bay for the growing number of patients. In Michigan that April, the infection rate in state prisons was 56 percent, with thirty-three deaths. A headline: "Prisoner Dies in Cell, Covid-19 Virus Spreads to 200 Inmates in Michigan." At a private prison in Tennessee with a population of 2,500, more than half of the inmates and staff caught the virus. At an Ohio state prison, nearly 2,000 of the 2,500 people incarcerated there tested positive. In the first year of the pandemic, according to the Bureau of Justice Statistics, almost 2,500 incarcerated people in the United States died from their exposure to Covid.

Apart from system-wide lockdowns, prisons did little else in those first months to protect the incarcerated. At Hill, no one was tested. No one had masks or cleaning supplies. Johnnie was sixty-seven and had sarcoidosis, an inflammatory lung disease. He was what the Centers for Disease Control and Prevention called at high risk for severe Covid illness. He walked to the shower holding a cloth over his face. When he had a chance to use the phones, he covered the receiver with a tube sock. Finally, he and the other men at Hill were issued two surgical masks and two plastic bottles of soap, the miniature hotel size. They were instructed to clean their own cells, while porters went around scrubbing the common areas with a disinfectant of such high bleach concentration that it erupted like little flames inside the nose and throat. There was an outbreak in Hill's health department. Johnnie heard rumors that men on the prison's quarantine wing were returned to population too soon, or that men who transferred into Hill didn't quarantine first. He heard that more than a hundred men at the prison were sick. Johnnie wasn't tested until the last day of 2020. Eventually, the guards started coming around with thermometer guns. But Johnnie feared the COs most of all. They were the only ones traveling between the outside and the prison. He heard that guards tested positive but still worked their shifts. He imagined them on their off days wearing MAGA hats and treating personal protective equipment as if it violated their constitutional rights.

Johnnie was right to worry about the guards. In facilities across the country, they were infected at high rates. In Missouri, sick guards led to the closing of county jails. So many COs fell ill with the virus in New

Hampshire and Ohio that the National Guard was called in to keep the prisons running. North Carolina was forced to shutter four of its prisons because it could no longer staff them, leading to mass transfers to other crowded facilities. Due to staffing shortages, California, Michigan, and Wisconsin had to consolidate their prison populations as well, increasing the risk of the virus spreading from facility to facility.

Beyond the daily health threats, everything in prison during the pandemic was worse. For people with mental illness or substance abuse issues, the lockdown meant no group therapy. The isolation, while necessary to stay safe, put everyone on edge. Food was delivered to cells. People couldn't exercise on the yard or congregate in the dayroom. There was no school or church. Depression, always lurking, grabbed hold of people. At Hill, men were let out of their cells two at a time to shower. They were allowed to go to the commissary to buy supplies every few weeks. Visits were forbidden. Johnnie missed his work shifts, which had at least provided movement and activity. He was supposed to be in battle mode, but he couldn't even meet with his think tank. People at home were trying to cope with their own changed worlds, with children out of school, with the lack of work or the new dangers of a service job. The absence of contact with loved ones inside strained relationships that in normal times already had built-in strains. Little problems grew to seismic proportions. Johnnie couldn't check in daily with his granddaughter to make sure she was okay.

Even in Johnnie's darker moments, when he tried to temper Darlene's expectations, protecting her from the heartbreak of another parole rejection, he'd believed that the best parts of his life were yet to come. He had to. But the pandemic left him less sure. A black spot appeared in his thoughts. Johnnie had lost so much over the past fifty years. The deaths of his mother and aunts and uncles, his daughter, siblings, friends. He often told himself he'd become impervious to suffering. He was like wood when it's petrified into stone. Now guys on Johnnie's wing fell sick and shivered through the night, calling for the guards who ignored them. Johnnie would repeat like a mantra that he had already lost everything. But there was plenty more to lose.

* * *

JOHNNIE'S DATE WITH the parole board was scheduled for the end of 2020. But the medical lockdown extended for weeks and then months, with Covid cases only growing in and out of prison. Several months into the pandemic, the Prisoner Review Board had yet to restart its operations. No system was set up to hold hearings remotely or to interview parole candidates via video conference. Most of the parole boards in other states also heard far fewer cases that year. But not all boards. Oklahoma's parole commissioners met more frequently in 2020 than they had in 2019—and their denial rate also climbed. Iowa created a special second parole board during the pandemic to speed up hearings, since overcrowding in prisons was a matter of life or death. Iowa's special board, however, ended up denying most petitioners, and the total number of people granted parole in the state in 2020, with two boards operating, increased by only 4 percent. Florida, in 2020, released just 1 percent of its parole candidates. The discretionary parole rate in Alaska fell in 2020 to historic lows, from as high as 66 percent in 2015 down to 16 percent.

Johnnie again applied for executive clemency. "Two bites of the apple, not just one," he said. It was a long shot. Governors and presidents, as chief executives, have broad and mostly unchecked constitutional powers to commute a sentence to a less severe punishment or to grant an outright pardon, which forgave a person for an offense and released them from any ongoing or future penalties. Executive clemency corrects nothing structural about the criminal system, but it could be used effectively to address specific cases of malfeasance or injustice. Barack Obama, in the last two years of his presidency, in 2016 and 2017, did use clemency at least to cast a light on a systemic problem, commuting the sentences of over 1,600 people in prison, most of whom were serving long terms for nonviolent drug offenses. In Illinois, in 1994, after years of pressure from activists and lobbyists, a Republican governor, Jim Edgar, granted clemency to four women who were convicted of murdering men who had battered and abused them.

But governors and presidents use their clemency powers sparingly, and almost always at the end of their terms, when they are done campaigning and no longer fear the political consequences of being labeled weak on crime. Jan Brewer, Arizona's Republican governor from 2009 to 2015, granted thirteen pardons in her entire tenure, twelve of them on her last day in office. An exception was Kate Brown, Oregon's governor from 2015 to 2022, who used her power to grant commutations or pardons more than a thousand times long before her last weeks in office, at which point she also pardoned forty-seven thousand people with past convictions for small amounts of marijuana possession and commuted to life in prison the sentences of the seventeen people on the state's death row. "We are a nation of second chances," Brown insisted. Clemency was also deployed transactionally to reward donors or to serve a politician's own interests. Bill Clinton (457 total executive clemencies granted), in his final hours as president, pardoned a wealthy financier named Marc Rich, charged with racketeering and fraud, after Rich's family gave large donations to the Democratic Party and the Clinton presidential library. Trump (238 granted) reserved the power mostly as a reward for fellow celebrities or loyalists who protected him during his first impeachment and through numerous other investigations. Joe Biden, in his first year in office, didn't use his clemency powers once. In October 2022, though, he pardoned people who'd been in the federal system for simple marijuana possession, which affected about six thousand people, all of them already out of prison. Another constructive "first step," but also a small one that added to the reasoning that mercy stopped with nonviolent offenses.

Any official supporting Johnnie's clemency petition would face inevitable reprisals from police and victim advocates. But the extraordinary circumstances of the pandemic created an extraordinary opportunity to save the lives of people in prison. One solution to easing the spread of the coronavirus in crowded prisons and jails was simple: make facilities less crowded by releasing more people. There were 450,000 men and women in jails across the country who were awaiting trial, who hadn't yet been convicted of a crime but who nevertheless might face a death sentence from the virus if they remained herded together in lockup. Many of them could be sent home without endangering the public. The trials that they were awaiting weren't even taking place early in the pandemic. Similarly, people in prison whose sentences were soon to end could be sent home without any substantive difference to justice or public safety. Older men and women made up a fifth of all U.S. inmates. They were, because of their age and the poor health created by long prison sentences, the most susceptible to severe illness or death from the coronavirus; they were also the least likely to reoffend. Most of them could be released with little crime risk. There was even a chance because of the pandemic to go beyond the cautious advance of the First Step Act, to take bolder action, to remake the American prison system. It was an opportunity to think of people convicted of violent crimes differently, to revisit the risks and rewards of alternatives to long-term incarceration.

What's remarkable, though, given the scale and gravity of the pandemic, was how few people were allowed to leave prison. The data was indisputable: doing nothing during a deadly pandemic put everyone working and living in prison at dire risk. The number of deaths in prison jumped nearly 50 percent from 2019 to 2020. Yet overall more people were released from state and federal prisons in the United States in 2018, before the rise of Covid-19, than in all of 2020. Jail and prison population numbers that fell in the first months of Covid-19's spread had mostly returned to pre-pandemic levels by the summer. In federal prisons, there were thirty-one thousand requests for compassionate release in the thirteen months after March 2020. A total of thirty-six were approved. At a federal women's prison in Texas, where Covid had infected hundreds and killed six, 346 of the 349 people requesting early release were rejected. In Louisiana, in the first months of the pandemic, the state considered 1,100 incarcerated people for compassionate medical parole and released sixty-three. Oklahoma released twelve. Alabama, the state with the most overcrowded prisons, granted compassionate parole to only five people in all of 2020. Nevada freed none. Pennsylvania's Democratic governor issued an executive order demanding that his prisons identify people suitable for immediate release. But the order excluded anyone whose crime involved violence, drug trafficking, or a number of other offenses, ruling out nearly everyone. Greg Abbott, the Republican governor of Texas, offered no pretense of protecting people in prison from a virus whose threat he steadily denied. He issued an executive order prohibiting the release of anyone in prison and jail for a violent crime or with a history of violence. More than ten thousand people in Texas prisons who had already been granted parole remained locked up as they waited to take a class required for release that wasn't meeting because of the pandemic. Twenty-six of them ended up dying in prison from Covid-19.

Early in the pandemic, the CARES Act, which delivered billions of dollars in unemployment benefits, forgivable business loans, and other emergency assistance, lifted nearly thirteen million people out of poverty, the biggest, fastest change in the country's history. This economic stimulus bill also permitted the federal Bureau of Prisons to transfer more than eleven thousand incarcerated people to home confinement, thus reducing the risks from Covid. In December 2020, in the last weeks of the Trump administration, the Justice Department issued a legal memo trying to return many of these people to prison. But this cohort of released people also served as proof of how much more could have been done during the pandemic. In August 2022, the Bureau of Prisons reported that of the eleven thousand sent home, only seventeen committed another crime. That's a recidivism rate of .15 percent. Anyone would feel safe with those numbers. Of those seventeen crimes, moreover, most were minor, and drug related. Only a single one was for a violent offense, an aggravated assault. It was evidence that reimagining long sentences and early release made sense.

Johnnie had one other potential bite of the apple. He and Garber were petitioning for a resentencing hearing based on the 2012 *Miller v. Alabama* U.S. Supreme Court decision. In *Miller*, the Supreme Court ruled that mandatory sentences of life without parole for juvenile offenders were unconstitutional because young people were fundamentally different from adults. In the 1980s and 1990s, an idea took hold that children who committed murders and other violent crimes were molded by their mostly inner-city environments into super-predators and were beyond repair. So they were locked up for the rest of their lives. The Supreme Court in *Miller* found that the opposite was true—juveniles, because of their lack of maturity, possessed a "heightened capacity for change." The decision recognized the advances in neuroscience that showed a teenager's developing brain was constitutionally different from that of an adult. Adolescents weren't fully in control of their impulses and reasoning; they were more likely to take unwise risks and be adversely influenced by peers. And in the coming years, over long incarcerations, they would literally grow up. It took another

Supreme Court decision, *Montgomery v. Louisiana*, in 2016, to make Miller retroactive to people already serving time in prison. Each state then had to pass laws determining how to apply the *Miller* ruling, and much of the advocacy and legal debate centered around who exactly qualified for a claim.

In 2012, there were 2,500 people serving the exact sentence of life without parole in state and federal prisons in the United States who had been under eighteen at the time of their offense. But there were thousands of others who weren't technically juvenile LWOPs but whose punishments amounted to the same thing. They'd been charged as adults, given mandatory consecutive terms, their sentences enhanced because of the involvement of guns or gangs or any number of escalating factors. They were serving de facto life sentences. Johnnie fell, possibly, into this second category. Illinois defined a de facto life sentence as forty years or longer. Johnnie had served fifty years in prison for a crime he was convicted of committing at the age of seventeen. His indeterminate sentence meant he already came up for parole. He wasn't an LWOP. But in her petition, Garber tried to demonstrate that his chances with the parole board were effectively nonexistent. After three decades of parole hearings, Johnnie had never received a single vote in favor of his release. Eleven times, the parole board elected to put off his next hearing for three years. Garber described how the board's record showed that it was hostile to those convicted of crimes against law enforcement. Craig Findley had stated publicly that he didn't think Johnnie or his codefendant would ever get out of prison. Johnnie's accomplishments over the past quarter century, moreover, were a vivid illustration of the science behind *Miller*. He'd matured.

Garber told Johnnie that the courts could drag out his *Miller* appeal for years, and during Covid-19 they were going to be even slower. She believed, however, that he would eventually win and qualify for a resentencing. She also expected the victory to prove hollow. The Supreme Court ruling made unconstitutional only the automatic requirements that triggered juvenile life without parole. The ruling returned discretion to the judiciary. Meaning, any judge considering a new sentence could still deliberate and issue a life sentence. Evan Miller, the named plaintiff in the landmark 2012 ruling, was still in prison. When he was fourteen, Miller, who is white and from a tiny Alabama town, killed his mother's drug dealer, beating the man with a baseball bat before setting him on fire. In 2017, an Alabama county judge heard his resentencing appeal. Miller, then twenty-eight, was incarcerated in an "honor dorm" and had used his time in prison to study welding. He apologized to his victim's family at the hearing: "I'm sorry once again for stealing the joy from your lives." Witnesses testified to the violence, drugs, and neglect that dominated Miller's childhood. He'd been in and out of foster care; he'd been physically abused by his stepfather and had attempted suicide several times before his crime. The judge deciding on a new sentence took no action. Years passed. It wasn't until 2021 that the judge finally resentenced Miller—life without parole.

JOHNNIE CONTINUED TO wait for news about his scheduled parole interview—when it would happen and whether it would be in person or not. In the meantime, he asked Darlene to marry him. He typed out the proposal and made a recording of it by reading it over the phone to another person. The prison system limited each call to a maximum of thirty minutes, and often much less time than that. It took several days for Johnnie to record the entire thing. Johnnie began his proposal by setting the scene, asking Darlene to imagine a romantic evening that he could create only in words—a luxurious meal, flowers, their families looking on and waiting anxiously for Johnnie to get on one knee and reveal the ring. Johnnie compiled an extensive playlist to accompany the proposal. Marvin Gaye and Anita Baker, Teddy Pendergrass, the Four Tops, René and Angela. He didn't have access to any of the music. So at the moment he wanted a song played, he named the artist and the album, hoping Darlene would pause the recording and find the accompanying music. He detailed each chapter of their intertwined lives, starting when they were children hanging out in front of the buildings at Cabrini-Green and roller-skating together.

Darlene said yes.

13

Twenty Is Plenty

"You need a shirt? You straight? There some shoes back there. You a size ten?" In St. Leonard's basement, in a musty room overflowing with donated clothes, Michael sized up a recent arrival to the halfway house. Michael pointed to the dark suits and pants squeezed onto racks and piled high on shelves. Garbage bags packed with unsorted items formed outcroppings along the walls. People needed clothes when they got back from prison, sometimes everything from head to toe. St. Leonard's provided. It outfitted its residents for more dressy occasions, too, for job interviews, church services, reunions with their families. Each time a new cohort finished the Road to Success employment training, St. Leonard's held a graduation ceremony. The graduates could find suits and ties in the basement as well.

The guy Michael studied now was barely in his twenties, and as slender and skittish as a fawn. He stood at the threshold of the room waiting for instructions, his face locked in consternation. Finally, he spoke.

"Do I have to bring 'em back?"

"Naaahhh," Michael sang out magnanimously. "They're *yours*."

Michael wore a white baseball cap with the brim cut off, an ironed gray T-shirt, and a long measuring tape draped around his neck like a scarf. He volunteered in the St. Leonard's basement, working by himself for several hours a day. He arranged the donated items and made sure residents and employees didn't take more than their share. Each new arrival could pick out three pairs of pants, three shirts, shoes, and a belt. Michael was basically in charge, he said, and he created a little space for himself in a corner, with a small table, a radio, and a sewing machine.

Michael's phone chimed, and he put it on speaker. It was Joyce, his ex-wife, calling from a suburb of East St. Louis. After Michael's release, it had seemed natural to both of them to lean on each other again. They were in their sixties; they had grown children and grandchildren together. The decades of no communication were in the past. Joyce had given Michael the sewing machine, and she'd visited him in Chicago, staying with him in his apartment.

"I got a customer back in the back," he told her. "I'm working."

"You in class or you doing this or that. I'm about to get jealous. I'll call you later." They talked multiple times a day.

"I appreciate it."

"Nah, you call *me*," Joyce said, trying a different tack, before ending the call.

Michael's customer, the kid just back from prison, held up a white button-up shirt for Michael's approval. Michael shook his head. It was a woman's blouse. Michael went over to a rack and pulled a different top.

"Match them up with the pants," Michael said as he placed items on the young man's outstretched arms. "That's perfect," Michael chimed. "You batting a thousand. You lucked out." It was as if Michael turned a key—the young man's face opened. He smiled. And then just as suddenly, it was gone. He bowed his worried face.

"Wassup?" Michael asked.

"How you tie a tie?"

Michael enjoyed the work. He wanted to do his part at St. Leonard's, to contribute to a community that had given him so much. But he also liked outfitting folks. People dressed up for who they wanted to become. New clothes, even ones that weren't technically new, were the hope of a fresh start. Michael told whoever ventured into the storeroom that by looking sharp they were most of the way there. People were going to be drawn to them. And what people would see wasn't a convict, an ex-felon, a violent offender. They'd be looking at a well-dressed human being.

Another man strode into the basement storeroom and announced that he was forty pounds heavier than when he last wore anything but state-issued prison clothes. Everything he owned garroted him. Michael told the guy to pick something out, and he could alter it to make it work.

"It might cost you a little bit," Michael said. "But, you know, we straight. Go for it."

Michael had started a business tailoring clothes. It was another reason he liked working in the basement: a constant flow of customers. Michael wasn't trying to extort anyone. A cleaners down the block might charge fifteen dollars for a hem. Now *they* were robbing people. Michael charged three dollars. Some nights he stayed up to four in the morning in his apartment making alterations. As he had in prison, he found ways to earn money by figuring out what was in demand.

Michael's phone rang again; he put it on speaker. It was RJ, calling from another building at St. Leonard's.

"What's up, creep?" Michael said playfully. RJ was working with Michael, delivering and picking up clothes.

"I'll be over there in a minute, chump." RJ had cataracts and had problems seeing, which also affected his hearing and equilibrium. But out of prison, he eventually had surgery on his eyes. He said it was like the world was brand-new. RJ had given Michael a baseball cap to customize for him. He wanted the brim cut off and shortened and then reattached. It was RJ's style more than forty years earlier, before he'd gone to prison. He didn't like how a hat today was all blocky and too big, like a stew pot on your head. But Michael hadn't gotten around to doing it.

"I get treated the worst, and I'm the eldest and no respect," RJ told him.

"I know you're more patient than those other guys."

"You think I am."

Another guy entered the storeroom, greeting Michael as Taboo. He had a wine cask of a body, a giant barrel with stubby legs and arms. Stating what was plain to see, he said finding clothes that fit was a problem.

"It's going to be hard to match you up," Michael agreed. He guessed the guy wore a fifty-two jacket. Michael could adjust the sleeves, bring in the waist on some pants, hem up the bottoms. "I could have you fitted like a glove."

Michael's phone rang—one of his daughters, Corlette, calling from

East St. Louis. She had also gotten into the habit of checking in with him daily. He told her he was helping some customers with clothes.

"My clothes are getting too small," Corlette said. Why wasn't he getting her something new to wear?

"You need to start getting on that track." Michael was always telling his family to take up running. He called it therapeutic. If they ran, he preached, they'd not only get fit; they could also work through their problems.

"I don't know about all that," Corlette said.

MICHAEL WAS OUT on parole, trying to make something of his second chance; Johnnie, in prison, was waiting anxiously for his next shot. The men in Stateville who'd been on the debate team were still trying to give everyone locked up in the state that same chance. It didn't matter in Illinois whether someone grew old in prison, earned college degrees, no longer posed a risk to the public—without parole there was no viable mechanism to contest an extreme sentence. Oscar "Smiley" Parham was free, but the Hail Mary of his clemency was the exception that proved the rule. And Parham's clemency reduction had not actually been enough to free him. The governor commuted his sentence, but from life to a whopping seventy years, of which Smiley would have to serve half. He had spent thirty years in prison so far; he would have to serve another five. His initial plea deal in 1988 would have had him serve a total of five and a half years. It took another push by advocates to get the state's attorney where the crime occurred to further reduce Parham's sentence so he could go free. The prison disbanded the Stateville debate team in 2018. The men couldn't practice or host another public event. Katrina Burlet, their coach, couldn't enter any Illinois state prison. Debate for them was never the point. What they wanted was a real opportunity to be considered for release. In 2019, a few of them formed an organization called Parole Illinois. The group's mission was to expand parole eligibility to everyone imprisoned in the state.

Debate had prepared them to talk about parole policy. They now knew more about the issue than just about anyone. They'd become experts. As organizers, though, they were inexperienced and at a disadvantage.

Other criminal justice reform groups had spent years building grass-roots and institutional support. No politicians owed the guys in Stateville any favors; no elected officials worried much about blowback from a constituency of disenfranchised prisoners and their families. The Covid-19 lockdowns made the work that much harder. Without visitors, members of Parole Illinois couldn't lobby or persuade face to face. They could call only people on their preapproved phone lists, and it could take weeks to add a new name. Joseph Dole, a Stateville debater who became the Parole Illinois policy director, mailed a handwritten note to all 277 members of the Illinois General Assembly. Ten wrote him back. Shari Stone-Mediatore, a philosophy professor at Ohio Wesleyan University, got to know Dole after teaching one of his essays on abolishing solitary confinement. She now agreed to serve as the Parole Illinois managing director. She figured out how to set up a website. Membership shot up to over 2,100 incarcerated people. But because the prison messaging system didn't allow group emails, sending 2,100 separate messages took much of a day's work. Relatives of the incarcerated and other volunteers on the outside helped, and two women locked up at the largest female prison in Illinois joined the fledgling board. Parole Illinois raised enough money to hire an organizer part-time. Smiley had gotten a job in a Chicago suburb, as a mentor at a foundation specializing in prison reentry. He started speaking as well at churches to build support for Parole Illinois, telling his own story and those of the other men on the debate team, talking about how Jesus had also been over-sentenced.

One of the politicians who attended the public debate had introduced a parole bill in the state legislature; if passed, it would apply only to people convicted after it became law, meaning anyone currently incarcerated wouldn't be eligible. Raul Dorado, another member of the debate team who went on to lead Parole Illinois, dismissed the proposed bill as a betrayal. In 2019, Illinois extended parole consideration, after ten years of imprisonment, to most people who were twenty-one or younger when they committed their crimes. But the Youthful Parole Law wasn't retroactive either, helping no one already in prison. In a statement published in the political magazine *In These Times*, Dorado wrote that any parole legislation "must be retroactive to include the people who for decades have shouldered the burden of mass incarceration."

The Parole Illinois demands weren't outlandish pipe dreams. Many legal scholars and criminologists now agreed that whatever prisons were supposed to accomplish—whether it was incapacitation, account-ability, rehabilitation, or deterrence—it could be achieved within two decades. The Sentencing Project, a nonprofit focused on criminal legal reforms, argued that the United States should follow the lead of other countries and cap prison terms at twenty years, barring exceptional cir-cumstances. Vera Institute of Justice called for a maximum twenty-year sentence for adults and fifteen for anyone up to the age of twenty-five. The Robina Institute suggested that parole consideration should come at the latest after fifteen years of incarceration. "Fifteen years is a long time to do time," Edward Rhine, who directed Robina's Parole Release and Revocation project, said. The Model Penal Code of the American Law Institute, a century-old organization led by judges, law professors, and legal experts, also proposed reviewing long sentences for resen-tencing or release after fifteen years. The American Bar Association urged every criminal justice system in the United States to give people in prison a "second look" resentencing after ten years.

Parole Illinois was proposing something similar. "In 20 years, most young adults age out of crime," the group's literature announced. The group wanted everyone who had served at least twenty years in an Illi-nois prison to be entitled to a parole review. "Twenty is plenty." Parole Illinois pointed out that it was a bipartisan issue, that both Bernie Sanders and Lindsey Graham, the far left and the far right in the U.S. senate, said they wanted to bring back parole. In 2020, there were about 2,500 people incarcerated in Illinois who had spent the last two decades in prison, but thousands more with long sentences would eventually surpass that mark. Parole Illinois wasn't suggesting that people con-victed of violent crimes suddenly be set free. The group wanted only that a parole board look at each person as a full human being and con-sider the actual risks and benefits of restoring his or her freedom. Parole Illinois wanted everyone in prison, without exceptions, to at least have an opportunity to show a parole board why they warranted a second chance. The parole board could simply reject those deemed dangerous or unreformed. The bill "does not let everyone out. Nor does it entail an emergency scramble to release people," Parole Illinois explained in one of its policy flyers. "Instead, it provides a regular and merit-based system of review, which utilizes the existing Prisoner Review Board and requires that candidates earn release by demonstrating their readiness to rejoin society."

As far as the problems with parole that led people in the 1970s to try to abolish it, most of them remained. The focus above all else on the original crime. The bias and lack of oversight. The mistaken belief that boards could predict future crime. The pretense that long prison sentences somehow served the interests of crime victims. The purposelessness of the whole project of corrections. Parole still reflected the practices of the entire justice system as well as the country's values around crime and punishment. After spending years tangling with the California Adult Authority, Keith Wattley, of UnCommon Law, believed the parole system beyond salvation: "This subjective parole process cannot deliver fairness or justice, so we're seeking to dismantle it and replace it with something that can. In the meantime, while we have this one, we want to get as many people out successfully through parole as we can."

For many in a growing prison abolition movement, they worried that reforms like those proposed by Parole Illinois legitimized an inherently racist and dehumanizing carceral system by trying, incrementally, to better it. *Instead of Prisons: A Handbook for Abolitionists*, published in 1976, stated, "Imprisonment is morally reprehensible and indefensible and must be abolished." Johnnie's hero, Angela Davis, wrote in her 2003 book, *Are Prisons Obsolete?*, "The most difficult and urgent challenge today is that of creatively exploring new terrains of justice, where the prison no longer serves as our major anchor." Davis said that in abolishing the prison system no one alternative form of punishment would fill its massive footprint. Prison abolitionists today work on the local level to close prisons and jails one at a time. They look to alternative forms of accountability, such as restorative justice and pretrial diversion programs, and they believe that the enormous public investment in policing and punishment could be channeled into support systems that treated crime at its roots. The prison abolitionist group Critical Resistance lists among the many things that could be funded instead of prisons and jails to help keep communities safe: substance abuse treatment, mental health initiatives, free healthcare, job training, food and housing security, and after-school programming. Ruth Wilson Gilmore, one of the founders of Critical Resistance along with Angela Davis, often said, "Prisons are catchall solutions to social problems."

The imprisoned people working for parole reform in Illinois didn't have the luxury to be abolitionists. The two million people currently locked up in prisons and jails in the country couldn't wait for the revolution. Parole was undoubtedly flawed. But it offered a chance to be seen and judged and released. Parole Illinois proposed safeguards as well to make sure an expanded parole process was better. Finding ways to get people out of prisons and jails is also a central tenet of the abolition movement. Abolitionists in New York worked closely with a group called RAPP, Release Aging People in Prison, which was part of a coalition pushing for an Elder Parole Bill before the New York legislature that would grant the right to a hearing to anyone fifty-five and older who had served at least fifteen years in prison. In a virtual abolitionist workshop during the pandemic, Angela Davis talked about advocating for incremental reforms with Kathy Boudin, the former Weather Underground activist who spent twenty-two years in prison for a robbery that killed two police officers. Boudin said that when she was in prison, abolition seemed like a fantasy: "We just need some sanitary napkins. Give us enough toilet paper. You know, I can't imagine getting rid of the prison system." Boudin, who died from cancer in 2022, at age seventy-eight, was paroled in 2003, and helped found a center at Columbia University focused on ending mass incarceration. In the Zoom with Davis, Boudin said it was now clear to her that envisioning a future without prisons and helping imprisoned people in the present were inseparable. Abolition, rather than an absolutist concept, was a continuum. "We're working on trying to change the parole system so that it's fairer, and we're working on trying to get people out who are elderly. But we have an *analysis* of the system—that it's deeply tied to white supremacy, that it's deeply tied to something that's larger than just the criminal justice system." Abolition, she said, "is really about the need to change the larger system that criminal justice sits in."

Parole Illinois also recognized that transformational change to the criminal justice system seemed more in reach than at any time since 1971 and the uproar after the massacre at Attica. In May 2020, a video went viral of a Minneapolis police officer killing forty-six-year-old George Floyd. The white officer kneeled casually on Floyd's neck, for an agonizing eight minutes and forty-six seconds, as Floyd, a Black man, six-four, 220 pounds, cried out for his mother before being asphyxiated. The police report of the incident identified Floyd as "the suspect," not a "victim." But his death led to protests against police brutality that spread across the country—becoming the largest mass protests in United States history. Floyd's murder seemed to force a national soul-searching of the racism and inequality that permeated not only the criminal justice system but also that "larger system that criminal justice sits in." In June 2020, the U.S. Congress introduced the George Floyd Justice in Policing Act, a law to counter police misconduct, excessive force, and racial profiling. U.S. cities and states instituted police reforms, banning chokeholds and removing police officers from public schools. Many municipalities announced that they would reduce police budgets and increase spending on alternatives to policing, such as mental health first responders and community-led violence interrupters, in effect heeding a rallying cry to "defund the police."

In Illinois, the state legislature's Black Caucus, a group of 30 out of 177 senators and representatives, managed to use the energy and outrage from the Floyd protests to push through an array of reforms that touched every stage of the criminal legal process. The 764-page omnibus bill represented the country's most concrete and extensive fulfillment of the summer's demands for structural change and racial justice. The new laws in Illinois made it official misconduct for a police officer to turn off a body camera or to misrepresent the facts of a police incident. It gave judges more leeway to sentence people to lesser terms, to probation, or even to conditional release, thereby rolling back the mandatory minimums imposed in the 1980s and 1990s. The legislation also undercut draconian three-strikes laws, changing who counted as a habitual offender. It added more ways for incarcerated people to earn good-time credits, and, once out, it granted those on mandatory supervised release additional freedoms to work and to leave home without risk of a parole violation. The omnibus criminal justice reform bill required prisons to report the deaths of those in custody, which, *oh my god!*, was not previously required, and it ended the practice of prison gerrymandering, making sure that the tens of thousands of people incarcerated in Illinois were counted for census purposes as residents of their previous "free" addresses. Most notably, the bill put an end to cash bail in Illinois, so that wealth and poverty weren't the factors determining who remained in jail pretrial. People who couldn't afford bail wouldn't feel compelled to cop to a plea deal whether they were guilty or not.

Most of the members of the state's Black Caucus agreed philosophically with the Parole Illinois proposal—changing the bail system involved confronting many of the same outsize fears of releasing anyone from lockup and marshaling similar facts about racial and economic disparities, wasted resources, and misconstrued risks to public safety. But the lawmakers decided not to include parole reform in the omnibus bill. The margins as far as passing the bill had been razor-thin, even without the addition of retroactive parole eligibility for the entire prison population.

The members of Parole Illinois had no other choice but to try again. They spoke to state lawmakers who said they might support a parole reform bill in the future if it didn't include those convicted of the most serious offenses, such as certain sex crimes or multiple murders. Up to then, the guys in prison had been inflexible on carve-outs that excluded anyone from expanded parole eligibility. They reiterated that parole was not a get-out-of-jail-free card. It was a way to assess who was and wasn't fit to release. But now they made concessions. They'd take that carve-out if it meant relief for the other 2,500 who had already done two decades, and for the many more who would soon reach that milestone. "Who knows how many years it'll take to get 100 percent," Joseph Dole said. "And there's a hundred people dying in here every year, so it's kind of desperate times call for how can we get the most people out of prison the quickest." They agreed as well that parole priority would be given over the first several years after the bill's passage to those in prison who were fifty-five and older. That group was more likely to suffer from poor health and be at risk from Covid. And the bill's supporters knew, too, that older inmates seemed less threatening to the public.

The proposal secured new legislative sponsors, and in February 2021
a revised version of the Earned Discretionary Reentry bill was introduced in both chambers of the Illinois General Assembly. The proposal
could come up for a vote as early as the fall of 2021.

MICHAEL'S SON DROVE in from Massachusetts, and the two of them
headed downstate together to East St Louis. Michael didn't have to
tell his parole officer about the trip. He was off electronic monitoring,
and he wasn't leaving the state. But Michael didn't alert many in his
family either. He had not been home in a half century, and he hoped to
sneak in and get his bearings. He didn't want a big to-do. It was enough
on this first visit to spend time with his daughters and Joyce. "I'm re-
acclimating," he'd tell them each time they urged him to come. It was
counterintuitive to them that Michael needed more time apart: he'd
been in prison for forty-six years, and now he was free. The separation
was supposed to be over.

Michael had been slowly reconnecting with his family, albeit on his
terms. His grandkids visited him in Chicago, and Michael took them to
LEGOLAND in the suburbs. On his daily calls with Joyce, he gave her
advice on how to repair her car, explaining what she would owe beyond
the deductible on her auto insurance, and he encouraged her to leave an
unfulfilling relationship. It was problem-solving, he said, which is what
he'd mastered in prison. He repeated to one daughter who, in middle
age, continued to mourn what Michael's absence did to her, that she
couldn't get stuck in the past. She'd call him late at night, teary, and he'd
tell her, "You got to put history where it belongs. That time is gone."

Michael's drive to East St. Louis with his son took more than four
hours, and they traveled through the night. When Michael was incarcerated, he looked forward to medical appointments or anything that
took him beyond the prison walls. In the vans he would press a sheet
of paper to the window, hoping the drivers in other cars saw it. "I'M A
LONELY HEART," it read, along with the address of the prison and his
identification number. A guy locked up with Michael at Mt. Sterling
told him once that he had a girlfriend, and she had a friend who might
be interested in meeting someone. The girlfriend's friend's name was

Amelia. "My heart is searching," Michael wrote her. "I'm looking for a companion." He handed the letter to the guy who said he'd give it to his girl who would share it with Amelia. "If her friend don't want it, tell her to pass it on to another person," Michael said. He had no other way of finding connections in the outside world.

"Daddy's home!" his daughters shouted when Michael arrived.

The next morning, Michael borrowed a car and drove around East St. Louis to look for familiar sites. He didn't have a license. He'd never had one, not even before his arrest at age twenty. A ticket or accident and he'd come in contact with the law. Anything could happen. But he wanted to explore by himself. East St. Louis was nearly unrecognizable. The buildings, the highways, the streets, none of it was the same as in 1974. But Michael refused to look at a GPS or a map. He was supposed to know his hometown. Plus, he liked the feeling of sitting behind the wheel and guiding the car. He passed a police officer and waved. Then he started to see signposts that triggered memories. The way he came up Tenth Street and took a right on State. The block where Sears used to be, which was now a bank. The spot where the gym had been. Where the library once stood. He navigated by ghostly absences. He didn't try to find the Delisa Lounge, the tavern where he shot Richard Schaeffer. The lounge was gone, as was his aunt's house around the corner and nearly every other house on her block, each of them razed at some point and now gone to field. Driving on State Street, Michael passed a tattoo parlor, a pawnshop, churches, a mosque, the shuttered headquarters of a Black newspaper. The open businesses were few and far between, many of the buildings boarded up and crumbling. A stretch with a new Walgreen's, McDonald's, and Dollar General stood out like an oasis. When Michael was a kid, East St. Louis was home to seventy thousand people, already down from a peak of more than eighty thousand. There were now only eighteen thousand residents left. Michael's daughters and Joyce had joined the exodus. They lived in the surrounding suburbs.

Despite his precautions, word spread of Michael's arrival. That night he found himself at a fish fry in his honor. Most of his extended family was there. Nearly the entire clan on his mother's side. Cousins Michael never met leaned in next to him and snapped selfies. Older relatives, anyone who knew Michael's deceased mother, commented how much he looked like her. The same fair skin, the same doleful eyes. By visiting East St. Louis, Michael was introduced to his great-grandson. A woman pushed the small child toward Michael. "He's responsible for the name you got," she told her son, who was also named Michael and who stared blankly at Michael Henderson.

At the fish fry, Michael retreated to the kitchen. He needed space to process, to think. *Know everyone before they know you.* He tried to busy himself by cleaning a few dishes. But his mother's sisters shooed him out. He had no business cooking or cleaning when everyone was there to celebrate him. This was a day for his family to get to know him.

14

Institutional Interview

Early on a Wednesday, Johnnie was let out of his cell at Hill Correctional Center, and he started the walk to the prison's school building. He hadn't been there in some 250 days. There were still no classes. The barbershop next door was closed. Hill remained on lockdown. Across the country, the pandemic continued to rage. The previous day alone, 1,300 Americans had died from Covid-19, and the numbers were again climbing. Within weeks, the virus would be killing more than four thousand people in the United States each day. Johnnie passed a couple of friends on work assignments, guys he hadn't seen since before the quarantine. He barely recognized them. They'd grown long beards that hung from their faces like shrouds. Johnnie had changed some as well. He hated to admit it, but the lockdown, the lack of movement—"Covid weight." It was November 4, 2020, and after several months of coronavirus delays Johnnie was heading to his virtual interview with a member of the Illinois parole board.

He slept a total of three hours the previous night, probably less. He was on edge, of course. Whoever popped up on the video call would later report back to the full board in Springfield, sharing his or her first-hand impressions of Johnnie and offering a recommendation for or against parole. If the person who spoke face-to-face with Johnnie didn't trust him, couldn't recognize him as worthy of release, why would anyone else on the Prisoner Review Board? But that wasn't the main reason

Johnnie had stayed awake until dawn. The day before was Election Day. Johnnie was as gripped by the national drama of the presidential race between Trump and Biden as anyone. All night he watched in his cell as results trickled in. Johnnie was exclusively MSNBC, sticking with the network's data analyst Steve Kornacki, in his khakis, as he updated ballot counts in each critical district. Johnnie couldn't look away. Like much of the country, on either side of the political divide, he could no longer disentangle a sense of his own fate from that of Trump's. Johnnie's well-being, his mood, depended on the day's news. For him, the election was a referendum not only on Trump's demagoguery, on his abusive pronouncements, on his fictions, his attacks on just about every democratic norm. But it was somehow also tied to Johnnie's own parole chances. By four thirty in the morning, Biden had inched ahead in Wisconsin, had moved into striking distance in Georgia, North Carolina, and Pennsylvania. Johnnie finally turned off the television and shut his eyes, hoping it bode well for his own fortunes.

Johnnie and Sara Garber had spoken two days earlier, and they'd gone over last-minute preparations. Garber was on maternity leave, and in the preceding weeks she'd put limits on how many times Johnnie could contact her outside their scheduled attorney-client meetings. Otherwise, he wanted to phone or email every time he was struck by a new strategy or insight. She'd already crafted a 135-page argument for Johnnie's release and presented it to the parole board. She'd processed thousands of pages of court testimony, fifty years of imprisonment, an entire lifetime, and turned them into a cohesive narrative arguing for release. Every board member was sent a copy of the parole petition. It included twenty-one attached evidentiary documents. There were letters in support of Johnnie's parole from the Jewish Council on Urban Affairs, the Inner-City Muslim Action Network, the Chicago chapter of the National Lawyers Guild, the union in Chicago representing musicians, the Puerto Rican Cultural Center, and numerous other organizations. Johnnie had approached staff at the prison to write letters on his behalf. He asked the guards who supervised his mentorship program, who oversaw the health classes he taught, who thanked him daily for volunteering to bunk with men who were mentally ill. They all said no:

it was against regulations, as if the goal of a correctional facility in the United States were not to rehabilitate and try to return people to society.

But Johnnie did get a new slate of character letters from people locked up with him. One guy wrote, "Khalif is one of the men I can always count on positive feedback inspiration." Another explained that Johnnie went around to everyone on their wing, making sure no one jumped on or took advantage of his cellmate who had psychiatric problems. A third, from a fellow longtimer, described a day before the pandemic when Johnnie was playing baseball, how Johnnie stroked a line drive and shot around the bases. "I couldn't believe that he still had that much speed left in those legs of his, but he's turning second and the ball is on its way to third, and I just knew he was going to be out." Johnnie, already in his sixties, in full sprint, dove headfirst as if leaping through a ring of fire. Safe! The man had been in prison with Johnnie for a decade, but only then did he realize something about Johnnie's bid. "It was more than just doing one day at a time that he has made it all these years," he wrote. "That slide said, go all out for the things that you love, give your all in everything that you do, and most importantly, never give up."

At the school building, Johnnie was greeted by two staffers with masks on. They said there was going to be a delay. Johnnie needed to come back that afternoon. He had waited three years for this moment. Garber had read through fifteen thousand pages of court transcripts and carefully assembled a lengthy parole packet. But the Prisoner Review Board, just starting up again in the pandemic, had assigned Johnnie's case to one of its members only that morning. The person, whoever it was, requested an extra ninety minutes or so to scan Johnnie's extensive file.

JOHNNIE HAD NO clue which parole board member would interview him. Those on the Prisoner Review Board were assigned cases according to a rotation as well as their availability and geography—someone who lived in southern Illinois wasn't going to travel all the way to Stateville, in the northeastern corner of the state, to conduct what was called an institutional interview, and someone based in Chicago wasn't going to drive 350 miles downstate to Menard. But videoconferencing meant Johnnie could pull any of the current fourteen. Garber said Johnnie's chances of getting released, as slim as they were, depended on which board member picked up the assignment. He could luck into someone like Edith Crigler, a social worker from Chicago, who tended to focus on who a parole applicant was today. "It's been how many years now? Forty? What more can people do in prison?" Crigler had said at a hearing before the lockdown. Or he could bad luck into someone like Joseph Ruggiero, a former criminal prosecutor who had the look of an American eagle—penetrating dark eyes, a heavy black brow, a white widow's peak. Ruggiero usually felt deeply in his bones that granting parole would deprecate the seriousness of a terrible crime and promote disrespect for the law.

Johnnie could also get Pete Fisher, who proudly called himself a "victim's advocate." Aviva Futorian, in her role as a parole watcher, had urged the governor's office not to reappoint Fisher and another board member, writing, "Neither of them really believes in the concept of rehabilitation, which I believe should be the basis of granting parole. Whether reporting on a candidate or questioning the reporter, each of them focuses on the original crime rather than on what the candidate has accomplished during his 40 plus years of incarceration." In a recent parole hearing, after the momentum had tilted toward release, Fisher reminded his colleagues that innocent people had been murdered. "I want to give voice to that, because it's like, let's not forget about all the victims here."

But Johnnie could also be interviewed by Lisa Daniels, who at that same parole hearing responded to Fisher by saying the victims weren't being forgotten, that they were well represented and spoken for. Daniels was far from the most vocal board member. She sat silently through entire cases, or offered opinions with a restrained decorum, as she mentally calculated when or how to intercede without coming across as contentious. But in responding to Fisher, she sounded like a fist pounding the table. Daniels said, "We can't change what happened. What we can do is we can pick up the pieces and move forward. And that's just the place I live from." In that heightened state, she started to tell the story of her son. "I asked for leniency for the man that murdered my son! Because of the fact that I understood that if my son was still here, I would want somebody to see his humanity. I would want somebody to see the fact that he was a human being, and he did something terrible that day that cost him his life."

At a moment when Americans with divergent backgrounds and ideologies were rarely discussing anything together, let alone their different views, when they didn't necessarily imbibe the same versions of reality, parole deliberations could seem downright exceptional. The board in Illinois, for all its imperfections, included a broad spectrum of beliefs about public safety and punishment. Board members together tried to hash out an application of justice. Fisher was one of three men then on the Prisoner Review Board with a background in law enforcement. Daniels was one of four members with training in practices of restorative justice. The restorative justice process, an alternative to incarceration for many offenses, brings together offenders and victims in an effort to resolve conflicts and repair harm. It often involves dialogue and negotiation and some form of reparative act. Ideally, the harmed person feels heard, and even to some extent healed by the process, and the offender has to undertake some form of accountability.

Of course, not all people who commit crimes want to participate in a healing circle or a restorative dialogue, and not all victims of crimes feel safe enough to trust in the restorative justice process. But many do. Danielle Sered runs Common Justice, which works to heal violent conflicts between young adults in New York without relying on the carceral system. She reports that 90 percent of victims of violent crimes—the "harmed party," Common Justice calls them—when given the option between the criminal legal system and restorative justice chose Common Justice. Even though the "responsible party" didn't get sent to prison, those harmed by a crime didn't feel cheated. They didn't feel victimized again. They didn't feel the person who victimized them was getting away with something. They didn't feel deprived of justice. On the contrary, in studies of restorative justice practices, 80 to 90 percent of the victims ended up satisfied with the outcomes. And the process avoids all the personal and societal devastation caused by prisons.

At parole hearings I attended, I often watched as victims testified to their ongoing anguish and trauma even after the person who hurt them had spent forty or fifty years in prison. "This is our twenty-third time in thirty-six years, and it's grueling," I heard a woman say about her family's embroilment in the parole process. She said the long indeterminate sentence the parole candidate had received of up to 150 years "gave us the promise that we would have that release, that we would be able to focus on recovery—that elusive hope of healing. And we've never, ever, ever been able to get past that because we've been constantly forced to relive this horror." The families continued to demand more punishment, despite its unsatisfying returns, maybe because that was the only option presented to them.

Restorative justice appealed to Daniels because a long prison sentence for her son's shooter had also offered her nothing she could use. Denying someone else freedom was never going to make her feel better. "I don't believe that prison heals people; I believe prison harms people," she would say. Her most recent tattoo: "Repair the Harm." Daniels thought about how she wanted the man who shot her son Darren to be held accountable. Rather than prison, she wished he had been asked to step in and be a surrogate parent to Darren's children, taking them to football games. She'd rather he came over after a snowstorm and shoveled her walk.

Johnnie figured that if he got anyone from the board to interview him who backed Trump, they might be salty the day after the election. They might not be in the most merciful of moods. But the person he dreaded the most was Donald Shelton, the retired downstate police officer. When Shelton had interviewed him a few years earlier, it felt to Johnnie like an interrogation.

"If Shelton taught me nothing else," Johnnie said now, "he taught me to choose my words wisely."

WHEN JOHNNIE RETURNED to the school building later that Wednesday, he took a seat and stared at a blank monitor. The AV tray and camera were ten feet from him. A staffer said his institutional interview was ready to begin. The feed went live. The first person Johnnie saw on the screen was his lawyer. Garber sat in front of a brick wall and several framed prints. Johnnie saw Darlene, in her living room in Kansas, sporting flamingo-pink eyeglasses. And there was Poppy, Aaron Quincy, Johnnie's twenty-four-year-old grandson, bearded and heavy-lidded, enveloped in a white cable-knit sweater. I was late to join. I logged in from home, in the room I used as an office throughout the pandemic. Johnnie, who tended to see everything, sent me an email the next day commenting on my bookshelves. "Man how in the world did you amass so many books smile."

A parole board member appeared above the words "PRB SPRING-FIELD HEARING OFFICE." His camera showed him from the neck up. A white man in his midsixties, he was bald and bull-necked, with a ruddy complexion and tight-set eyes. Johnnie didn't know him by sight. Garber did, and her heart sank. Pete Fisher, the retired police officer from central Illinois.

"I like to start off with finding out how everybody's health is," Fisher said by way of introduction. He added that checking on one another's well-being was more important these past twelve months than ever. "Under the status of our pandemic, whether it be political or real."

Even at her most pessimistic, when Garber thought there was no way Johnnie would make parole, she hoped that the person conducting the institutional interview at least treated him with dignity and recognized his achievements. There was grace in that. *The pandemic being political or real?* Now she feared the worst.

Fisher looked down as he scrambled through Johnnie's paperwork. He asked how old Johnnie was.

"Sixty-eight in a couple of weeks," Johnnie announced. Fisher was still looking down, distracted. He searched for something in the case file. Twenty seconds passed.

"You've got several accomplishments you've made . . ." Fisher trailed off. He sighed loudly. "I usually have this organized." He explained that he saw Johnnie's parole petition for the first time only that morning. He wished he'd been given the case sooner. He didn't like going into an interview cold. Usually, he had time to distill two or three critical questions about a case's history, questions he formed after reading through the massive file, ones he felt hadn't been answered before or had been answered but falsely.

Garber stepped into the silence, directing Fisher to page fifteen, where she'd outlined Johnnie's accolades. And then she started listing them. Johnnie's classes and degrees, his music and mentoring. At trial, Garber had to remind herself to slow down when she spoke. Now she wanted Fisher to know everything Johnnie had managed to do in prison, so she talked even faster, trying to cram it in. Johnnie taught classes on HIV, hepatitis, and prison rape. Garber described how Johnnie helped design Project Sound Off, for men like him who were older with distant or no out dates.

"And there's more and more," Garber said after eight breathless minutes. "It just goes on and on." She said, "Johnnie is one hundred percent committed himself to helping others." Then, realizing Johnnie had said little so far, she asked him how he was able to turn his life around in prison.

Johnnie asked the staffers in the room if he could remove his mask. They nodded. Johnnie, ten feet from the camera, appeared distant and small, his facial features a blur. He had prepared for months for this interview. He wanted to talk about the educators who had come into the prison and saw something in him that he hadn't seen in himself. As debilitating as prison was, as punitive and mean, he had learned to love reading and knowledge. He became a teacher himself.

"I did not want to see myself like the older cats I saw in the institution steady doing the same thing when they first entered the institution twenty, thirty years later," Johnnie said. "So I had to make a choice on my own." He stared straight ahead, his shoulders and neck still. "My self-worth taught me that there is *value* to my life. There is value to what I *do*. So let me get focused."

Fisher wanted to take the interview in a different direction. He said board members had felt in the past that Johnnie was remorseful only up to a point because he wouldn't take responsibility for the crime. Fisher's voice was deep and unhurried, dispassionately self-assured. He said to Johnnie that when small children break something they instinctively deny it, even though adults know they're guilty. "You want them to admit it," Fisher said. He was giving Johnnie an opportunity to fess up after all these years. "You know, we're not holding a confessional here or anything like that," Fisher said. But maybe there was something Johnnie wanted him to relay to the rest of the board. "From your lips to their ears, okay? Might be something that they want to hear." Then he offered a possible scenario. Fisher had read that Johnnie was in a gang in 1970, when the two officers were killed. "Maybe you were trying to look like a big wheel, okay? You were seventeen years old, I do know that. At seventeen, we may want to look like the man. So maybe that's what happened."

Fisher grew up in East Peoria, Illinois, in the middle of the state, a land of corn and soybeans and the factories that made the tractors to work it. He was a police officer in his hometown for thirty years, retiring as deputy chief, and then worked five more years in a neighboring suburb as chief of police. Fisher didn't know a lot about the parole process at that point. But he was friends with a former sheriff who'd served on the Prisoner Review Board, and the opportunity intrigued him. He was used to arresting people, sending them to lockup, and now he would be able to see people at the other end of the criminal system after years in prison. "And so it kind of came full circle for me," he'd explain. Fisher readily admitted that his background in law enforcement shaped his thinking on the parole board. "I realize I'm probably a little prejudiced for police officers and on their behalf," he'd say. "I'm 'you kill a police officer, you're gonna do your time.'" And when that time was an indeterminate sentence of a hundred or hundreds of years, he believed the original sentencing judge was trying to tell the parole board something through the decades. "This guy sat in the trial, so he knows what happened. So he's sending us a message: 'Do not let this guy go.'"

Garber interjected, taking the question about a confession of guilt. She summarized the prosecution's case against Johnnie at trial. In the parole petition she had sent the board, Garber managed to make the fifty-year-old case seem new. She wrote that she'd finally got hold of lost court records and police reports. She was the first person to read through the entire trial transcript in a generation. She'd also obtained the original autopsies of the slain officers. Father Dennis Kendrick, the priest who baptized Johnnie as a child and later prematurely read him his last rites after Johnnie's throat was slit, had requested them on a whim at the Cook County Medical Examiner's Office. Kendrick showed the autopsy reports to a medical examiner he knew, who pointed out that the trajectory of the bullets that killed the two policemen came from a horizontal position, from ground level. Johnnie and Knights were said to be waiting with rifles in a bathroom in a vacant sixth-floor apartment. Garber found the architectural blueprints of that Cabrini-Green tower. The bathroom window in that unit didn't even present a clear view of the ball field that the two police officers were crossing when they were gunned down. Garber told Fisher, "So when you line up these few pieces of circumstantial evidence, they fall and they fall and they fall."

But Garber knew that traveling back in time to the months surrounding the 1970 shooting, to the original crime, was not a winning move. It distracted from who Johnnie was today—that he'd served more than fifty years with a phenomenal prison record. It gave the board members an excuse to dismiss the parole petition, saying it wasn't their job to retry a case.

"That's where we end up each and every time," Garber went on. "You can ask him all you want, and he should feel free to say whatever he wants, but that's where we are with this. And I'm just urging, you know, you and the board to consider whether this case could be looked at without that burden, that requirement that he accept responsibility." She pointed out that at Johnnie's last hearing, in 2018, board members said on the record that they would consider voting for him if he admitted guilt. That requirement was unfair, she said. It trapped Johnnie. The case against him was shoddy. They could spend all day dissecting it. But Johnnie was convicted on the theory of accountability as a teenager and had spent the last fifty years in prison. Those three facts alone—teenager, accomplice, fifty years—plus his superlative record in prison over the last quarter century, should be enough to grant him his release, period, end of story. "I've done so much work to try to show that actually there are reasons to be questioning this conviction, and not to make it about that. But simply, if the board is going to require that, if some of the board members, then they should look closely at that evidence."

IN THE PAROLE petition that Fisher was seeing for the first time that morning, Garber wrote that Johnnie, as a teenage member of a gang from Cabrini-Green, had been kept in prison over the decades because he had been cast, as she put it, "as a monster from a monstrous place." She wanted to demystify Cabrini-Green, to tell a fuller story of Chicago public housing than one of infamy and mayhem, and by doing so to portray Johnnie as less boogeyman than human being. I had written a book about Cabrini-Green. (When I first interviewed Garber at her law offices, I saw a copy of it on her bookshelf, next to the scales of justice and posters of Angela Davis and Assata Shakur.) She sent me a list of questions. *Can you provide a brief history of Cabrini-Green and what it looked like to live there in 1970?* She quoted my responses in the parole petition and included my complete answers as an exhibit at the end of the document.

Garber asked me also to detail what were by then years of reporting on parole and on Johnnie. *What has your research and investigation included? Have you been able to locate any new information that would shed light on this case?* After my last book came out, in 2018, a man named Ted Pearson, of the Chicago Alliance Against Racist and Political Repression, reached out to me. He and Johnnie had become close friends, and Pearson asked if I would look into "a case of wrongful conviction on which our organization is working." I started going to parole hearings in Springfield, and I ended up attending nearly every hearing since the start of 2019. I traveled to western Illinois and met with Johnnie—Khalif. I'd read the fifteen-thousand-page trial transcript, the appeals, the police reports, the prison file, the minutes from past parole rulings, and the numerous letters of protest and support. I'd interviewed Johnnie a hundred times. He called from prison once a week or as often as three times a day. I'd interviewed his codefendant, George Clifford Knights, as well as Johnnie's original lawyer, police officers, district attorneys, members of the parole board, associates of Johnnie's in and out of prison, and those who were at Cabrini-Green fifty years ago when the crime occurred. I'd spoken with experts on parole policy as well as parole candidates and commissioners from numerous states.

On the video call, I told Fisher about the spate of violence by and against police in Chicago around the time of Severin's and Rizzato's shootings. About a documented pattern and practice of police misconduct that matched what was claimed by Johnnie's trial attorneys. I tried to track down three teenage witnesses, friends of Johnnie's, who recanted their testimony against him at trial. Two of them were dead. I couldn't find the third, Paul Williams, who was thirteen or fourteen in 1970 and known as Leprechaun because of his size. But Darlene, Johnnie's fiancée, was also one of the hundred or so young people at Cabrini-Green who had been taken in for questioning. The day the officers were murdered, she saw Johnnie playing baseball with his friends. She wasn't with him when the shots were fired. She was in her apartment with a girlfriend, washing clothes by hand. The girls heard the rifle blasts, stood on the tub, and looked out the bathroom window. They could see two bodies in the distance, and Darlene phoned the operator, who connected her to the police. Later, when Darlene was questioned at a police station, she overheard Leprechaun's screams as he was being interrogated by officers and saw him as he exited with his face red and swollen. I found another man who, as a boy at Cabrini-Green, signed a statement against Johnnie and said he still had no idea what he signed. He explained to me, "They told me what to say. I was young at the time. I was scared. They were talking about giving me a boatload of time."

I had no sense what Fisher was thinking as I spoke. He didn't offer comments. But I thought he would know better than most how to assess a police investigation, whether it was done well or badly. Johnnie and Knights hadn't communicated in forever, and yet their stories to me never contradicted each other's. I told Fisher how I spoke with people who lived at Cabrini-Green at the time of the shooting, and they almost all said the same thing about the unlikelihood of Johnnie and Knights being coconspirators. "The janitor?" more than one person said, unprompted. They couldn't see the two of them holding a conversation, let alone plotting an assassination of police officers.

I ended by recounting my efforts to get a statement from Billy Dyson. He was the rival gang member, in 1970, who testified that Johnnie had cornered him soon after the shooting and sort of admitted to the crime. "See how the Stones do it? Let's see if you all can get three." Johnnie insisted he never said it. But Dyson's testimony was seized upon at trial, as well as in later appeals and in decades of ensuing parole hearings, as proof not only of Johnnie's guilt but his total depravity. In 2020, Dyson was in his sixties and was still around Chicago. I learned that he worked for the Illinois secretary of state, Jesse White, a stalwart of the Cabrini-

Green community whose Jesse White Tumblers, famed for their high-flying acrobatics, was made up largely of local kids. I wanted to ask Dyson a simple question about Johnnie's brag. Did Johnnie really say it? If Dyson answered no, I wanted to ask whether the police and prosecutors had told Dyson what to say. Did they write a statement and make him sign it? Was his testimony coerced? I figured that, fifty years later, Dyson would feel free to tell the truth.

But Dyson didn't want to speak with me. I described to Fisher my efforts to persuade Dyson. I called Jesse White's office and pestered his staffers. I wrote and phoned the church where Dyson was a deacon. I sent a letter to Dyson's home. I tried several intermediaries. I went to a memorial for a nine-year-old from Cabrini-Green, a victim of gun violence, his celebration of life taking place in the very same park that Severin and Rizzato were crossing when they were gunned down. I was told Dyson would show. People played softball and grilled late into the night. But no Dyson. He agreed at one point to a sit down with another old-time Cabrini-Green resident. Then, before the meeting, Dyson canceled. He eventually made it clear to me that there was no way he would talk about Johnnie Veal. He told one person I had call him on my behalf that those teenage years, when he was in a gang, had nothing to do with who he was today. Like most people, he'd grown up, the intervening decades had changed him. The same was true of Johnnie, as well as just about anyone who'd spent decades in prison. But Dyson could choose to keep the distant past from boxing in the rest of his life. He thought bringing up that past might hurt him professionally today. In the outside world, Johnnie was a ghost. It was easier to keep it that way. Garber quoted me in the parole petition: "It's noteworthy that when Dyson declined, he didn't say he stood by his testimony. He said he didn't want to get involved. He feared that the political nature of a case involving the murder of a police officer, even fifty years later, could harm his present position with Mr. White."

Unlike Johnnie, I had been on Zoom regularly for the past year. I tended to look down on video calls in exactly the shifty way Johnnie had trained himself to avoid. I glanced up at my computer screen. Fisher was chuckling. There was nothing funny or ludicrous about a former state's witness fearing blowback decades later. I told Fisher that he saw with his own eyes the police officers who still showed up by the bus-load at every one of Johnnie's parole hearings. He knew about the police message boards and the protests, as well as the continuing notoriety of the case. I repeated myself, only less clearly.

"Hang on. Hang on," Fisher said.

"You're cutting out, Ben," Garber said. It turned out my Wi-Fi was glitching, and as I prattled on, Fisher was still waiting to hear whether Dyson ever spoke to me.

He said, "We didn't get the most important part."

DARLENE, IN HER testimony, was much more direct. "He's the love of my life," she told Fisher. "He is a senior citizen. So am I. It's not much that we could do, but kind of just live a quiet life here." Aaron Quincy described the bond he shared with his grandfather. Johnnie had been locked up for Quincy's entire life, times two, but they spoke every day, Johnnie guiding him and imparting life lessons. Quincy rocked back and forth, overcome with emotion. "For a man to be behind bars for fifty years, to show another individual how to adapt in a world of society, to become a better person, that's big. That's big," he repeated. "I know my grandfather is a good man."

Fisher said he remembered seeing Johnnie's family at a clemency hearing a couple of years back. "They were pretty impressive, all of them." A psychology professor named Tara McCoy had joined the video call as well. She'd met Johnnie at the prison when he was selected among several long-termers to help facilitate a class she taught. McCoy said she'd also studied Johnnie as part of her research into personality psychology. "What I have looked at with Johnnie," she said, "is that based on who he is today, and his identity, and the way that he phrases his experiences, those all correspond with positive mental health outcomes, as well as community outcomes such as pro-social behavior."

After listening to all this, Fisher did have a question for Johnnie about his teenage years as a member of the Cobra Stones. It was a question drawn from his career as a police officer, one I hadn't thought to ask. He wanted to know what sort of firearms Johnnie had used. Johnnie was open about his past gang involvement, and he answered without hesitation.

"Shotguns and handguns," he said.

"A shotgun is different than a rifle. You know that?" Fisher said.

"Oh, yes, sir."

"Have you ever fired any kind of rifle?"

"No."

"I didn't think so," Fisher said. The weapon used in the murders of Severin and Rizzato was a rifle fired at long range. "This is not a weapon of choice for gangbangers," Fisher continued, more to himself than to Johnnie or any of us. Eighty minutes into the hearing, he seemed to be chewing over the prosecution's case against a seventeen-year-old, forcing himself to taste its different flavors. "I think I have more questions now than I did before I even picked up the file."

Fisher returned to Johnnie's innocence claim. He said he would have to report back to his peers at a full parole hearing, and he wanted to make sure he got Johnnie's statement right. So Johnnie's assertion was that he never made those boasts to Billy Dyson?

"Let me give you a quick history lesson between me and Mr. Dyson," Johnnie said. "We are not the best of friends." The camera was still too far away to capture Johnnie's facial expressions, but he sounded more like his confident self. He kept his eyes locked on the screen, as he'd practiced, and with his hands he emphasized each word with nimble chops. He said he and Dyson were enemies at Cabrini-Green, and Dyson started dating someone who lived in the same high-rise as Leora, the mother of Johnnie's two children. Johnnie and a friend caught him over there one day and roughed him up. Not long after that, Dyson was picked up for questioning about the murders of the two police officers. Johnnie could only assume that Dyson put the spotlight on him, either out of revenge or expediency or both. Better Johnnie than him. Johnnie found it baffling that Dyson's testimony was given such credibility. "I always asked myself, why would I talk to my nemesis, someone that I have no type of bond with, no type of ties, and make a statement like that?"

Fisher offered as a conclusion that he was impressed by Johnnie. "You've done a remarkable job when it comes to rehabilitation. I think that you should certainly be proud of yourself," he said. "You wanted to be rehabilitated, and then you go ahead and do it, and you have people supporting you and standing behind you and are there. That's a huge thing." It was the positive recognition that Garber had wanted for Johnnie.

Fisher said he was still wrestling with what accountability meant in this case. "I'm not the easiest person to *turn* on these things," he said. But he'd listened to Johnnie today. "I've been in law enforcement for thirty-five years. It's probably skewed my vision a little bit." He said this with pride, not apology. "However, I've also interviewed thousands of people in my career and heard millions of stories. So like I said, I have more questions now than I did before I sat down. And I'm going to see if I can get answers to the questions. I'll give you my word on that. I've heard some very interesting facts today. Not statements. I've heard *facts*."

15

Second Chances

Michael was working in the basement at St. Leonard's after lunch one day, helping a guy find a belt, when in walked Eddie Williams, his running partner from prison. The sound of Big Kane's joyous greeting pounded the ceiling in the little storeroom and ricocheted. He reminisced about running laps around the yard with Taboo. Michael wasn't totally surprised to see Williams. He'd taught Williams how to make extra money in prison, how to make a store by buying from the commissary and reselling items to people back on the cellblock. He also encouraged him to apply to St. Leonard's, to follow Michael there after he got out. Michael thrilled in showing his old friend how far he'd come in such a short time.

At St. Leonard's, Williams also came to benefit from the programming. He graduated from Road to Success and the other classes. Unlike Michael, though, he couldn't wait to get out of there. St. Leonard's advised him to take it slow. But Williams bounced with the energy of someone who had to get started now. He wanted to work. He was still wearing an electronic monitor, which meant he had to be home between the hours of 7:00 p.m. and 7:00 a.m. It didn't matter. He applied for jobs.

"I believe I'm going to get fifteen dollars an hour," the big man would announce, as if speaking it into existence. Williams was, by his nature, upbeat. "You get what you put in. I know it's coming. I've got a positive attitude. It's going to work out."

In Illinois, as in every U.S. state, laws make it harder for people like Williams to find employment. With a criminal conviction on his record, he was ineligible to receive many professional licenses and business contracts from the state. He was restricted from working as a civil servant, as well as in health care and education. He couldn't work in private security. He couldn't drive commercially—not for schools or the elderly or churches or even for Uber or Lyft. Other states ban people with felony convictions from jobs as real estate agents, as nurses, as physical therapists, as barbers and beauticians. People are barred from many public sector jobs. In Florida, those with past felonies face restrictions from 40 percent of the most common jobs. All the restrictions are on top of the countless ways employers discriminate against those with a criminal record, or even those they assume had a conviction on their record. Employers simply said the job was filled or never got back to candidates or fired them citing other reasons. The Prison Policy Initiative estimated that a quarter of the millions of formerly incarcerated people in the country were unemployed, a rate five times higher than the population as a whole. The Urban Institute found that more than half of the people released from prison were jobless in their first sixteen months out. St. Leonard's helped with some of those barriers, training residents and also connecting them with the Chicago Transit Authority, FedEx, and other local businesses looking to hire. But the halfway house could help only the few who secured a bed there. It didn't change policies and practices that systematically excluded returning citizens from the pay and dignity of work.

The certificates Williams earned in prison were of little or no value to employers. The jobs available to him were mostly low-wage and the least desired even by people without a criminal record. But Williams was strong and exuded a buoyancy that made employers believe him when he said he would work hard. A month after arriving at St. Leonard's, he applied for a janitorial job at a hospital and for a spot on the assembly line at a Ford Motor Company plant. Thirty-seven states, along with many cities and counties, had passed "ban the box" laws in recent years, legislation prohibiting employers from asking about a job candidate's criminal history before at least considering his or her other qualifications. In 2019, the U.S. Congress enacted the Fair Chance to Compete for Jobs Act, which did the same for those seeking employment with the federal government or with government contractors. Most employers still did a background check. Discrimination remained. A study by the sociologist Devah Pager looked at hundreds of applicants for jobs in the service industry, as delivery drivers and warehouse workers, with the applicants distinguishable by race and criminal record. She found that 5 percent of the Black applicants with a criminal record were called back, compared to 17 percent for whites. But Black people without a criminal record were called back only 14 percent of the time, a rate lower than even the white people *with* a criminal record. Pager wrote, "High levels of incarceration cast a shadow of criminality over all black men, implicating even those (in the majority) who have remained crime free."

Williams didn't hide his background; he disclosed his felony convictions and prison history. He heard back from the hospital first. He was hired. Williams accepted the job on the spot. Then the Ford plant called—he could start orientation the following Monday. Big Kane felt he'd already given his word to the hospital, so he told a woman from Ford's human resources that his schedule wouldn't permit him to start at this time.

His first day cleaning the hospital was a success. He worked hard buffing floors. He showed up the second day ready to work even harder. But he was summoned into an office. The hospital had conducted a background check before hiring him and knew about his history. As part of an automatic credit union registration, however, Williams's past was searched again. He'd been flagged by their system. Most laws meant to help the formerly incarcerated didn't protect them long-term. The hospital wanted to keep Williams on. He'd proven himself. But the rules were the rules. Nothing they could do. It didn't matter that he'd passed up the Ford job out of some sense of loyalty and commitment. They let him go.

Big Kane felt like he'd been kicked in the head by a horse. His knees buckled. He tried to convince himself that God, the earth, karma, whatever, were all moving in the right direction for him. Everything was going to work out. He called the Ford plant to see if there was any chance their offer was still available. No one picked up. He called fourteen times.

He sent six texts. The next day he dialed the number ten more times. On his twelfth call, just as the office was closing for the weekend, the same woman he spoke to before picked up. Yes, she remembered him.

"Did you straighten out your schedule?" she asked. Williams assured her he had. He said working for Ford was too great an opportunity to pass up. The assembly plant was on Chicago's distant South Side. Williams started orientation that Monday. The auto plant was "felon friendly"— his criminal history didn't exclude him. He was soon hired full-time. He worked ten-hour shifts, assembling Ford Explorers and Lincoln Aviators, never missing a day, never coming late. Whenever he had the chance at overtime, he grabbed it.

In prison, he and Michael had talked of self-sufficiency, of living honorably. Michael liked staying at St. Leonard's. He'd been going down to East St. Louis more regularly. Michael returned for Father's Day, taking the train. He went back for the Fourth of July and then for a family funeral. Michael got a driver's license, at sixty-seven, and bought a used Hyundai Elantra to make the trip to East St. Louis on his own. Then, when the steering column proved faulty, he got another Hyundai that worked fine. He and Joyce started wearing wedding bands again, referring to each other as husband and wife. On one of his weekend trips, Michael brought RJ along with him to meet his family. RJ gave Joyce a painting as a gift. Michael spent Christmas down there with Joyce and his three grown daughters. But he also enjoyed being able to return to his own place at St. Leonard's and to the community there.

Williams was different. He wanted a private space to himself. He had a twenty-two-year-old son he wanted to move in with him. Williams was earning a steady income, and he got an apartment in the southern suburbs, less than ten minutes from work. He moved in on March 1, 2020. Fourteen days later the plant and everything else in the country shut down because of the Covid pandemic. Unemployment didn't kick in for Williams for eight weeks. He waited, unsure about making rent. But karma or whatever was on his side. Eventually, he got backpay, and the assembly line reopened that June. Some people didn't come back. Twenty-five workers operated in close quarters in Williams's section of the line. But they wore masks and protective goggles and Big Kane was going to work.

The first time Williams had been able to keep up with Michael in prison, he ran alongside him around the yard for two continuous miles. Michael had praised him, saying his discipline had paid off. Williams was starting to take control of the parts of his life that were his own.

BY THE FALL of 2021, the United States was in the critical early stages of a correction. Mass incarceration stood at a crossroads. The number of people in state and federal prisons had crested twelve years earlier, at 1.6 million. The ACLU Campaign for Smart Justice, which set a goal of cutting the U.S. prison population by half, had launched in all fifty states. Almost every state had reduced its prison numbers. Yet the changes remained on the whole modest. There were still 1.2 million people in prison in America. An analysis by the Sentencing Project showed that half the states had seen prison declines of less than 10 percent. At current rates, the Campaign for Smart Justice goals wouldn't be met until 2078.

Reforms to parole were part of this nascent correction. Many states that had curtailed parole eligibility in the "get tough" years were re-thinking those decisions. Maine, the first state to eliminate parole, in 1976, was looking into reinstatement. Virginia, too, was debating a proposal to reverse truth-in-sentencing laws that did away with parole and required anyone convicted of a felony to serve at least 85 percent of a sentence. Vermont, in 2020, established presumptive parole—automatic release without a hearing—for anyone in prison convicted of a nonviolent offense who completed a minimum term without a major violation. Tennessee and a dozen other states also implemented pre-sumptive release in some form for those convicted of most nonviolent offenses. The default became ending a prison sentence, rather than ex-tending it. The parole board in Rhode Island added its first ever formerly incarcerated member. Louisiana passed a law giving people sentenced to thirty years or more a chance at parole after twenty years, so long as they were at least forty-five years old. After Illinois passed legislation in 2021 that made it possible for people in prison with a terminal illness to apply for early release, Iowa became the only state in the country without a compassionate release statute. In Mississippi, in the spring of

2021, the governor signed into law a bill that expanded parole eligibility to everyone imprisoned in the state, excepting those convicted of murder, granting a hearing after either ten or twenty-five years, depending on the severity of the offense. After signing the legislation, Tate Reeves, the Republican governor, explained his reasoning on Twitter: "A measured approach to 2nd chances is good—a knee-jerk reaction can harm public safety." A bill up for consideration in Massachusetts proposed giving the more than one thousand people with LWOP sentences a shot at parole after twenty-five years of incarceration. The legislation would exclude anyone convicted of multiple murders or deemed criminally insane, but for eligible parole candidates it would also mandate a restorative justice program "in order to develop a plan of reconciliation."

It was amid these various reforms that the Stateville debaters again tried to bring back parole in Illinois. In October 2021, a special session was called in the Illinois legislature, and it offered another opportunity to vote on an earned reentry bill. As written, the proposed law would give just about everyone in prison in the state who had served twenty consecutive years a chance to appear before the parole board. It would reestablish discretionary parole in Illinois and end life without parole sentences. A state representative and a state senator sponsored the legislation and introduced a revised version of the bill in their respective chambers. Sixteen representatives signed on as cosponsors. A dozen added their names to the bill in the senate. Parole Illinois secured endorsements from forty organizations, including the ACLU of Illinois and the League of Women Voters. Newspapers in and around Chicago published opinion pieces supporting the bill. "There is no parole in Illinois. I did not know that until Katrina Burlet told me," a columnist wrote in the *Sun-Times*. An Illinois political newsletter called *Capitol Fax* picked up the story and conducted an online poll: "Should Illinois reinstate parole?" Of the more than eight hundred who answered, 69 percent said yes.

At a rally in Chicago that October, local celebrities endorsed the expansion of parole. The musician and philanthropist Common belted out, "Illinois, what are we doing? Other states are granting parole." Chance the Rapper added that the proposed parole legislation "gives those facing long-term sentences . . . an opportunity to prove they are worthy of a second chance." A group of supporters in Parole Illinois T-shirts headed down to Springfield and gathered outside the capitol building as the lawmakers were in session. The bill had to make its way out of the Senate Criminal Law Committee to come up for a full vote. But Parole Illinois had already secured promises of support from twenty-eight senators; they would need to win only two more Democrats who said they were on the fence or undecided in the fifty-nine-member chamber. And they believed passage in the Senate would spur on the House, where they were also close to the necessary majority.

Burlet met with the chairman of the Criminal Law Committee, John Connor, a former prosecutor who represented a senate district about an hour west of Chicago that included Stateville. Connor, a Democrat, didn't want the bill to make it out of committee. He didn't think it would get the votes. But Connor and another Democratic colleague in the room hadn't yet agreed to support the legislation. By Burlet's count, their two votes were all that was necessary for the bill to pass. Burlet said here they were, three white, privileged people; this legislation didn't affect them or their families directly. And yet there were thousands of mostly Black and Latino men who would likely die in prison without the law's passage. They had the power at that very moment to do something transformational. They could give those in prison an opportunity to prove their worthiness for release.

Senator Connor mentioned several times to Burlet the danger, in supporting the legislation, of Republicans ginning up Willie Horton–style attack ads, the type that featured a Democrat's face next to the face of a person out on parole, or really out on any form of release, who went on to commit another crime. The following year was an election year, the 2022 midterms. Connor himself was running for circuit judge. Anyone who voted to reinstate parole could be accused of wanting to free violent criminals. Connor wouldn't budge. He didn't let the parole bill come up for a full senate vote. He said Parole Illinois should try again, possibly after the election in the fall of 2022.

Connor wasn't wrong about the likelihood of attack ads, although that wasn't a reason not to do the right thing. In the governor's race in Illinois the next year, the Republican in the general election accused the Democratic incumbent, J. B. Pritzker, of turning "the Illinois Prisoner

Review Board into a violent offender advocacy agency." The governor in Wisconsin was set upon by opponents for appointing a parole board chairman who had previously founded a group opposed to truth in sentencing. "His goal was to be soft on crime and to release criminals back into society." During the height of the Covid-19 pandemic, New Jersey governor Phil Murphy had approved a public health emergency plan that allowed 7,600 people to leave prison up to eight months before the end of their sentence. Of those released, some had previously been denied parole. A state assemblyman said, "Clearly, freeing criminals who were determined to still be dangerous was more important to Governor Murphy than the safety of law-abiding people, but what else is new."

When Joseph Dole got the news in Stateville that the earned-reentry bill had failed, he said the lawmakers didn't understand the urgency. According to data collected by the Covid Prison Project, the number of Covid-19 deaths among those locked up in U.S. prisons would soon top 2,900. In Illinois prisons, the number of staff who tested positive for coronavirus would surpass 12,500; the incarcerated, 28,000.

"Why don't you guys just wait till 2023," Dole said, mocking the suggestion to try again in the future. "I'm like, sure, and watch a couple hundred more of my friends and colleagues die in here."

Once when Michael was downstate in East St. Louis, a director from St. Leonard's called him. It was during the pandemic, and Michael was at Joyce's, outside in the yard, washing his car. On the phone with the halfway house's director, Michael was giddy as he described where he was and what he was doing. The scene was out of some TV show set in the suburbs, with Michael cast as the father character. The solidity of place, the bonds of family, the leisure of tending to one's own property. To think not long ago he was prisoner number C-10609.

After the call, the St. Leonard's director spotted RJ in the halls and asked if they were going to lose Michael. Michael had his loved ones in East St. Louis. He had a life there. Why would he come back to the dank basement crowded with used clothes, the surroundings of men who continued to carry the bonds of prison with them in their gaits and gazes and strident words? RJ was one of the residents at St. Leonard's who sanitized the facility each day. He told Michael about the director's question, and Michael later assured her that he wasn't going anywhere. He said he was needed at St. Leonard's. He also felt connected to Chicago. When his family talked about Chicago, all they thought of was the gun violence and the gangs they heard about. They wanted Michael out of there. But Michael saw the opportunity. The majesty and the beauty and the people. He had made a life there for himself. "I'm making two homes, one in Chicago and one in East St Louis," he would say.

Michael signed up for the construction class at St. Leonard's. He learned how to build and demolish an entire house—a miniature one. When the class was over, he started working for a man named Paul who bought an abandoned two-flat on Chicago's West Side. Paul, who was white and had been incarcerated himself, was living on the second floor during the renovation. Michael and someone else from St. Leonard's, a friend who went by the name Seven Day, were there twenty to thirty hours a week, painting, drywalling, restoring the woodwork on the hundred-year-old building. Michael found the labor therapeutic, even relaxing. But he was also picking up valuable skills. Michael, as usual, had an entrepreneurial angle. He asked Paul if he could rent the first-floor unit when it was completed. Paul was interested in buying other distressed properties in the area, and Michael wanted to work on those buildings as well, rehabbing them and maybe managing the future tenants in the predominantly Black neighborhood. His bigger goal was to get a home of his own. He wanted Paul to teach him what he needed to know about purchasing a fixer-upper and renovating it. "I don't want to be relying on nobody. I want my own," Michael said. He'd be able to bring Joyce into his world.

Michael worked weekdays on the West Side two-flat, and every Thursday or Friday he drove to East St. Louis to spend the weekend with his family. He returned to Chicago at the start of the week. "I haven't stopped since I've been out," he said of the pace of his life. "I'm enjoying it to the fullest." He usually traveled through the night, three hundred miles, eating candy to stay awake and making it in under four hours if he gunned it. On one drive, he fell asleep at the wheel and woke up in a ditch, the car still speeding along, tall grass whipping all around him, like he was in the forest. It was pitch black out, and Michael didn't know whether he was on the left or right side of the highway, but he floored the accelerator and the car rose up and reentered the roadway without crashing into anything. Another time he was pulled over going ninety-eight miles per hour. He was fined three hundred dollars, and he had to take a ninety-five-dollar driving class that would cost him an additional six hundred if he didn't complete it. He was given thirty hours of community service, but that last punishment wasn't a big deal. Most of his life at that point was community service.

One day after work on the West Side two-flat, Seven Day took off and Michael rested for a while on the front stoop. Three neighborhood kids and their dog played on the sidewalk in front of him. Michael waved to a couple across the street who were returning home. There was a vacant lot next door, and Paul had decorated it with potted flowers. "I'm a prime example that the second chance works," Michael mused, thinking about his time in prison. "Some of the guys inside have given up. And if it wasn't for me preparing for this day, I'd have probably been lost back there too."

He said he was just one person. He couldn't speak for anybody else. But Michael wasn't shy about giving advice. "All you have to do is become a thinker. You have to think for yourself." He believed you could alter your life by the way you thought, by how you looked at things, whether bad or good. Michael's car was in the shop, and he'd borrowed Joyce's. He was getting ready for the drive to East St. Louis. He said, "I have a lot to give, and I know where I fit and how I fit."

16

The Case of Johnnie Veal

Early one morning in Springfield, in a hotel five miles from the Illinois state capitol, Pete Fisher removed a face mask made to look like an American flag and announced the start of a parole hearing. "This is the case of Johnnie Veal, number C-01600." The room fell silent as the former police chief spoke. It was February 25, 2021, sixteen weeks after Fisher interviewed Johnnie—and three years since the Prisoner Review Board last denied Johnnie's parole. Because of the pandemic, the board was meeting in the Crowne Plaza Springfield, a fourteen-story establishment tucked away along the interstate and hemmed in by a Red Lobster, a Holiday Inn Express, and a Hooters. Social distancing at the Crowne Plaza was not a problem. That morning it was nearly empty of both visitors and staff. Of its twenty-nine other conference rooms, none was in use. The members of the parole board sat a minimum of six feet apart from one another, around a ring of tables fringed in bunting, in the hotel's largest ballroom. The parole board was down from fourteen commissioners to twelve. One had recently left to take a job at an Illinois prison. Another retired, receiving his full state pension, and later reapplied with the hopes that he might be reinstated and earn a salary as well. For Johnnie to be paroled, that meant at least seven of the twelve board members present would have to vote in his favor. Fisher joked that he wasn't too good at math, but by his count this was Johnnie's twenty-second attempt at parole. "He's never received a favorable vote," Fisher said. "His projected release date is May the twenty-fifth of 2071."

Fisher wore a dark pinstriped suit, a purple shirt, and a purple tie. He put on glasses and read from a document on his iPad. Johnnie's case file was stacked in front of him a foot high. Fisher spoke without interruptions for seventeen minutes, hurtling back in time and giving an account of the 1970 crime. "The cause of death of Sgt. Severin was a bullet wound of the liver, the path of which was reported to be downward. . . . According to the investigation, Veal's gang, the Black P. Stones, had planned the execution for several days." Fisher believed that several of his liberal colleagues, when they presented a case at a parole hearing, didn't give the full picture of an applicant's crime and record in prison. Fisher felt they placed too much emphasis on the positive things a candidate had done, ignoring the rest. The board reviewed dozens of parole cases each year, as well as thousands of clemency petitions and parole revocations. Fisher wanted to offer his fellow board members a refresher on the facts, at least as they were established by the prosecution at trial. He recounted how Johnnie showed his friends the vacant sixth-floor apartment, how ninety minutes after the shooting Johnnie told a rival gang member named Billy Dyson that he was lucky, because Johnnie had also held him in his rifle's scope. Johnnie had insisted that neither of those things were facts—that they hadn't happened. Fisher said, "Veal then told Dyson, 'See how the Stones do it. Let's see if you can get three of them,' in effect challenging a rival gang to shoot three police officers."

In the back half of the ballroom, rows of chairs were split into two separate sections, like at a wedding. On one side, pieces of paper taped to the chairs read "Behalf," and on the other "Protest." The people on the Behalf side were mostly Black and wore red or black T-shirts displaying the words "FREE JOHNNIE VEAL." (A niece of James Severin, appearing on a right-wing radio program, would later characterize what Johnnie's relatives had worn: "His entire family dressed in their gang affiliation.") On the Protest side, the visitors were mostly white men, and they wore police uniforms or street clothes with visible badges. In 2018, twenty-five uniformed police officers had shown up for Johnnie's hearing. Under Covid-19 protocols this year, the Prisoner Review

Board was forced to cap the total number of visitors at fifty and required people to register ahead of time. Sixteen police officers were in the Protest section that morning. Hunched in a chair in front of them, in a Blue Lives Matter face mask, was John Catanzara, the president of the Chicago chapter of the Fraternal Order of Police. Catanzara said that if not for the coronavirus he would have brought a hundred police officers with him to protest the release of a convicted cop killer. Catanzara, a vocal Trump supporter, had been elected to lead his union even though the Chicago Police Department had stripped him of his police powers for filing a false report against the police superintendent. He'd been charged with violating a number of other department rules as well, among them posting racist and incendiary remarks on social media, using excessive force, and engaging in partisan political activity while on duty. Catanzara had recently defended the January 6, 2021, insurrection. Trump supporters who denied the legitimacy of a presidential election that saw Biden win by seven million votes had attacked the U.S. Capitol Building with Congress in session. Catanzara said the worst crime that occurred that day, in his estimation, was trespassing. As far as blue lives mattering, the insurrection killed one Capitol police officer and led to the death of four others by suicide. Catanzara later apologized for his remark, even as he continued to make his own claims about a stolen presidential election. Moments before the start of Johnnie's hearing, Catanzara said there was a reason why an assault against a law officer was worse than one against an average citizen, and why the likes of Johnnie Veal should never go free. "We are the line between good and evil," he said. No one else but a police officer, he went on, was going to stop the person trying to kill a baby. No one else would get in front of a domestic or a bank robbery. "If we are attacked, then nobody is safe."

Fisher continued to read from his prepared remarks, describing his interview with Johnnie. He said he wished "Inmate Veal" had been closer to the camera, that he seemed a long way off, but overall he found Johnnie to be respectful and engaged. He praised Johnnie's accomplishments in prison. He talked about Johnnie taking care of mentally ill men, working as a mentor and peer educator, and designing a curriculum for lifers. Fisher said Johnnie had remained close with family and friends. That he had places to live if paroled, including with his fiancée in Kansas. As Fisher had promised during the prison interview, he related Johnnie's innocence claims. Fisher displayed little emotion as he read. "A lot of the interview was spent with attempts to relitigate the case, which is not the purpose or duty of this board." He said a court found Johnnie guilty, not of shooting the two police officers but of planning their executions. And yet Fisher offered that he now wondered whether the courts got it completely right. He said of his interview with Johnnie, "It did manage to again raise several questions and issues with this case."

Then Fisher came to the end of his prepared remarks. He asked if board members had any questions before they started to deliberate. He held off giving a recommendation to grant or deny parole.

WHILE FISHER PRESENTED Johnnie's case at the Crowne Plaza Springfield, Johnnie remained in his cell in Galesburg, Illinois. Galesburg was home to Knox College, which, in 1858, hosted one of the seven debates about slavery that year between Stephen Douglas (pro) and Abraham Lincoln (con), and it was the birthplace of the poet laureate Carl Sandburg. "Freedom is a habit / and a coat worn / some born to wear it / some never to know it." The prison's isolation rules because of Covid meant Johnnie couldn't make his way to the phones to call anyone for a parole update. He thought it better anyhow not to distract his people who were at the hearing. He wanted their minds focused on the battle in the room and whatever it required of them. He had an attorney call scheduled with Garber in the afternoon. Until then, all he could do was wait. So he watched MSNBC on his thirteen-inch television and let himself get lost in the news of the country. The Manhattan district attorney had got hold of Trump's tax returns. New Jersey legalized weed. Congressional Republicans were already condemning the stimulus checks that went out to people during the pandemic, the ones that reduced poverty in record numbers, calling them, along with other unemployment benefits and money for schools and vaccinations, a boondoggle. A 9/11-type commission was forming to investigate the January 6 attacks on the Capitol. Johnnie wondered, "How can you send me to the joint and prosecute us to the full extent of the law, and for treason and espionage you slap them on the wrist?"

Johnnie had waited years for this day. He was supposed to be in full action mode. And yet in the lead-up to his parole hearing he'd had to fly blind. Communication with the world outside was limited. No visits. Restricted phone use. Each email had to be approved by the Department of Corrections and took days. He found himself always playing catch-up. He wanted—needed—as many people at the hearing as possible, and for the past weeks he'd tried to reach his family, to fine-tune plans, to figure out who among his people would go to Springfield and who would break his heart. Johnnie's sister had health issues and wasn't able to attend. His son said he couldn't do it. Darlene had surgery. She'd scheduled the procedure back when it looked like the parole hearing would be remote, and she wasn't well enough to travel. Then, at the last minute, they scrambled to find her a plane ticket, but the only flights from Kansas had five-hour layovers in Dallas and would be too wearying. Johnnie told her not to worry. They'd missed Valentine's Day together. But he'd be home with her by Easter. Their plan was to get married within two weeks of his release, even if it meant missing out on a big wedding because of the coronavirus. "Nothing else will step between us again, so we doing it ASAP," Johnnie said. Maintaining the dream was important for both of them. Envision it, and it might come true.

Two of Johnnie's grandchildren said they'd be at the hearing to speak on his behalf. But then there was a cold snap, negative temperatures, and almost two feet of snow. Lawanda Starks, Little Peaches, wasn't sure her car could make it from Milwaukee, or if she could rent one, or if she wanted to drive with other people since she was a new mother and didn't like her baby being around anyone during the Covid pandemic. Aaron Quincy didn't know whether he could get off work from his job delivering packages for Amazon. It fell to Johnnie to find friends who could offer rides and arrange lodging. He had to ensure that Starks had a working cell phone. "A lot is riding on this, make sure your logistics is great," he'd say. Then in the middle of these efforts, the prison changed its phone system, and Johnnie suddenly couldn't reach anyone—his calls went straight to voice mail. The emails he sent weren't delivered—he later heard it might have been because of a new ban on emoji. It felt like everything was working against him. He needed to make real-time decisions, and he was trapped in the alternate universe of prison time.

Johnnie had recently started a twelve-week correspondence class called Aim Higher. It covered anger management, family dynamics, and cognitive behavioral therapy. He was several weeks into the lessons, and he certainly hoped he wouldn't get to finish the course. But it had been available and he couldn't sit idly. He was also one of seven people at his prison who volunteered to be a Covid vaccine ambassador, trying to convince the incarcerated population to take the shot that was then becoming available. Many people in the prison still weren't ready to trust their captors. They talked about the Tuskegee experiment, the government program started in the 1930s that infected Black men with syphilis and studied how the treatable disease killed them. And closer to home, men incarcerated at Stateville during World War II had been used as lab rats, exposed to malaria and treated with experimental drugs, in exchange for promises of time off their sentences. Johnnie was all for the Covid vaccine. He decided he would need to take either the Moderna or the Pfizer. That one-shot vaccine wasn't going to be strong enough for the kinds of viruses he was exposed to in prison.

Garber had been trying to lower Johnnie's expectations. In New York, the state parole board had recently voted to release a man named Herman Bell, a seventy-year-old former Black Panther and Black Liberation Army member who had been in prison since 1973 for the murder of two police officers. Carol Shapiro, a New York commissioner who voted to parole Bell, explained her vote: "He radically transformed his life, he was an older man, and I just didn't see any purpose in keeping somebody who worked so hard to change himself in prison. I think he was as remorseful as one could be." The political reprisals were swift. The police union described Bell as an "animal" and said he deserved the equivalent of a life without parole sentence. Democrats called for endless retribution as well. The governor at the time, Andrew Cuomo, condemned the parole decision, and New York City's mayor, Bill de Blasio, said, "Murdering a police officer in cold blood is a crime beyond the frontiers of rehabilitation or redemption." Shapiro soon resigned from the New York parole board because she didn't think the other commissioners believed people in prison who changed their lives deserved to go free. The parole board in Illinois had voted for release recently at a higher rate than at any time in the past thirty years. But a police case was a different matter. Garber said Johnnie had a chance to make parole. He could also get zero votes and a five-year deferment until his next hearing. Those were the two extremes. But she said there was also a gray area in between—a longer game. If he got even one vote this time, that would be progress, setting him up for future hearings.

Then Johnnie had gotten a ticket. His first in years. He snuck off to the phones, making a call when he was supposed to be somewhere else. "Driving on the wrong side of the highway," Johnnie called it. Nothing out of the ordinary. The COs didn't mind, especially since Johnnie was not someone they worried about. But a new correctional officer was assigned to Johnnie's wing that day—maybe because of how many guards had come down with Covid, or how many were calling in sick. He wrote Johnnie up. The infraction was minor. But it felt to Johnnie like the end of the world. He'd slipped. He gave the parole board another reason to say he wasn't rehabilitated and to deny him.

Johnnie told Garber and everyone else in his circle that they didn't have to worry about him. Win, lose, or draw, Johnnie said he knew how to get back up and continue to do what was necessary. "When the wind blows, I just try to keep standing," he said. He thought of it like surviving a bout with Covid. "I have seen so much tragedy and setbacks, I have built up an immune factor to it." It wasn't true, of course. He could feel depressed and defeated. But he didn't want anyone's pity. What he did want from his supporters was a promise that if the decision didn't break his way they would call Darlene as soon as possible since he couldn't. "She can't take the punches like me," he said. Darlene had invested so much into his parole chances. Johnnie worried how she'd respond to the disappointment of a setback. "It may shatter her."

AT THE HEARING in Springfield, Garber saw that there might be reasons for some optimism. Three years earlier, Findley had doomed Johnnie's already meager chances by talking about another Chicago police officer who'd been stationed at Cabrini-Green—Commander Paul Bauer was killed in the line of duty days before Johnnie's 2018 hearing. Johnnie, apparently, had some forever role in the perils of Chicago and Cabrini-Green. The morning of February 25, 2021, Cabrini-Green was again on Findley's mind. He brought with him to the hearing a copy of my book *High-Risers*. Garber took that as a good omen. Findley was at least contending with a fuller narrative about Johnnie and his home.

Then as the board members began to discuss Johnnie's case, Edith Crigler removed a bejeweled face mask, straightened a pair of red eyeglasses, and praised the lengthy parole petition that Garber had sent to each of them. Crigler was moved by the power of the storytelling.

"It almost reads like a novel," she said.

Crigler had been absent during Johnnie's 2018 hearing, and so didn't cast a vote, but she'd been on the board long enough to have voted against his release on other occasions. Now, she made clear, she was convinced to vote otherwise. "I'm not trying to try the case again. But there really are so many different things that don't hold up under close examination," Crigler told her colleagues. "For me, there's just too many discrepancies." Crigler felt that the punishment was at last enough. "And the fact that even if he did plan this, which I don't believe he did, he was arrested and convicted on accountability. He's been in jail over fifty years. . . . He has an excellent, in my opinion, institutional adjustment. And one of the strongest parole plans that I have seen in a long time."

Johnnie was going to get his first ever vote for parole. Progress. No matter the outcome, Garber would be able to tell Johnnie that. She started a mental tally. One vote for parole, zero against.

The next person to speak was Virginia Martinez. She was one of the board members Garber considered a must if Johnnie had any chance at seven votes. She was a conflicted no in 2018. Three more years had passed. Martinez would soon end her tenure on the Prisoner Review Board, stepping down, at the start of 2022, to write a series of children's books called Adventures with Abuela. At Johnnie's hearing in 2021, she said she'd been reading up on the science behind the Supreme Court's *Miller* ruling. There'd been a shift nationally on holding people accountable for the rest of their lives for crimes they'd committed as teenagers. Young people lacked impulse control; their brains weren't fully developed. Martinez said that Johnnie epitomized the *Miller* decision.

"As time went by, he grew up in prison," she asserted. "He has, in fact, shown that he has become rehabilitated." She wasn't committing to a yes vote. But she said she was prepared to take into consideration his growth and change in prison, to weigh that as part of her decision.

For Garber, the possibility of another vote felt like a win. Martinez recognized Johnnie's age at the time of the offense and all he'd done since. On the heels of Crigler's endorsement, momentum was building. Garber thought the impossible might be happening.

"Who else seeks recognition?" Findley asked from the center of the conjoined tables. The chairman waited for replies. But no one else sought recognition. The other members on the board were silent. Garber turned to Daniels, the board's most vocal proponent of second chances. Garber turned to one or two of the other board members who seemed like potential yeses. No one spoke. There was no momentum. Maybe it was the presence of the police officers. Or the politics of the high-profile case. Or maybe the rest of them still thought the crime beyond redemption.

A FEW WEEKS earlier, Kim Foxx, the Cook County state's attorney, sent a seventy-page letter to the members of the Prisoner Review Board detailing why her office continued to oppose Johnnie's release. The arguments against parole were mostly cribbed from a dozen similar protest letters sent by Foxx's predecessors, rehashing the crime with some colorful embellishments that without eyewitnesses or confessions or material evidence were largely speculative fiction. "Veal armed himself with a .30-30 Winchester rifle and Knights had a .30-30 Savage rifle," the two of them waiting and then *both* firing "a volley of shots." Johnnie was convicted by that office, in 1971, not of firing any shots but of helping to plan the attack. This year's letter referenced the rehabilitation clause of the state constitution, which stated that the purpose of a prison sentence was restoring someone to "useful citizenship." But it went on to say that "protecting society from a dangerous criminal must take precedence," asserting that Johnnie still posed a threat to the public. The protest letter went to great lengths to discredit Garber's parole petition as a desperate effort to relitigate evidence that was already decided at trial and confirmed on appeal. It called me out by name, since I was cited throughout the petition as an authority on Johnnie's case. How could Ben Austen claim any special insight "even though he was not on the jury and indeed is researching this case many years later"? During Foxx's tenure, her office had vacated over 175 past cases that were deemed wrongful convictions, correcting wrongs *years later* and doing so also without having attended the trials. That's exactly what research can do. "Mr. Austen's opinions on the credibility of witnesses are, quite frankly, irrelevant," the letter stated.

Kim Foxx was among a new wave of district attorneys who believed they could use the power of the top prosecutor's job to combat racial bias in the criminal legal system and reverse decades of excessive punishments perpetrated by previous DAs. Like Larry Krasner in Philadelphia, Rachael Rollins in Boston, and Chesa Boudin (the son of Kathy Boudin) in San Francisco, Foxx embraced the role of "progressive prosecutor," a title that to most still seemed an oxymoron. There were only a couple of dozen of them out of the 2,300 state's attorneys nationwide. Foxx was a former resident of Cabrini-Green herself and the first Black woman district attorney in Cook County. In her first five years on the job, she led an office that sought reduced or no charges for many low-level offenses, raised felony thresholds, and increased the number of defendants diverted away from prison and into drug treatment or counseling. Foxx supported both bail reform and the legalization of weed. These were the types of changes that Finland used to radically reduce its overreliance on incarceration.

On the day before Johnnie's parole hearing, in fact, Foxx decided to do something that she had been considering for a while. She announced that her office would no longer offer recommendations on parole cases, either to oppose or support release. She called the practice of state's attorneys weighing in with a recommendation a relic of the tough-on-crime past. She explained what was fact: current prosecutors had no new information on cases that were tried years before; no insight into how parole candidates had spent their time in prison, whether they were rehabilitated or remained—as she or one of her assistant district attorneys had written of Johnnie weeks before—"a dangerous criminal." Her office would still notify victims and provide factual materials, but beyond that, Foxx said, the Prisoner Review Board was much better positioned to make determinations about everything that had transpired since the case was presented at trial. The Los Angeles district attorney, George Gascón, another progressive, had recently established the same policy of ending parole recommendations. In Illinois, Findley said Foxx's decision was "well-reasoned," adding, "It is unnecessary for her to do more than speak to the crime itself." John Catanzara said Foxx wasn't doing her job. "We don't have a state's attorney," the head of the police union said.

When Garber was given an opportunity at the hearing to address the members of the parole board, she thought about the timing of Foxx's decision. Why did it have to come *after* the DA had opposed Johnnie's release and recommended that he not get another hearing for five years? Foxx's letter objecting to Johnnie's parole had closed by stating, "Veal has established a continued inability to abide by the rules of the Illinois Department of Corrections, even after all this time." It felt to Garber like another stroke of bad luck. She was already battling heartbreak. That morning, as she went over last-minute preparations in her hotel room, Garber got a call about Robert Jones, RJ, Michael Henderson's buddy. RJ was at a Walmart in Chicago the night before when he collapsed. He was taken to a hospital. He didn't survive. RJ was seventy-eight. Garber tried to remove RJ's death from her thoughts, to focus on Johnnie, but it felt connected.

"This crime is horrendous," Garber began. She sat at a table facing the board members. She was allotted only a couple of minutes to speak. "And the loss is immeasurable." She had been preparing what she wanted to say in this moment since Johnnie's last hearing in 2018. It was her final chance to try to convince any of the board members to vote in Johnnie's favor. Garber said that if all they were there to talk about was the crime, then they could end the hearing right now—there was nothing more to add. But she knew that the board believed in second chances. "That this board knows that people are more than the worst thing they've done or been accused of doing, even if that thing is horrible." Garber was trying to appeal to Daniels, who often used that exact line. Garber mentioned Martinez and her remarks about Johnnie growing up in prison and the sea change in thinking about adolescents who commit crimes. Garber

needed both of their votes. She talked about how Johnnie had entered
Stateville as a teenage member of a gang, and how over fifty-one years
he'd changed his life, how he now worked fiercely to change the lives of
others. Garber said Johnnie was unshaken by hopelessness and despair,
more proof that he was no danger to the public if released.

The police officers in the room stared straight ahead, refusing to
look Garber's way. One officer muttered several times, "Bullshit," saying
it like he was spitting out the actual thing. For those seated on either
side of the ballroom, the decision about Johnnie's parole was an obvious
one. The Behalf side knew who Johnnie was now. He was a stabilizing
force in their lives, a guide, a mentor. Starks got to address the board
members, and she said her grandfather called her all the time, checking
in on her, comforting her, pushing her to do better. "My grandad's voice
motivated me in so many ways," she said. The Behalf side had no doubt
it was long past time to let Johnnie go.

For the Protest folks, the calculation was no less certain: you're convicted of killing two police officers, whether as the actual shooter or the
one plotting the executions, and you never get to live free again. "This
man is a monster," James Severin's twenty-four-year-old great-niece said
of Johnnie during a break at the hearing. "No matter how many years
have passed, we can't forget what he did and why he's in jail and why he
needs to continue rotting the rest of his life in jail. There's no forgiving
that. There's no changing. He can't be a 'better person.'"

It was up to the board members to determine which of these perspectives won out. Fifty-one years of incarceration. Sixty-eight years
old. However the board members made up their minds, it wouldn't be
because those numbers were unusual. During this past half century of
mass incarceration, extremely long prison sentences in the United States
became part of the culture. Punishing to the full extent of the law when
the laws had shifted drastically, following the guidelines when those
guidelines had become aberrations, these obscured any honest and just
consideration of the costs and benefits of depriving people of their liberty for extensive periods of time. Many of the board members said that
Johnnie's case caused them consternation. They weren't sure what deserved the most weight. The original crime, the pain of the victims, the
time in prison, his rehabilitation, his age at the time of the offense, his

remorse or lack of it, the possibility of recidivism. Other variables must have also come into play—the fear of political consequences, the ire of the police, their own personal experiences and opinions.

Garber ended by mentioning RJ. She took a deep breath. The parole board had released RJ in 2018, after forty-one years of incarceration. Garber told the board that RJ had died the night before. He lived free after his parole for less than thirty months.

"He reminded me this morning that we cannot wait to do the right thing," she said. "We cannot wait, even until tomorrow. I'm asking that this board do the right thing by Johnnie Veal and grant him parole."

Jean Severin Cabel, the niece of James Severin, asked the board to do the right thing by her uncle and the families of the two slain police officers. Severin Cabel was sixty-four, and she'd been coming to parole hearings most of her adult life. "The bottom line is we show up," she announced to the parole board. "It's our family tradition to maintain the honor of two cops who were willing to step out of their squad car." Severin Cabel wore a replica of her uncle's Chicago Police Department badge on a chain around her neck. She now lived in Florida, and she'd made the trip, amid the pandemic, arriving that morning at the Crowne Plaza ballroom ninety minutes before the start of Johnnie's hearing, explaining that she was always the first to show, another demonstration of her vigilance. When Fisher again recounted the crimes, Severin Cabel wept. She did every time. But she said enduring the story of her uncle's death was the least she could do. He never had another chance to do anything. And why? Because he put on a police uniform and tried to help the Cabrini-Green community. The indeterminate sentences given Johnnie and Knights meant that Severin Cabel and her relatives had to mobilize year after year to protest their release. "We suffer, the victims' families are suffering. Please remember all this," she pleaded at the hearing.

Severin Cabel told the board that she was a scientist, a protein biochemist, and she reviewed the fifty-year-old autopsy reports and saw no discrepancies. She couldn't believe the facts of the case were being questioned after all these years. It seemed to her pathetic, but also part of a larger upheaval in the country. "Is it politics?" she demanded to know. "Is it the swing to the left and everything in its path gets to be rewritten?" She didn't specifically mention the protests after the murder of George Floyd, or the election of Joe Biden as president, or the removal of Confederate monuments, or the emergent efforts to address the racism and inequality deeply rooted in the country's institutions. But she said the world had been turned upside down. Law and order had become insults. There seemed to her to be more sympathy for a person convicted of murder than for a slain police officer. It seemed to her that political whims of the moment were being allowed to undo facts. It seemed to her that the very notions of right and wrong that held society together were suddenly up for grabs. Severin Cabel said Johnnie Veal at the time of the crime might have technically been a youth, but he was just shy of eighteen and a seasoned gang member. "This was not some child, an innocent child," she told the board.

She said that with everything going on in the country right now, much of the public wanted her and her relatives to feel ashamed for being a cop family. But they wouldn't. Many in law enforcement subscribed to a worldview in which humanity was divided mostly into two distinct categories, sheep and wolves, the defenseless and the merciless. Police officers constituted a third category: they were the sheepdogs, predators themselves, but ones who were righteous and necessary to guard against the violent wolves. Sgt. Severin's niece said, "We are very proud to be associated with the sheepdog that keeps the wolf from the door."

Crigler asked Chairman Findley if she could respond. With the microphone in hand, Crigler assured Severin Cabel that her opinions on this case didn't stem from an anti-police bias. Crigler said that she, too, was part of a proud police family. Her uncle, Sgt. Clifford Crigler, had been one of the few Black police officers stationed at Cabrini-Green at the same time as Severin and Rizzato. She knew about the walk-and-talk beat from him. Crigler's husband, who was now deceased, had also been a Chicago police officer. And now her son was a police officer. Addressing all of the police officers in the ballroom, Crigler said, "I want you to know that we respect what you do." She added pointedly, "When you show other people humanity." You could both love people working in law enforcement and recognize that policing needed to be reformed. Crigler said that she texted with her son every day before he went on duty. "I say, 'Be safe, and I love you.' And I'm saying to all of you all, 'Be safe, and we love you.'"

Shelton, a retired police officer himself, followed Crigler, weighing in for the first time that day. He had arrived hours before the hearing, in multi-pocket work gear, and crawled beneath the tables. A do-it-yourselfer in his sixties, he wired the room's sound system before readying himself by changing into a dark blue suit. He now said he wanted to explain why he was voting against Johnnie's release. (Garber updated her tally: one vote for parole, one against.) Shelton said he'd voted in the past to free a person who killed a police officer. "It was a painful decision for me," he added, but he was willing to do it. Not for Johnnie, though. Shelton said it happened each time the parole board convened: they declared they didn't want to retry a case, but then they heard information calling a conviction into question. That was retrying the case, he announced. Shelton was not infrequently guilty of it himself; no one on the board dug as deeply into a parole petitioner's past or the vicissitudes of an ancient trial than he did. His voice rose with indignation. Shelton saw no evidence to support Johnnie's innocence claim. "We keep drifting off into, 'There are all these reasons to think now that there's something wrong with the trial,' and we are *way* too far down the road to make decisions like that."

Fisher said he was ready to make his official motion. He agreed with Shelton, his colleague seated next to him, and he was recommending to deny parole. (One for, two against.) Fisher said the decision was a difficult one. He said Garber's parole packet was probably the best he'd ever seen. Fisher believed that Johnnie had found ways to live productively in prison and that Johnnie was no longer a threat to reoffend. Fisher wanted the rest of the board to see that portrait of Johnnie. The bottom line for him, though, was that he didn't learn anything new that fundamentally altered his understanding of the crime. The only thing that had changed, he said, was time. I later asked Fisher why the questions he had about the conviction weren't enough to make him reconsider Johnnie's guilt. He said he thought the police work and the prosecution from fifty years ago were "kind of messed up," but that didn't change his certainty that Johnnie was mixed up in the murders, just not in the way they were able to prove at trial. The details might be fuzzy, he believed, but the fact of Johnnie's guilt, for him, remained clear.

Fisher read his recommendation like a storyteller reaching the moral of a tale. "Considering all the facts of the case, and the accomplishments notwithstanding, being an old sheepdog myself, I personally am not yet able to support parole for Inmate Veal."

JOHNNIE WOULD LEARN what Fisher had said at the hearing. That after everything, after their interview, after the autobiography Johnnie wrote, after the extensive parole petition and Johnnie's long list of achievements, Fisher reverted to the same stock language used at every hearing, like they were transported back to 1988. "To grant parole would certainly deprecate the seriousness of this offense and would show disrespect for the law." Fisher had also added that Johnnie's conviction likely kept him from being murdered himself. "The life that he was leading outside of prison probably wouldn't have allowed him to live very long," Fisher had announced as he gave his recommendation to deny parole. "If you're a family member, that should console you a little bit."

When Johnnie heard that, he had to admit Fisher wasn't entirely wrong. So many of the kids Johnnie grew up with hadn't made it. His best friend Steve Jones had been killed in Darlene's Cabrini-Green doorway. And Timothy Walker. June. Hood. Chicken. Johnny B. Baby Frail. All dead. And Kokomo. Lonnell Gates. Lucius. Bonnie and Pudding Tate, sisters whom Johnnie ran track with. "My broken heart," he said. The list went on. Johnnie's brother Glen, older by a year, was murdered by someone who robbed him only months after Johnnie was taken into custody. At Cabrini-Green, Johnnie was marked for death. Guys were gunning for him. He had a giant X on his back. If one of the aims of incarceration was incapacitation, removing someone from the streets at the ages when they were most prone to violence, then in that respect, at least, Johnnie's bid did that. But he also knew that prison was way more dangerous than the streets. The outside seemed tame by comparison. Prison was a constant fight to stay alive. Twenty-four hours a day in harm's way, the risk and the trauma accumulating. There was no consolation in that.

Fisher had also said the only thing that had changed about Johnnie's case was time. But all that time had to count for something. Fifty-one years. Any benefits of incapacitation were long past. You could cut Johnnie's time in prison by more than half and he'd already have aged out of those wild years and been rehabilitated. Another twenty-five years on top of the twenty-five didn't deter crime. No one on the streets hesitated before pulling a trigger because Johnnie Veal was growing old in prison. What did endless incarceration accomplish? What more could Johnnie do? And the Severin and Rizzato families felt no more whole after fifty-one years than they had after twenty. They needed healing that the justice system and Johnnie's life or death in prison couldn't provide.

AT JOHNNIE'S PAROLE hearing, for all the buildup, the vote came suddenly. Craig Findley, the board chairman, was still thinking about Cabrini-Green. "Well—" He began to address the room and then paused, forming what he wanted to say. "Over the years, and to the dismay of my wife, I would occasionally drive through Cabrini-Green on our way to Cubs games." They lived in central Illinois, in a quiet town, and Cabrini-Green, Findley said, "was as foreign to me as anything." His words had a soothing quality, like a grandparent putting a child to bed. Findley was a former politician, newspaperman, and government official—the trips to Chicago were opportunities to gather new information. Once he joined the parole board, in 2001, and started to hear cases, many of which originated in places like Cabrini-Green, if not in Cabrini-Green itself, he had more reason to try to bridge the divide of incomprehension. "I would occasionally walk through the Cabrini project," he went on, "because I could never understand what it would be like to grow up as a child in that world. I could never understand what it would be like to be a police officer without a vest walking into that world every day not knowing if they would walk home at night." He had read Garber's petition carefully. He had read my book on Cabrini-Green. Findley could have elaborated as he had at Johnnie's 2018 hearing, repeating the testimony of police officers who had once worked at the public housing complex, or recounting the words of a Chicago police chief who said Johnnie, as a child, burned his older brother with a flare, or describing the interminable suffering of the Severin and Riz-zato families. He could have given an account of more recent assaults on police or of demands to defund policing more generally. But he chose not to.

"Whether Mr. Veal earns his parole or does not—and my position on this has been consistent through the years—this case will never be far out of my thoughts." Findley would not vote for Johnnie. (One vote for parole, three against.) But he had nothing more to add to try to sway his peers. That was a decision in itself. "Would you please take the roll," he instructed.

Martinez ended up voting in favor of Johnnie's parole; Ruggiero, the former criminal prosecutor, against. (Two to four.) Daniels had been subdued throughout the hearing, but she was for parole, and Wayne Dunn, the retired school guidance counselor with the heavy Southern accent, said Johnnie, with his fifty-one years of incarceration, many of them as a model prisoner, had done about all he could to make amends. He voted for release as well. (Four, four.) Another board member, whom Garber had deemed a toss-up, looked downward when his name was called, going into some internal place for what felt like five minutes. When he resurfaced, he uttered something inaudible. *What did he say?* He said no to Fisher's recommendation—meaning he approved parole. (Five to four.) A Republican, who was a former probation offi-cer and former counselor at a juvenile detention center, had asked Gar-ber to explain Johnnie's most recent disciplinary tickets. Johnnie had feared that this lapse would come back to haunt him. Here it was. Gar-ber described Johnnie's infraction, putting it in context. "He was using the phone during a break at work." The board member decided to vote to release Johnnie. (Six to four.) And so did the two remaining board members.

"There being eight affirmative votes," Findley said without fanfare, "parole is granted to Mr. Veal."

"Oh. My. Fucking. God," Garber was already saying before the last vote was counted. "Can you fucking believe this?"

"I feel so weak to my legs right now," Starks cried.

"He's coming home!" a friend who'd been mentored by Johnnie in prison bellowed.

Someone put a call in to Darlene, who started pacing her home in Kansas. "I'm just walking back and forth," she said. She didn't know what to do with herself. She and Johnnie were finally going to start a life together in earnest. It was hard to grasp the new reality. "I'm just walking back and forth."

Shelton, on his way out of the hearing for a short recess, stopped to offer Garber his praise. "You did a great job on the petition. You really did."

Findley, too, complimented her. "You were brilliant today."

Aviva Futorian, standing next to Garber, demurred. "I was prepared to tell you what you could do better for next year."

Garber, still stunned, shook her head. "I can't believe RJ is dead."

On the other side of the room, Jean Severin Cabel headed out, led by a phalanx of police officers. She felt like the vote had stolen something from her. Her entire adult life she'd been guarding against this moment. It was part of her purpose, a job she inherited from the generation before hers and one she was supposed to pass on as well. She believed she failed her family.

JOHNNIE WOULDN'T HEAR the outcome for hours. When Garber called him, Johnnie picked up the receiver of the prison phone steeling himself for the blow. He cried at the incredible news. He thought of everyone and everything he'd lost over fifty-one years. But soon he composed himself. Johnnie didn't like breaking down in front of anyone. Then the gears of his mind started to turn, the teeth catching, and he was contemplating the challenges ahead. He was back in what he called "battle mode." How would he live in the free world after so much time in prison? How would he find work and pay his bills? How would he need to reinvent himself again?

Parole Plans

Pete Fisher would tell me later that he knew even before the hearing started that Johnnie would make parole. He had no intel. What he had was a hunch. It was based on the progressive mood in the country, on the marches since the summer protesting abusive policing, on recent political elections and the mainstreaming of many criminal justice reforms. Fisher believed these disruptions were a bad thing. "We can't be so laxed with crime," he told me. But in retrospect, I was struck as well by Johnnie's timing. For more than a decade, the United States had chipped away at mass incarceration. In small and slightly larger ways, more people came to recognize that this country's fifty-year social experiment of increasing the prison population like never before, of locking up one in four of the world's incarcerated people, was a madness that had only come to seem normal. It was expensive and cruel, with little evidence that it made us safer and all sorts of proof that it destroyed generations and communities of people. By Johnnie's hearing, the U.S. prison population had fallen to 1990s levels, although it was still nowhere near what it was in the 1970s. The George Floyd protests, in beaming a light on deep structural inequities in the criminal system, seemed, at least for a time, to speed up the dismantling process. In my reporting for this book, I felt like I was witnessing these changes in real time. In interviews or at hearings or in legislation, I noted a shift, a general acceptance that even individuals convicted of violent crimes could change, that everyone deserved the possibility of a second chance. The opportunities for people to leave prison expanded. And I observed more and more parole applicants go free.

Looking back now, I can see that I wasn't reporting from inside a dismantling—it was more like a jag in a much longer story of punishment and prisons in this country. First steps lead to decarceration only if other steps follow. Johnnie's window of opportunity, in fact, was small. If his hearing had been just a few months later, there would have been no way he made parole. Johnnie's codefendant, George Clifford Knights, who was six years older, with no history of gang involvement and few disciplinary tickets in prison, had a hearing in 2022. He received two votes in favor of release. By then, the country was already being whiplashed by a tough-on-crime reversal. It was like a repeat of the years after Attica, the opportunities for real transformational change in this country being as rare as they are fleeting.

With violent crime higher in the second year of the Covid-19 pandemic, people in the United States stocked up on guns in record numbers, and Republicans leaned into a fevered vision of "American carnage." At a time when more white Americans were buying into theories of their racial "great replacement," the lock-'em-up alarms were again sounded. The George Floyd Justice in Policing Act died in the U.S. Senate. Chesa Boudin, San Francisco's progressive prosecutor, was ousted in a recall. In the two months leading up to the 2022 midterm elections, Republicans across the country ran more than a hundred thousand ads that drummed up fears of crime and cities, of Black and brown people, and of anything but unmerciful punishment. It was a jarring return to the politics and rhetoric of the 1980s and 1990s. One Wisconsin Democrat had supported an effort to cut the state prison population by half, which an attack ad explained "would mean releasing over 10,000 criminals right into our neighborhoods—10,000 reasons your family would be in more danger." *Our* neighborhoods, *your* family—these specters of dread imagined a class of victims that had nothing to do with protecting the communities and people most affected by crime.

At the same time, many Democrats distanced themselves from criminal justice reforms. "We should all agree the answer is not to defund the police," President Biden repeated in his first State of the Union. "It's to fund the police. Fund them. Fund them. Fund them with resources and training." In the last weeks of campaigning before the 2022 midterms, Democrats actually outspent Republicans on ads referencing the "police." If the less-disastrous-than-expected results of those midterms suggested a shrewd political strategy by Democrats, they didn't point to sound policy, to what was right or good for people. Spending on policing and prisons had never really dipped, and nationally it was still higher than the entire military budgets of all but two countries—China and the United States. There were still millions more caught up in the carceral system than in the 1970s, at the start of the mass incarceration era.

With the country seized again by a punitive backlash, all forms of early release from prison or jail were cast as existential threats, as if the very idea of a second chance was anathema to American values. Bail, electronic monitoring, clemency, probation, diversion programs, compassionate parole were all targeted. And discretionary parole came under attack as well. Parole reforms failed in New York and Virginia. The five members of the Oklahoma parole board who oversaw a mass commutation were removed and replaced by two retired district attorneys, a retired police officer, a former prison warden, and a retired federal probation officer. In Mississippi, a new parole board chairman was installed in 2022, a former project procurement manager with the oil giant Chevron, and release rates plummeted—in less than a year, the state prison population was up by roughly two thousand people.

In Illinois, the Prisoner Review Board was decimated. Johnnie's release, along with the parole of a couple of others, fueled a series of reprisals. "They are cold-blooded killers who should have never lived a free day after their conviction and sentence. These monsters are the true faces of evil," the Republican leader in the Illinois House, a former prosecutor named Jim Durkin, proclaimed. Not only was the Parole Illinois bill tabled, but Durkin proposed new legislation that would make it much harder for any of the dwindling C-Numbers to get released. Then the Illinois Senate refused to confirm appointments to the parole board. Republicans denounced the commissioners who'd voted for Johnnie as anti-victim and pro-criminal; most Democrats remained silent. A political ad slamming Illinois governor J. B. Pritzker featured Jean Severin Cabel . . . and Johnnie. "Jean Cabel is still incensed more than a year after the Illinois Prisoner Review Board released convicted cop killer Johnnie Veal. . . . Punish J. B. Pritzker for releasing a cop killer." State senators wouldn't renew the terms of others on the Prisoner Review Board. One board member submitted his resignation before a sure no vote. In 2022, the state parole board dropped to six members. Without a quorum, they couldn't hold hearings. Eventually new members were approved, ones who wouldn't be "laxed with crime."

Johnnie, when he saw his name dragged through the news again, lamented, "I look at this Willie Horton thing, and I see myself with that same poster tag on me about criminal justice. 'Don't parole this guy.' 'I should have been locked up the rest of my life.' 'Don't let criminals go free.' 'Get tough on crime.' I say, ain't this something. Déjà vu."

AT THE FIFTY-YEAR mark of mass incarceration, the country can't afford to pendulum back and forth in this way between reforms and punitive reprisals. Locked in that cycle, we ignore the extent to which our destructive practices around crime and punishment are recent creations of the decades after civil rights. This is not normal. This is not okay.

I'm more convinced now than ever that parole is central to a correction, to a change in the country's values. Reinstating parole and expanding eligibility are not *the* solutions to rolling back our devastating overreliance on imprisonment. The parole process is still arbitrary and subjective; it remains a contest between who can tell a better story, with the story of a past crime always starting in the lead. But parole does offer an essential release valve. It's a system of second chances that gives people in prison, and particularly those convicted of violent crimes and serving extreme sentences, an opportunity literally to be seen and heard. More parole would give hundreds of thousands of people a shot at being returned to useful citizenship. A parole consideration is a way to contend with their humanity in a legal system that too often ignores it. More broadly, it's also a way to question what incarceration is supposed to accomplish, and to see the ruthlessness and wastefulness in a process that denies our mutual responsibility.

Parole reforms have the potential as well to usher in a range of other necessary changes to the criminal legal system. Any expansion of discretionary parole would wind up repeating the mistakes of the last half century if conditions in prisons weren't also improved. There need to be effective educational and rehabilitative opportunities. A better carceral system focused not on vengeance and permanent punishment but on the possibility of everyone going home would begin to prepare people for their release from the first days of their incarceration. It would put in place effective ways to heal and protect those harmed by violent crimes. Such a system wouldn't work either if those released on supervision were set up to fail.

Other countries do all this without a system of discretionary parole, by holding people accountable while still valuing their humanity and caring for those hurt by crimes. And that's the ultimate goal here as well. More parole is not the point. Parole could be a pathway to radical change and its own obsolescence.

ON ONE OF Michael's trips to East St. Louis, he stayed with his second-oldest daughter, Corlette. Joyce and his children sometimes argued over who would host Michael, and at that point he was still alternating between their different homes. But he had to admit, he enjoyed staying at Corlette's. For starters, she was a good cook. Michael was particular, too, about how he liked a house kept. Ever since juvie, when the guards made him bounce dimes off his bed, Michael had been meticulous. If all he had was a few square feet in which to sleep and eat and shit, he was going to make that space pristine. Now that he was out, he couldn't abide dishes in the sink or dust on the windowsills. Corlette shared Michael's need for order.

Michael brought his running gear with him, and he woke early the next morning to get in some laps. It was dark still, and Corlette drove him to a city park. Michael stretched, as he always did, and then he started around the path. On one side of the running trail was a baseball field, and on the other a street with clapboard houses. Michael began behind home plate. He passed a dugout, turned before a fire station, and jogged around the outfield and a scoreboard. He tired faster these days, but he enjoyed being back in the rhythm of running, the discipline of it, the structure. He could lose himself in a run, enabling his mind to roam. Corlette, who was in her fifties now, stuck around. She told her father she wanted to get in better shape. She walked around the field as Michael jogged.

Michael rounded the park, sidling up to his daughter every few minutes. They traded playful barbs. Michael liked to mess with Corlette about her habit of taking selfies, calling her vain. She teased him, too, for being short or for not calling more when he was back in Chicago. Then Michael continued on. Up Third Street, around the fire station and the outfield again, down Second Street, until he caught back up to his daughter. It continued like that. He ran. They walked for a spell. He ran some more.

When Michael thought about the process he'd been through, coming up before the Prisoner Review Board for thirty-five years, he believed everyone in prison should have the possibility of a second chance. He didn't think the parole board should let everyone out. Prison hadn't turned Michael into an abolitionist. He knew guys inside who seemed to find pleasure in hurting others. Maybe the conditions in prison had cultivated the worst in them; people forced to live as if they were less than human might end up acting that way. But they were also the ones who had made Michael's bid harder. Still, parole could give even them a reason to do better. They might find a higher purpose to their prison time.

Michael wouldn't wish his experience on anyone. He'd made choices, bad ones, and he'd given most of his life to repay them. Forty-six years in prison. No one needed that. Whatever the point of incarceration, it had, for him, been achieved long ago. Locking him up for five decades served no just purpose. Michael wasn't one to wallow in regrets, in what could have been, and he stopped his family when they went down that path. But he couldn't ignore his time in prison either. He couldn't forget it. To do so would be to deny his own existence. To not consider how prisons and punishment had defined the past half century. He knew there was no point to that much time locked up. But he talked about his journey so the next years might be different.

After thirty minutes of jogging, Michael stayed with Corlette longer before beginning another lap. He lingered, acting like it was for her benefit, to walk together so they could catch up. But the truth was he also needed the rest. They strolled a quarter of the way around the field, and then he trotted off. In prison, Michael ran ten miles a day, on average, for more than twenty years. What was that? A hundred thousand miles? More? Running alone in prison, he often envisioned a day like this one. His family with him as he jogged, the freedom of movement and their company. He tried to recall if he'd seen an image like that in a movie or on television. A father jogging and enjoying a morning with his daughter. But the experience was his own. Here he was living it.

ON MAY 7, 2021, Johnnie stood in the lobby of a small Galesburg hotel, thanking his family and friends who had helped him outlast his incarceration. Johnnie's sister, his son, his grandchildren, his great-grandchildren, and a dozen other relatives and supporters filled the space next to the reception desk, a nook that included little more than a few tables and a microwave. "I am blessed," Johnnie said. "I have a team. I have a family, and I got a generation that knows nothing about me. I got to take the time to educate them about me and my dos and don'ts, my approaches in life, my focus."

Johnnie had been out of prison for less than an hour, and he was giving a speech that he had practiced in his head for years. Even at this moment, sentimentality was not his thing, and Johnnie started calling out the family members who, in his estimation, forgot about him, the ones who wrote him off as a double murderer or a lost cause. "I forgive you for all the shortcomings that you didn't do," he said. "I cannot carry that baggage into my future. I cannot carry disappointment into my future."

Johnnie wore a mustard-colored shirt with a collar like a paper airplane and baggy pants a couple of sizes too large. Earlier that morning, two of his friends at Hill Correctional Center, Mousy and Ty Brown from Texas, had picked the outfit for him to wear. Johnnie hadn't worn street clothes in a half century, and he didn't know his sizes. He changed out of his prison uniform. "How I look?" he asked. "You look fly," Ty Brown assured him. Johnnie walked out the prison gates a free man, and his family, cheering, lined up to be photographed with him. "We're not on prison time anymore!" his son roared. Bumpy was fifty, and he'd lived his entire life without a father on the outside. The two of them had never been close. But the day represented a fresh start. Bumpy presented his dad with a watch to make this point about the shift. "We on family time!" he yelled. Others teased Johnnie: "Who dressed you? You look torn up."

Johnnie's granddaughter drove him from the prison to the hotel, the others following in a caravan. Johnnie told her to stop the car right away, to pull over. He leaned out and vomited. Johnnie had been still so long that thirty miles per hour was warp speed. Johnnie was paroled on February 25, 2021, but he remained in prison until that morning in May. After the board voted to release Johnnie, he was informed that it would take up to forty-five days to complete the paperwork and processing for him to go to Darlene in Kansas. He could go somewhere in Illinois and leave prison within days, but once he was out it would be harder to secure an interstate compact. Johnnie had spent the last eighteen thousand days in prison. He was ready to burst. With every additional hour in a cell, he was at the mercy of guards and any of the other men locked up at Hill. His freedom could be snatched from him in any number of ways, and he was more likely to catch Covid and die from it. But Johnnie decided to wait.

The Kansas Department of Corrections approved his transfer. A parole officer spoke to Darlene, saying that Johnnie could take two days to travel by train from Illinois. If he was released from prison on a Thursday or Friday, he wouldn't have to check in to register in Kansas until the following Monday. He and Darlene could have the weekend to themselves. After forty-five days, however, the Illinois Department of Corrections rejected Johnnie's move. The prison system said Johnnie couldn't be paroled to Darlene's because they weren't married. It made no sense. If that was the policy, why not tell him seven weeks earlier? He and Darlene would have married immediately. And they were planning to wed as soon as he got there. Why not let them? So in May, after Johnnie's reunion with his family at the Galesburg hotel, after a meal together at a Chinese buffet, after a first dance with his granddaughter, Johnnie would go live by himself in a two-hundred-square-foot one-bedroom in an industrial suburb north of Chicago.

In the coming months, Johnnie landed a job as a machine attendant, the overnight shift, manufacturing plastic tops for eighteen dollars an hour, nineteen dollars after his first raise. He lost that job but eventually found another one manufacturing plastics. He paid taxes for the first time. He volunteered with a ministry of churches called Love INC, delivering donated household goods and furniture to people in the area in need. He got permission from his parole officer to visit Darlene in Kansas, Johnnie's first time on a plane. He helped pack up her place, and she moved to the Chicago area to be with him. They were married in an online ceremony, kissing right before their internet connection stalled. That year, his son, Bumpy, died of a drug overdose. Friends of Johnnie's from prison died as well.

Johnnie wasn't always sure what about him was institutional behavior and what were his own predilections. His entire adult life up to then the two were never separate. He stocked his first apartment with walls of food, bricking up the refrigerator and freezer with chicken cutlets and steaks, filling the cabinets and whatever space existed on top of them with canned goods and pastas and juice. It was as if he couldn't trust there would ever be more. His bedroom was only two steps away, but he bought a second fridge for the six-by-eight space, like he was re-creating a prison cell. He sometimes slipped up and called Darlene his cellie, and he couldn't help himself, he fully dressed the moment he hopped out of bed, readying himself for any situation, even though it made Darlene feel like they couldn't relax. They moved into a better apartment, and then a better one after that. He had to figure out Wi-Fi and credit scores and Zelle and Sam's Club and public transportation. He voted for the first time. Darlene, furious at the Republicans' deceptions, particularly about Johnnie, got them to the polls the moment they opened. "It felt good that my vote contributed to silencing the BS politics of the day . . . smile," Johnnie texted. Nothing about his life resembled the five-alarm myth of the cop killer on the loose.

In the very first hours after Johnnie's release, while he was still at the little Galesburg hotel near the prison, he delivered a warning to his family. He wouldn't let them jeopardize the rest of his life. "Don't get around me if you living follies. If you into dumb stuff, if you're not on my page, miss me." He promised that he was going to be there for each and every one of them, but they couldn't just show up. "If you don't got my phone number, it's a reason you don't have it." And when they were together, they better come correct. "I will hurt your feelings, and I'll make you cry, but I love you."

That was also part of the speech Johnnie had been preparing for years. That was the message he wanted to convey. They were all family, but there had to be rules going forward. People were expecting Johnnie to fall down and fail. St. Leonard's had rejected his application, he guessed because his case was still too political. He told his family, "I got the Fraternal Order of Police and everybody else breathing down my neck, talking about, 'Where am I going?' 'What am I doing?'" These unseen attackers were convinced that he had vices, that his true nature as a felon would emerge. They wanted to catch him in a parole violation. Johnnie was certain of it. He told his loved ones that he had no margin for error. He couldn't make even a single mistake. If he slipped up or did something stupid, he would go back to the joint and die there. He was free for now, but not enough had changed. Did they hear him? Did they understand?

"I'm still fighting for my life."

ACKNOWLEDGMENTS

I want to thank above all everyone who spoke to me for this book, who shared their stories and ideas and answered my numerous questions. There are too many people to name here. Most of them are featured prominently in the preceding pages; others are not. Some talked to me at length even though we didn't agree about critical aspects of the criminal system. I am indebted to them all. This work of nonfiction would literally not be possible without the cooperation and trust of so many. As a reporter and writer and fellow human being, I try never to take that exchange for granted.

I am grateful to others who played pivotal roles in the long process of making this book. Ted Pearson of the Chicago Alliance Against Racist and Political Repression wrote an email imploring me to look into Johnnie Veal's—Khalif's—case. Maya Dukmasova, a friend who has written incisively about parole and criminal justice, passed along that note. The incomparable Mary Schmich, who featured the Severin family in one of her *Tribune* columns, provided early guidance. Sara Garber generously shared her time and resources—and also led to my meeting Michael Henderson. Bill Healy has been an invaluable partner in the reporting, understanding, and telling of this story. I'm thankful to the board members and staff of the Illinois Prisoner Review Board. And to Parole Illinois members, both inside and outside prison, who talked extensively with me about their campaign to get parole eligibility reinstated for all incarcerated people in the state. Erisa Apantaku, Natalie Frazier, Elaina Katz, and Heena Srivastava assisted with research. The talented Kelly Hui stepped in to fact-check and improved the book in countless ways.

What a gift to have friends read parts of this book as I was drafting them. Khalil Gibran Muhammad read the entire manuscript, offering suggestions as well as his vast knowledge of the criminal justice system; he also talked regularly with me about these important issues, often on the podcast that we host together, *Some of My Best Friends Are. . . .* My other best friend, Sascha Penn, steered me clear of a failed first chapter and then stuck with me, as he always does, every step of the way. I can't thank Audrey Petty enough for our morning coffee "writers' club." Adam Ross and Alex Kotlowitz each read early chapters and then continued to share their writerly genius. Michael Fischer's careful read of the entire manuscript was invaluable. Thank you, also, to my friend and longtime editor at the *New York Times Magazine*, Claire Gutierrez; to my sister, Jacqueline Stewart; to my mother-in-law and close reader, Carol House; to Lisa Lee; to my colleagues in the University of Chicago Creative Writing Program; and to Jon Lowenstein for his photography and kinship. I am deeply grateful to be part of the Prison + Neighborhood Arts/Education Project—and for all I learn from the students at Stateville and from my fellow instructors. A special thanks as well to the friends and family who kept me company and kept me sane over these past four or five years.

I received a reporting grant for this book from the Fund for Investigative Journalism, and assistance from the Jeff Metcalf Internship Program at the University of Chicago's Careers in Journalism and Creative Writing. As a senior fellow at the Invisible Institute, I was given financial support, as well as all kinds of collegial support, particularly from Jamie Kalven, Alison Flowers, Maira Khwaja, and Andrew Fan. I am extremely thankful that Impact Justice included me on its trip to visit prisons in Finland and Norway, and I owe a debt to each of the criminal justice experts from the United States who were also a part of that journey—every one of them taught me a ton.

That I have Chris Parris-Lamb as my literary agent still feels like a coup. He has had my back for more than a decade; he's a trusted reader, sounding board, and friend. I'm grateful to Sarah Bolling, Joy Fowlkes, and everyone else at the Gernert Company. I was immensely fortunate to end up with such a brilliant editor in Nadxieli Nieto. I've relied on her encouragement, guidance, and wisdom. Kukuwa Ashun and the entire team at Flatiron have been amazing. Sarah Murphy and Meghan Houser believed in this book and helped breathe life into it.

I have been reminded time and again while working on this project how profoundly fortunate I am. *How could I not?* To have my liberty. To have my health. To have such a loving family. This book is dedicated to them. Danielle, my wife and my partner since forever; our phenomenal children, Lusia and Jonah. My parents, Ernestine and Ralph. My brother, Jake.

BIBLIOGRAPHY AND NOTES ON SOURCES

This is a work of nonfiction. It's based on hundreds of interviews and more than four years of reporting and research. I attended nearly every parole hearing held by the Illinois Prisoner Review Board from the start of 2019 to the fall of 2022, some of them remotely during the Covid-19 pandemic. I visited prisons, halfway houses, and clemency hearings. I witnessed many of the events depicted in these pages.

In retelling the prison and parole sagas of Johnnie/Khalif Veal and Michael Henderson, I interviewed the two of them more than a hundred times. I spoke to their friends, family members, and lawyers, to people who knew them in and out of prison, to parole board members, police officers, public officials, and those who either championed or vehemently opposed their release. I was also like Donald Shelton, the parole commissioner whose tireless research into each case I describe in the book. I, too, combed through the thick accordion files, filled with fifty years of documents, that the Prisoner Review Board kept on Michael and Johnnie/Khalif. I read ancient police reports, prison records, the minutes of past parole hearings, and numerous letters of protest and support. I learned more about their criminal cases from trial transcripts, appeals, and writs of habeas corpus. The parole petitions their lawyers submitted included detailed accounts of their achievements in prison. Additionally, the stories of their crimes and punishments played out, to different extents, in the news and in public. I'm thankful to Bill Healy, once again, for tracking down files on Johnnie Veal in the Chicago History Museum's "Red Squad" collection, the undestroyed records, mostly from 1963 to 1974, of the Chicago Police Department's surveillance of alleged "subversives."

Because parole, at the back end of the criminal system, is the result of every decision and policy choice that precedes it, this book is also a history of American prisons, of sentencing laws and mass incarceration. In order to tell that expansive story, I interviewed parole candidates and parole commissioners from different states. I spoke with lawyers and nonprofits dedicated to assisting parole applicants at their hearings. I talked to policy experts, lawmakers, organizers, lobbyists, victims and their advocates, and restorative justice practitioners. I spent time with members of Parole Illinois, both inside and outside prison. I had the great fortune of visiting prisons in Finland and Norway with the nonprofit Impact Justice, meeting in these countries with incarcerated people, guards, wardens, and government and nongovernmental officials who drafted national carceral policies.

A couple of other notes. Unless otherwise indicated, I used the Bureau of Justice Statistics for prison, parole, and probation figures. I learned more about David Fogel from a collection of his papers held at the University of Illinois Chicago. I'd also be negligent if I didn't mention several other organizations whose work on criminal justice issues I found instructive and guiding: Illinois Prison Project, Injustice Watch, John Howard Association (and Aviva Futorian's parole watching!), Louisiana Parole Project, The Marshall Project, Parole Preparation Project, Prison + Neighborhood Arts/Education Project, Prison Policy Initiative, Restore Justice, Robina Institute of Criminal Law and Criminal Justice, the Sentencing Project, Square One Project, UnCommon Law, Vera Institute of Justice, and others I'm surely forgetting.

I benefitted greatly from the generosity of many journalists, researchers, academics, practitioners, and people impacted by the criminal system. If someone exploring these issues would like to know more about my research to advance their own work, I'd be happy to pay that generosity forward.

* * *

The following published sources were especially useful in the writing of this book:

Abrahamson, Shirley S. "Redefining Roles: The Victims' Rights Movement." *Utah Law Review* 3 (1985): 517–67.

Alexander, Michelle. *The New Jim Crow: Mass Incarceration in the Age of Colorblindness.* New York: New Press, 2010.

Allen, Danielle S. *Cuz: The Life and Times of Michael A.* New York: Liveright, 2017.

American Friends Service Committee. *Struggle for Justice: A Report on Crime and Punishment in America.* New York: Hill & Wang, 1971.

Aviram, Hadar. *Yesterday's Monsters: The Manson Family Cases and the Illusion of Parole.* Oakland: University of California Press, 2020.

Bazelon, Emily. *Charged: The New Movement to Transform American Prosecution and End Mass Incarceration.* New York: Random House, 2019.

Brockway, Zebulon R. *Fifty Years of Prison Service: An Autobiography.* New York: Charities Publication Committee, 1912.

Callaway, John D. "Father James G. Jones: A Pilgrim's Progress." *Chicago Scene,* January 1963.

Carrington, Frank. *The Victims.* New Rochelle, NY: Arlington House, 1975.

Carrington, Frank, and George Nicholson. "The Victim's Movement: An Idea Whose Time Has Come." *Pepperdine Law Review* 11, no. 1 (1984): 1–13.

Cavender, Gray. *Parole: A Critical Analysis.* Port Washington, NY: Kennikat Press, 1982.

Citizens' Inquiry on Parole and Criminal Justice, Inc. *Prison Without Walls: Report on New York Parole.* New York: Praeger, 1975.

Coates, Ta-Nehisi. "The Black Family in the Age of Mass Incarceration." *Atlantic,* October 2015.

Davis, Angela Y. *Are Prisons Obsolete?* New York: Seven Stories Press, 2003.

———. *If They Come in the Morning: Voices of Resistance.* New York: Third Press, 1971.

Davis, Kenneth Culp. *Discretionary Justice: A Preliminary Inquiry.* Baton Rouge: Louisiana State University Press, 1969.

Fogel, David. *". . . We Are the Living Proof . . .": The Justice Model for Corrections*. Cincinnati: W. H. Anderson, 1975.

Fogel, David, and Illinois Law Enforcement Commission. *Flat-time Prison Sentences: A Proposal for Swift, Certain, and Even-handed Justice*. Chicago: Illinois Law Enforcement Commission, 1975.

Foucault, Michel. *Discipline and Punish: The Birth of the Prison*. New York: Vintage Books, 1979.

Frankel, Marvin E. *Criminal Sentences: Law Without Order*. New York: Hill and Wang, 1973.

Garland, David. *The Culture of Control: Crime and Social Order in Contemporary Society*. Chicago: University of Chicago Press, 2001.

Gonnerman, Jennifer. "Prepping for Parole." *New Yorker*, November 25, 2019.

Gottschalk, Marie. *The Prison and the Gallows: The Politics of Mass Incarceration in America*. New York: Cambridge University Press, 2006.

Henderson, Lynne N. "The Wrongs of Victim's Rights." *Stanford Law Review* 37, no. 4 (April 1985): 937–1021.

Hinton, Elizabeth. *From the War on Poverty to the War on Crime: The Making of Mass Incarceration in America*. Cambridge, MA.: Harvard University Press, 2016.

Kim, Alice, Erica R. Meiners, Audrey Petty, Jill Petty, Beth Richie, and Sarah Ross. *The Long Term: Resisting Life Sentences, Working Toward Freedom*. Chicago: Haymarket Books, 2018.

Kohler-Hausmann, Julilly. *Getting Tough: Welfare and Imprisonment in 1970s America*. Princeton, NJ: Princeton University Press, 2017.

Kushner, Rachel. "Is Prison Necessary? Ruth Wilson Gilmore Might Change Your Mind." *New York Times Magazine*, April 17, 2019.

Lappi-Seppälä, Tapio. "Sentencing and Punishment in Finland: The Decline of the Repressive Ideal." In *Sentencing and Sanctions in Western Countries*, edited by Michael H. Tonry and Richard S. Frase, 92–150. New York: Oxford University Press, 2001.

Lichtenstein, Alex. "Mass Incarceration Has Become the New Welfare." *Atlantic*, September 16, 2015.

Maghan, Jess. "The Dilemmas of Corrections and the Legacy of David Fogel." *International Journal of Offender Therapy and Comparative Criminology* 41, no. 2 (1997): 101–20.

Martinson, Robert. "What Works? Questions and Answers about Prison Reform." *Public Interest* 35 (Spring 1974): 22–54.

Medwed, Daniel S. "The Innocent Prisoner's Dilemma: Consequences of Failing to Admit Guilt at Parole Hearings." *Iowa Law Review* 93 (2008): 491–557.

Miller, Reuben Jonathan. *Halfway Home: Race, Punishment, and the Afterlife of Mass Incarceration.* New York: Little, Brown, 2021.

Monroe, Rachel. "The War on Murder: Sharon Tate and the Victims' Rights Movement." *Los Angeles Review of Books*, March 31, 2013.

Morris, Norval. *The Future of Imprisonment.* University of Chicago Press, 1974.

Muhammad, Khalil Gibran. *The Condemnation of Blackness: Race, Crime, and the Making of Modern Urban America.* Cambridge, MA: Harvard University Press, 2010.

Murakawa, Naomi. *The First Civil Right: How Liberals Built Prison America.* New York: Oxford University Press, 2014.

National Congress on Penitentiary and Reformatory Discipline. *Transactions of the National Congress on Penitentiary and Reformatory Discipline, Held at Cincinnati, Ohio, October 12–18, 1870.* Albany, NY: Argus, 1871.

Nelson, Stanley, and Traci A. Curry, directors. *Attica.* Showtime Documentary Films, Firelight Films, Topic Studios, 2021. 1 hr., 56 min.

New York Executive Advisory Committee on Sentencing. *Crime and Punishment in New York: An Inquiry into Sentencing and the Criminal Justice System: Report to Governor Hugh L. Carey.* Albany: The Committee, 1979.

Pager, Devah. *Marked: Race, Crime, and Finding Work in an Era of Mass Incarceration.* University of Chicago Press, 2007.

Peters, Thomas, and David Norris. "Reconsidering Parole Release Decisions in Illinois: Facts, Myths and the Need for Policy Changes." *John Marshall Law Review* 24, no. 4 (1991): 815–41.

Petersilia, Joan. *When Prisoners Come Home: Parole and Prisoner Reentry.* New York: Oxford University Press, 2003.

Pfaff, John F. *Locked In: The True Causes of Mass Incarceration—and How to Achieve Real Reform.* New York: Basic Books, 2017.

Pick, Grant. "No Mercy." *Chicago Reader*, February 15, 1996.

Reamer, Frederic G. *On the Parole Board: Reflections on Crime, Punishment, Redemption, and Justice.* New York: Columbia University Press, 2017.

Reitz, Kevin R. "The Disassembly and Reassembly of U.S. Sentencing Practices." In *Sentencing and Sanctions in Western Countries*, edited by Michael H. Tonry and Richard S Frase, 222–58. New York: Oxford University Press, 2001.

———. *American Exceptionalism in Crime and Punishment.* New York: Oxford University Press, 2018.

Rentschler, Carrie A. *Second Wounds: Victims' Rights and the Media in the U.S.* Durham, NC: Duke University Press, 2011.

Rhine, Edward E., Joan Petersilia, and Kevin R. Reitz. "The Future of Parole Release." *Crime and Justice* 46, no. 1 (2017): 279–338.

Rothman, David J. *Conscience and Convenience: The Asylum and Its Alternatives in Progressive America.* Boston: Little, Brown, 1980.

Sered, Danielle. *Until We Reckon: Violence, Mass Incarceration, and a Road to Repair.* New York: New Press, 2019.

Shuwerk, Robert P. "Illinois' Experience with Determinate Sentencing: A Critical Reappraisal Part 1: Efforts to Structure the Exercise of Discretion in Bargaining for, Imposing, and Serving Criminal Sentences." *DePaul Law Review* 33, no. 4 (1984): 631–739.

Simon, Jonathan. *Governing Through Crime: How the War On Crime Transformed American Democracy and Created a Culture of Fear.* New York: Oxford University Press, 2007.

———. *Mass Incarceration on Trial: A Remarkable Court Decision and the Future of Prisons in America.* New York: New Press, 2014.

Slater, Dashka. "Can You Talk Your Way Out of a Life Sentence?" *New York Times Magazine*, January 1, 2020.

Statman, Alisa, and Brie Tate. *Restless Souls: The Sharon Tate Family's Account of Stardom, the Manson Murders, and a Crusade for Justice.* New York: HarperCollins, 2012.

Sullivan, Larry E. *The Prison Reform Movement: Forlorn Hope.* Boston: Twayne, 1990.

Taylor, Flint. *The Torture Machine: Racism and Police Violence in Chicago.* Chicago: Haymarket Books, 2019.

Thompson, Heather Ann. *Blood in the Water: The Attica Prison Uprising of 1971 and Its Legacy.* New York: Pantheon, 2016.

Thompson, James. 2014. Interview. July 31 (Interview Session 08). Governor Jim Thompson Project. Oral History Program. Abraham Lincoln Presidential Library.

Travis, Jeremy, Bruce Western, F. Stevens Redburn, and National Research Council Committee on Law and Justice. *The Growth of Incarceration in the United States: Exploring Causes and Consequences.* Washington, D.C.: National Academies Press, 2014.

Useem, Bert, and Peter Kimball. *States of Siege: U.S. Prison Riots, 1971–1986.* New York: Oxford University Press, 1989.

Von Hirsch, Andrew, and Andrew Ashworth. *Principled Sentencing.* Boston: Northeastern University Press, 1992.

Von Hirsch, Andrew, and Committee for the Study of Incarceration. *Doing Justice: The Choice of Punishments: Report of the Committee for the Study of Incarceration.* New York: Hill and Wang, 1976.

Von Hirsch, Andrew, Kathleen J. Hanrahan, National Institute of Law Enforcement and Criminal Justice, and Center for Policy Research. *Abolish Parole?: Summary of Report Submitted to the National Institute of Law Enforcement and Criminal Justice, Law Enforcement Assistance Administration, U.S. Department of Justice.* Washington, D.C.: U.S. Government Print Office, 1978.

Von Hirsch, Andrew, Kay A. Knapp, and Michael H. Tonry. *The Sentencing Commission and Its Guidelines.* Boston: Northeastern University Press, 1987.

Von Hirsch, Andrew, Julian Roberts, Anthony E. Bottoms, Kent Roach, and Mara Schiff. *Restorative Justice and Criminal Justice: Competing or Reconcilable Paradigms?* Portland, OR: Hart, 2003.

Western, Bruce. *Homeward: Life in the Year After Prison.* New York: Russell Sage Foundation, 2018.

Wilson, James Q. *Thinking About Crime.* New York: Basic Books, 1975.

INDEX

ABOUT THE AUTHOR

Ben Austen is a journalist from Chicago. He is the author of *High-Risers: Cabrini-Green and the Fate of American Public Housing,* which was long-listed for the Andrew Carnegie Medal for Excellence in Nonfiction and named one of the best books of 2018 by *Booklist, Mother Jones,* and the public libraries of Chicago and St. Louis. A former editor at *Harper's Magazine,* Ben is the cohost of the podcast *Some of My Best Friends Are.* His feature writing has appeared in *The New York Times Magazine, GQ, Wired,* and many other publications.